CALIFORNIA DREAMS
AND AMERICAN
CONTRADICTIONS

UNIVERSITY OF NEBRASKA PRESS | LINCOLN

CALIFORNIA DREAMS AND AMERICAN CONTRADICTIONS

Women Writers and the Western Ideal

MONIQUE MCDADE

© 2023 by the Board of Regents of the University of Nebraska

Part of chapter 3 previously appeared as "Sui Sin Far's Genre of Intervention: The Sketch and the 'Real' in Realism and Naturalism," *Studies in American Naturalism* 16, no. 1 (Summer 2021): 78–96.

All rights reserved

The University of Nebraska Press is part of a land-grant institution with campuses and programs on the past, present, and future homelands of the Pawnee, Ponca, Otoe-Missouria, Omaha, Dakota, Lakota, Kaw, Cheyenne, and Arapaho Peoples, as well as those of the relocated Ho-Chunk, Sac and Fox, and Iowa Peoples.

Library of Congress Cataloging-in-Publication Data
Names: McDade, Monique, author.
Title: California dreams and American contradictions: women writers and the Western ideal / Monique McDade.
Description: Lincoln: University of Nebraska Press, [2023] | Includes bibliographical references and index.
Identifiers: LCCN 2022022524
ISBN 9781496232960 (hardback)
ISBN 9781496235282 (epub)
ISBN 9781496235299 (pdf)
Subjects: LCSH: American fiction—West (U.S.)—History and criticism. | American fiction—Women authors—History and criticism. | American fiction—19th century—History and criticism. | American fiction—20th century—History and criticism. | West (U.S.)—In literature. | Progress in literature. | BISAC: LITERARY CRITICISM / Women Authors | LITERARY CRITICISM / American / Regional | LCGFT: Literary criticism.
Classification: LCC PS374.W4 M36 2023 | DDC 813.009/92870978—dc23/eng/20221202
LC record available at https://lccn.loc.gov/2022022524

Frontis: Julian Myles on Unsplash

Set in Monotype Ehrhardt.

For Ryan, Harper, and Emerson.

From start to finish, you three were on the front lines of this obsession. I owe you.

CONTENTS

Acknowledgments   ix

Introduction: A Frontier Ethic and the
American Paradox   1

1. "Autoethnographic" Heroines:
   María Amparo Ruiz de Burton's Sentimental
   Novels, *Who Would Have Thought It?*
   and *The Squatter and the Don*   35

2. The Liberal Fantasy: Helen Hunt Jackson's
   Sentimental Advocacy in *Ramona*   79

3. Sui Sin Far's Genre of Intervention: The
   Regional Sketch and the "Real" in Realism   117

4. An Autobiography of Western American
   Integration: Eva Rutland and Her
   Alternative Politics of Respectability   153

Conclusion: Joan Didion's Sacramento and
Arlie Russell Hochschild's "Deep Story"   199

Notes   217

Bibliography   239

Index   245

ACKNOWLEDGMENTS

As a scholar of literature, I understand that books are cultural products. But writing *California Dreams and American Contradictions* taught me first-hand just how interwoven texts are with their cultural moments. I started this project prior to the 2016 presidential election. Back then my vision was to think about western American women writers for the alternative ways they perform domesticity in literary texts. Unsurprisingly to me now, in the wake of the 2016 election, this project became my outlet for all the earth-shattering disappointments and anxieties I and many others experienced. The women writers I was working on started to speak to me in new ways. Their archives suddenly seemed full of the same frustrations I was feeling, and their dissatisfactions with dominant society reflected my own despondency with American institutions at the time. It seemed clear to me that we had not listened critically enough to the stories these women were telling, and yet they were also stories that appeared unfortunately timeless. Needless to say, this project became an obsession for me because it felt like the only action I could take in what was increasingly becoming a desperate time. So I must start off acknowledging the power of literary texts and thanking the women writers included in this book for reaching through the centuries to assist another woman in need.

In addition, I recognize my good fortune to have found myself at the University of Nevada, Reno (UNR), during the construction of this project. UNR proved to be a supportive environment as I worked out my ideas for early versions and later transformed this project from the dissertation stage to the final published monograph. I want to thank Katherine Fusco for reading countless bad drafts over the years and for offering guidance as I steered this project through its different iterations. I also want to thank Daniel Morse for encouraging me to get more technical and theoretical and for teaching me that I was capable of that kind of work. I am also grateful for all the early help I received from Jennifer Hill, Meredith Oda, and Daniel Enrique Pérez and for the generous advice Ashley Marshall and Michael Branch offered as I prepared this book for publication. I am indebted to UNR's Graduate Student Association for awarding me the research grant that made the fourth chapter of this book possible.

Along the way I also had help from several people outside of UNR. The countless discussions I had at the Western-American Literature Association's annual conferences and at the Society for American Women Writers' conferences over the last few years have greatly impacted this project. I must thank Ginger Rutland for the conversation we had in 2016 about her mother, a conversation that directed me to Eva Rutland's archive in Eugene, Oregon. I am also forever grateful to Helen Lee for the formative experiences I had in her classrooms at California State University, Sacramento. Helen was the push I needed to realize my potential, and there is no amount of thanks I can give that will ever repay her fairly.

Finally, I could not have completed this project without the unwavering support of my family. My parents, Colleen and Chris Isaacson, have kept me confidently humble as I tackled something that never seemed possible for me as a first-generation college graduate. I thank my grandmothers, Edwina Pama and Roberta McDade, for giving me their grit and creativity. Ryan Arnold reminded me each day that what I was doing mattered. And my children, Harper and Emerson, both came into this world at foundational points in this project, and their marks are forever upon it.

CALIFORNIA DREAMS AND AMERICAN CONTRADICTIONS

Introduction

A Frontier Ethic and the American Paradox

THE DREAM OF PROGRESS

In her 2003 memoir, *Where I Was From,* Joan Didion recalls the eighth-grade graduation speech she delivered to her Sacramento, California school in 1948. She begins the speech, as all Didion's beginnings must, with "our great-great-grandparents, [who] were pushing America's frontier westward, to California."[1] The speech is ripe with images of California's pioneers jettisoning "homes and security" for the "the biggest cities in the west" and the "greatest dams in the world."[2] Didion's young voice rings through perhaps some of her earliest documented writing as she describes how much "California has accomplished" and celebrates California's staunch dedication to progress.[3] "It would be easy for us to sit back and enjoy the results of the past," eighth-grade Didion tells her audience, "but we can't do this. We can't stop and become satisfied and content. We must live up to our heritage, go on to better and greater things for California."[4] Young Didion captures a California character forever on the move toward something better. Didion also articulates a California always on the run from "the results of the past." In retrospect, Didion finds irony in her eighth-grade speech as it tries to find an "our" and a "we"—a shared heritage—in an audience of California children largely arrived in the state as a consequence of the 1930s Dust Bowl rather than the 1849 gold rush. But as she tries to make her readers understand, "Such was the blinkering effect of the local dreamtime that it would be some years before I recognized that certain aspects of 'Our California Heritage' did not add up."[5]

The California dream is a dream of progress. The dream envisions a utopic society in which the dispossessed are reinvented and the inequities that plague other regions of the nation are cured by an affirmation of the American work ethic. As such, "progress" here refers to the relentless belief that America, while good in theory, has yet to be achieved and that it is in the West, and in California in particular, that America will finally be realized. But as Didion points out, somewhere along the way the California dream degenerated into a "dreamtime," a calcified version of the dream paralyzed in the past and, by Didion's twentieth-century moment, useful only for selling postcards of a "vintage" California complete with palm trees, ocean waves, and snow-capped mountains.

California represents a particularly gripping American enigma because progress implies an always in-flux state. To be "in progress" means to be in between what was and what is hoped for in the future. In addition, to "have made progress" is to indicate movement away from some unwanted state of being but to also admit that there is still more to be desired. Articulating the American West through a rhetoric of progress traps the region's identity within an always incomplete history. As such, the discourse of progress enables the region to perceive itself as separate or as having moved on from other regions and their histories while it also stops the West from ever becoming settled. Because the West is misperceived as a new beginning and even the start of a new America, eighth-grade Didion is proud of the California dream and understands it to be progressive. But older Didion is critical of the dream and experiences California progress as a false promise, detecting "a terrible secret, a kernel of cyanide," at the center of the western American story.[6] For this reason, critics have said that "Didion is in love with her disillusionment,"[7] but this is not the whole truth. Didion is in love with the *nation's* disillusionment, for Didion's body of work reveals the ways the West's story is the nation's story.

California Dreams and American Contradictions is interested in the ways American literature participates in disseminating narratives of progress and tracks literary histories that intervene in those narratives. In this book, I follow a genealogy of western American women writers who compete with the literary histories behind Didion's calcified California dream of progress. Specifically I evaluate literary products by María Amparo Ruiz de Burton, Helen Hunt Jackson, Sui Sin Far, and Eva Rutland as they engage with and reinterpret American notions of progress and, thereby, western American regional identity. Didion offers a helpful starting point because in her mid-twentieth-century moment, she is writing in and about an American West that is finding it increasingly difficult to sustain the very narratives of progress that brought her family West in the mid-nineteenth century.

JOAN DIDION'S WEST: A PLACE OF SPEECHLESSNESS

Didion's writing career documents a twentieth-century western American identity crisis as she confronts the contradictions and the fantasies upon which the American West asserts itself as distinct from the rest of the nation. In the 1970s Didion writes that she had begun to feel restless in California. She says she had a "dim and unformed sense . . . that for some years the South and particularly the Gulf Coast had been for America what people were still saying California was, and what California seemed to me not to be: the future. . . . I did not much want to talk about this."[8] Perhaps it is Didion's Californian refusal to be "satisfied and content" that drove her South to find a new "future" in a region she associates with the past, but after spending a month traveling through the American South, Didion returned to California to realize "that the story doesn't matter, doesn't make any difference, doesn't figure."[9] Of course, the story Didion says "doesn't matter" is the story of western American progress and of the sacrifices Anglo-American pioneers made on the trail and that Didion's family imagines they continue to make as they resist satisfaction and contentment in their own twentieth-century California. But on her trip South, Didion listens to a southern voice "convinced that they have bloodied their place with history" while she tries to reconcile that in the West, "we do not believe that anything we do can bloody the land, or change it, or touch it."[10] And while Didion prefers not "to talk about this," she notes the South's "dense obsessiveness" with talking about "race, class, heritage, style, and the absence of style" to "keep the wilderness at bay."[11] Didion applies the wilderness metaphor here—a metaphor that conjures an American exceptionalism out of an American anxiety—to frame her critique of a southern "obsessiveness" with what Didion perceives to be things of the past. But the metaphor is misplaced and implies more about Didion than it does the southern community of which she is writing. If, in Didion's twentieth-century context, the wilderness represents some past chaos thoroughly contained by Anglo-American progress, then the South does not subscribe to such narratives. The past is imbricated in the South's present and future, and it is clear to Didion that the South remains close to its past in a way the West fundamentally does not. In using the West's metaphor of the wilderness to think about southern "obsessiveness," Didion reveals that even as she tries coming to terms with the fact that the story "doesn't matter," she continues searching for the story nonetheless. For stories *do* matter to Didion, and they matter because they provide the fodder that fuels the California dream. But these same stories are personally heartbreaking to Didion as she begins to recognize that in writing about the West, she is "trying to place [herself] in history" and that she has "been looking all [her] life for history and [has] yet to find it."[12] When Didion says the stories don't matter, she is working to articulate her own misplacement within the western American stories that raised her. I argue that Didion's sense of misplacement—or, to put it more precisely, Didion's process of un-recognition in western American narratives—is what ignites Didion's desire not to talk.

And Didion's body of work is fraught with not wanting to talk. As prolific as Didion is as a writer, her works resist speaking or, at times, express an inability to speak with exactitude. In *South and West*, for instance, she actively runs away from speaking to the connections between the "bloodied" South and her golden West. "And so," Didion says "instead of talking about it I flew south."[13] What makes Didion's work so "sharp," as President Barack Obama suggested when he awarded Didion the 2012 National Medal of Arts and Humanities, is that it is immersive. Didion writes from within the cultural space she is investigating, but she also always keeps her own sense of dis-belonging at the center of her critiques. She is driven by her speechlessness to fly South to find the words she cannot locate within her own histories in Sacramento.

I use the term "speechlessness" intentionally. Speechlessness, as I use it, is different from "voicelessness." It does not imply that women cannot speak but that for the women in Didion's linguistic culture—including Didion herself—the words do not exist, and so they choose to remain silent rather concede to half-truths, others' truths, or problematic expectations. I follow Patti Duncan in arguing that speechlessness is a site of feminist empowerment because it confronts dominant culture about its dismissal of women's experiences. Duncan challenges an activist rhetoric that uses terminology like "speak up" and "find your voice" as a language of resistance. Rather, Duncan argues, "it is not simply that silence can and must be replaced with speech (any silence, any speech)," but "both speech and silence must be continually interrogated for their meanings, both explicit and implicit."[14] It is assumed that in a U.S. context where "freedom of speech" is especially provocative, speaking out is connotative of power and remaining silent is the demarcation of powerlessness. But such a discourse leads to victim blaming and reinforces a Ben Franklin–like narrative that views individuals as wholly in control of their own outcomes. But speech is limited, and as Duncan and others have suggested, whoever controls language controls its access and limitations. For Didion, the western American narrative that underwrites her identity as a woman in the West is controlled by the white male language of the frontier. As such, her access to language is restricted, and the words available to her are besieged with meanings that support the Western myth, a myth that she is actively working to unravel. As such, Duncan helps us to see that "silence functions as a way of saying (and of unsaying) and is related to ways of seeing (unseeing) and knowing (unknowing), but it is useful only in contexts of other silences, whereby it signifies resistance rather than voicelessness."[15] Didion's silence is her un-recognition in western American narratives—her "unsaying," "unseeing," and "unknowing"—as her speechlessness calls attention to the silenced narratives buried under national and regional narratives of Manifest Destiny, American exceptionalism, and progress.

To demonstrate the high stakes involved in Didion's speechlessness and to set up a framework the rest of *California Dreams and American Contradictions* will use to complicate intersectional notions of speechlessness, I want to consider Didion's first published novel, *Run River* (1963). Although it has not received as much attention as her other novels, *Run River* is the first instance of Didion's speechlessness. It is not surprising that Didion's literary career begins with an intensive exploration of her western American environment. Marked by its cyclical structure and its treatment of California's post–World War II transformation, the novel tells the story of two families, the Knights and the McClellans, of Sacramento's landed aristocracy. Both families have, like Didion herself, ancestral ties to the first Anglo-American families of California, including the Donner-Reid Party. The novel begins in August 1959 with Lily McClellan (previously Knight) discovering her husband, Everett McClellan, has just shot her lover on the banks of the Sacramento River behind their hops ranch. After the first four chapters, readers are shuttled back in time in a section titled "1938–1959," in which Didion recounts Lily's and Everett's early courtship, their Reno marriage, and detailed accounts of their domestic life together in these years. The last two chapters return to that moment in August 1959 when Lily walks down to the riverbank to find her husband standing with a gun over the dead body of her lover. The novel ends with a second gunshot, sounding the moment in which Everett, Lily's husband, ends his own life.

Many critics have noted that while good in theory, "Nothing 'happens' between the first and second shots fired."[16] Or, as in Guy Davenport's 1963 *National Review* article on the novel, critics have questioned the purpose behind Didion's first novel: "But what do they mean? The details of a pattern are organized and organization is principle. What's that principle?"[17] When critics claim that "nothing happens," they are activating a rhetorical violence against Didion and the semi-autobiographical characters she represents in *Run River*.

When critics question Didion's principles in the cyclical structure of the novel, they participate in an institutional devaluing of women's experiences, and they normalize a patriarchal literary establishment that dictates industry norms. These critics attempt an institutional silencing of Didion's deeply feminine expressions in *Run River*, but because the privileged Didion embodies that western American myth of progress, the establishment also leaves room for her to revise her narrative. For instance, in a 1963 review from the *New Yorker*, the reviewer writes: "Miss Didion's first novel shows her to be the possessor of a vigorous style that is wasted on her characters—some Sacramento River ranchers and their aimless wives and discontented daughters . . . but her book gives promise of what she can do when she settles down to dealing with men and women instead of being content to describe human leftovers."[18] This early review applauds Didion's talent as an author at the same time that it derides her for her chosen subjects—the "human leftovers" represented by the "aimless wives and discontented daughters." The reviewer critiques the novel's centering of what they clearly understand to be insignificant characters living lives in equally insignificant places. In naming her characters "human leftovers," the reviewer pushes women's experiences to the fringes of regional and national histories.

The real problem these critics have with Didion's first novel is that rather than celebrating the rugged cowboy and his reluctantly adaptive Victorian schoolmarm or the broad expanse of space and opportunity in the West, Didion features the unsatisfied housewife in her claustrophobic western American environment. She presents a reorientation to the western American myth, one that does more than simply place the woman at the center of the narrative—a move that by this point is unsurprising. Didion intervenes by depicting the West as an unsustainable myth and demonstrates how western American women bear the burden not only of their own oppressed experiences within that myth but, by the twentieth century's changing western American terrain, that of their husbands' fall from grace as well.

Lily and Martha in *Run River* are antithetical to the strong pioneer woman archetype featured in a number of western American narratives dating back to Mary Hallock Foote. The female pioneer character is a Victorian woman who has adapted genteel society to meet the grueling demands of life in the "Wild West." In most cases she is a woman who is somewhat reluctant to travel West but who does so anyway in support of her husband's economic ambitions. As Amy Kaplan argues, the pioneer woman's constitution is offended by the rugged western environment, but she soon comes to domesticate and tame this environment, modeling it into the image of respectability.[19] As such, the pioneer woman trope is central to narratives of western American progress and the California dream. Victoria Lamont's recent book *Westerns: A Woman's History* builds upon this to show how the pioneer woman eventually transitions into the western American woman, a figure who is well adapted to her environment and even challenges male domination there. Lily and Martha are neither of these. By *Run River*'s mid-twentieth-century moment, Didion shows how the pioneer woman and the western American woman have degraded into the frail, opaquely resigned relics of this history. With her female characters Didion questions the long-term consequences of a western culture that asks women to adapt to inflexible masculine environments, and she unsettles histories of California progress by failing to see the point in their existence. While Lily follows a set of historical expectations by marrying another member of Sacramento's pioneer elite, Martha pushes against these expectations and seeks access to a new, modern iteration of the California dream. In the end, neither woman appears adapted to her environment. Martha commits suicide in the Sacramento River behind her home, and after her husband takes his own life on the banks of the same river, Lily walks back up to the house, wondering "what she would say" to her children.[20] She wonders what to say to her children because it is not just the news of their father's suicide she must break to them. She must also relate to them the historical circumstances that have depleted their inheritance and failed to deliver to them the promised western ideal. Lily's grief is thus substituted by a speechlessness. In the very last lines of the novel, Didion's narrator tells us that Lily "did not know what she could tell anyone except that he had been a good man. She was not certain that he had been but it was what she would have wished for him, if they gave her one wish."[21] Lily's uncertainty at the end of the novel, though it is projected onto her husband, is really directed at the vague "they" who have refused her "one wish" and who have sidelined her to the local color background of western American narratives. *Run River*'s conclusion marks a certain western American paradox that women live out through a rhetorical unease with the tensions between the region's histories and their own lived experiences. The absence of language here indicates the cultural environment's failure to account for Lily and Martha rather than Lily's and Martha's failure to adapt to their environment.

Consequently *Run River* depicts women in a number of sacrificial positionalities to the nation and national identity. Upon first read *Run River* may appear to be about the "nothing" happenings "between the first and second shots fired," but the novel is really about Lily's and Martha's inheritance of a specifically feminine burden. As their mothers die or age out of their roles as matriarchs, Lily and Martha are left to care for their ailing and impotent fathers, their insubstantial husbands and lovers, and their vulnerable sons and nephews. Didion's female characters absorb the loss these men face as their role in American society is overrun in the post–World War II era by a new masculinity and a new national identity codified in a globally expanding capitalist economy and a technological military presence on the world stage. It is an era in which Theodore Roosevelt's rugged masculinity and pioneer spirit are being replaced by Franklin Roosevelt's welfare state and an international, rather than simply a national, consciousness. Whether Didion's female characters are sacrificing themselves to marriages that push the genealogical and regional pioneer narrative just a little further, as with Lily, or incurring the brunt of the enigmatic transition from that pioneer history to a mid-twentieth-century California grounded in real estate and land speculation, as Martha does, Didion is tuned into the ways women pass these burdens down a female genealogical line to protect and shield the family's men from the ineffectiveness they come to represent by *Run River*'s critical 1959 moment.

In part *California Dreams and American Contradictions* works to showcase the systemic mechanisms wielded against women and women of color writers as they attempt to write their West in the long nineteenth century. As I will go on to show in the following chapters, Ruiz de Burton, Jackson, Sui Sin Far, and Rutland are not writing revisionist narratives, nor are they rebuking dominant western myths entirely. Like Didion, who rearranges popular narratives to provide new orientations—both gendered and historical—to regional and national identities, the women gathered here compete with western American narratives in real time as these narratives are being negotiated and settled in leading periodicals and publishing houses. The first thing *California Dreams and American Contradictions* acknowledges is that the women writers I evaluate are part of this literary land grab in the West and that, as much as they are being ridiculed by literary institutions—as we see with the reviews of Didion's *Run River*—they are also participating in the literary takeover of the West. As such, dominant literary trends recognize Ruiz de Burton, Jackson, Sui Sin Far, Rutland, and Didion as threats to homogenous national narratives regardless of how buried their works have become or how lashing public reviews of their works have been. This complicates our understanding of how women writers have engaged with literary trends and influencers and offers new points of entry into their literary agendas.

THE PATTERN OF FORGETTING

Didion is a clear example of how compounding motivations challenge gendered narratives of the West while also recreating other imperialist plot structures. As much as *Run River* exercises caution against the "redemptive" West trope, it also internalizes what I refer to as a pattern of forgetting. As indicated, the California dream is but a manufactured narrative of progress. The dream is built upon founding American stories of freedom, equality, and opportunity, but it is also a dream supported by what the narrative forgets. Take, for instance, Didion's sense that she is part of a "family, or a congeries of families, that has always been in the Sacramento Valley."[22] Even while she recognizes that some "might protest that no family has been in the Sacramento Valley for anything approaching 'always,'" Didion submits to a grandiose "always." "But," Didion continues, "it is characteristic of Californians to speak grandly of the past as if it had simultaneously begun, *tabula rasa*, and reached a happy ending on the day the wagons started west. *Eureka*—'I Have Found It'—as the state motto has it."[23] In a literary moment like this, *California Dreams and American Contradictions* admits complexity and engages with the overlapping histories of oppression located in the evasive language Didion uses here to talk about her histories but to talk around the histories hers submerges. I argue that, like the "unsettled and unsettling" Africanist presence Toni Morrison locates at the center of American literature,[24] the California dream tells the story of an "unsettled" and conquered region. If Didion and her "congeries of [pioneer] families" speak to a history of California redemption, then this redemption is filtered through the families that really had *always* been in the Sacramento Valley or at least those that had been there for centuries before her. Didion's "always" is both a point of criticism—"no family has been in the Sacramento Valley for anything approaching 'always'"—and a site of institutional forgetting as Didion fails to mention that there are in fact families that had been in the region for something closer to "always." As a writer herself, Morrison "came to realize the obvious: the subject to the dream is the dreamer."[25] As such, Morrison recognizes that for the Anglo-American writer writing their own dream, the "fabrication of an Africanist persona is reflexive; an extraordinary meditation on the self; a powerful exploration of the fears and desires that reside in the writerly conscious."[26] Didion's "always" is a reflexive move against competing "fears and desires" that "reside" within Didion and her western American pioneer history. The "always" is an expression of desire as it establishes a place for the dispossessed pioneers who suffered through the crossing to arrive at the promised land. But it is also an expression of fear for the stories that fell victim to hers. This fear is evaded—"no family has been in the Sacramento Valley for anything approaching 'always'"—but as Morrison argues, this "evasion has fostered another, substitute language" or, in Didion's case, a substitute history, "in which the issues are encoded."[27] The forgetting is institutional, supported by the inherited stories on which Didion grew up and reinforced in the continued manufacture of adapted western American motifs in the twentieth century.

 The kind of institutional forgetting we see in Didion's work also appears in a notable pattern throughout the works of Ruiz de Burton, Jackson, Sui Sin Far, and Rutland. In shape, the pattern is a circuit of oppressive exchange in which these western American women writers underwrite certain inequitable narratives as they attempt to make other narratives more expansive. As Didion's *Run River* indicates, national histories and the intimate histories of families become united in an agenda to maintain a quickly disintegrating myth about American exceptionalism and Manifest Destiny. Benedict Anderson offers a framework for understanding the consequences of western American myth making when he suggests that historical narratives play an important role in codifying national identity. However, Anderson also recognizes that this history must be read "*genealogically*—as the expression of an historical tradition of serial continuity"[28]—at the same time that it must also be read as a strategic history that relies on "forgetting" the fact that national formations and identities are imagined.[29] This strategic history is one that attempts to homogenize an otherwise diverse regional history. We see the strategic historical amnesia at work in Didion's eighth-grade speech when she uses "we" to speak to her class. The "we" is a mechanism of forgetting as it attempts to homogenize a western American origin myth. In the "we" assumption there is also an active forgetting of other cultural knowledges and a refusal to acknowledge different pathways for arriving west.

California Dreams and American Contradictions calls attention to the homogenizing moments in American literary ventures and showcases how Ruiz de Burton, Jackson, Sui Sin Far, and Rutland combat that homogenizing effort. Each of these women writers "arrived" in the American West by a different pathway. While Jackson comes closest to affirming Didion's western American pioneer myth, Ruiz de Burton is writing at the same time to problematize the "always" to which Didion clings and the meaning of the "crossing." For Ruiz de Burton "arrived" by remaining where she was; she "arrived" when the American West came to her in the form of the Mexican-American War. And then there is Sui Sin Far, who emigrated to the United States from Britain, relocated to Canada, and eventually found her way west as she sought out a livelihood as a writer. Even Rutland, an African American writer I am introducing into academic conversations for the first time, documents a mid-twentieth-century western American arrival by way of train from the South just as the civil rights movement is ramping up. As is evident from this quick synopsis, there is no viable "we" when it comes to how these women writers "arrived" in the American West.

Their stories are unique and reliant on their specific intersectional existence. Likewise, their reasons for being in the West and the dreams they invest in the West are different.

And yet *California Dreams and American Contradictions* recognizes that while Didion misused her "we" in her eight-grade speech, there remains a commonality among the women writers collected in this book. In paying tribute to the intersectional histories each of these women writers documents through their literary products, I call up the "othered" histories from the interstices of dominant national and regional narratives to piece together a shared female ecology of the West. Regardless of, or perhaps in spite of, the hopelessness and rejection many of the women I include in this book express at important points in their writing, there is also an awareness of female continuity and shared history. By "shared history" I do not mean the same history. As I mentioned above, I am aware of the intersectional experiences that make each woman's positionality to the nation unique and their speechlessness differently articulated. I do not shy away from the contradictory and often oppressive aspects of their literary works. Instead I argue that in the sample of western American women writers addressed here, there is an affinity in their responses to overarching national and regional literary dictates and a kinship in the stories they tell.

LIBERALISM IN THE WEST AND THE CONSENT OF THE GOVERNED

Put succinctly but far from simply, the kinship I find among Ruiz de Burton, Jackson, Sui Sin Far, and Rutland is rooted in their specific positionalities to an American liberal selfhood. As Stephen J. Mexal argues, the American West is central to the ways John Locke and Thomas Hobbes theorized classical liberalism's central tenets, such as individual rights and freedom. Mexal points out that both Locke and Hobbes refer to the American frontier as a wilderness and that this is held in contrast to an elevated, progressed state rooted in the consent of the governed. In opposition to Didion's instincts, Mexal suggests that "the stories we tell about the American West *matter*" because they are stories that open "the possibility for alternate political realities" and that articulate the "consent" in the "consent of the governed."[30] In tracing a mostly white male canon of western American frontier writers writing in the West's bourgeois literary magazine *Overland Monthly*, Mexal concludes that "liberal selfhood is actually *produced*. It is written into existence for some but not for all, and admitting this means recognizing the role that luck and contingency play in producing the liberal self."[31] While I agree that liberal selfhood is produced and that literary texts are central to that production, the women writers collected here would not consider this political work to emerge out of "luck," nor would they accept gendered, racial, and cultural "contingencies" as productive critiques. Instead Ruiz de Burton, Jackson, Sui Sin Far, and Rutland acknowledge the determined and determinant literary mechanisms that actively generate the circumstances of "luck" and "contingency." Therefore, I argue that dominant national literatures coalesce to define "consent" and to determine a spectrum of "consent" that subsidizes nationally prescribed histories and narratives.

In classical liberal terms, "consent of the governed" refers to a government formed out of the people's approval. The people give their consent to allow the government to form and to govern. In the United States' democratic republic, consent is expressed through the vote and indicates a willingness—a consent—to sacrifice certain individual freedoms to ensure the productive and efficient operation of the state. Like freedom and equality, the consent of the governed is another American concept deeply ambivalent and contradictory. At the start of the nation and well into the twentieth century, women, slaves, and people of color were denied the vote, and their consent was thereby not only not given but also not considered necessary to the nation's operations. *California Dreams and American Contradictions* begins at that important juncture when, in facing the Civil War and its aftermath, the nation was reinterpreting liberal personhood, including whose consent mattered and what consent meant. In many ways, the West became a region to reimagine women's civic roles in the nation. In her book *How the Vote Was Won*, Rebecca Mead argues that the West offered an optimal environment for women's suffrage. Noting that women in the West secured the vote by 1914, Mead criticizes those women's suffrage studies that center the East and posits that women in the West modeled successful campaign strategies that would go on to help women in the East secure the vote in 1920. As such, Mead suggests that women suffragists in the West helped "create a progressive political environment" in the West.[32] Throughout her book, Mead documents many of the contradictions and oppressive exchanges that occurred on the path to western American women's suffrage. And yet Mead still capitulates to a sense of the "progressive" American West. Although her argument "reintegrates this important region into national suffrage history" and "recognizes suffrage racism and elitism," it remains indebted to the myth that the West is progressively distinct from the rest of the nation.[33]

In contrast, I argue that western American "progressive" identity is toxic. One cannot tell the story of western American progress—whether that progress be about women's suffrage or "free" statehood—without recalling the instances of tradeoff where one oppressed group achieves liberal acknowledgment by the put-down of another oppressed group. In other words, the story Mead tells of white western American women taking advantage of anti-Black, anti-Chinese, and anti-Mexican racism in the West to persuade white men to give them the vote is not a progressive story. It is counterintuitive to progress if one group has to solicit freedoms on the condition that the freedoms of another be further withheld. And yet these are the stories the West tells about itself in order to uphold the western American ideal.

The western American women writers included here offer alternative narratives, ones that evidence all the ways the ideal is engineered and disseminated to appease ordinary Americans in exchange for their consent. In their adaptations of dominant genres, tropes, and literary modes, these women writers grapple with the unstable and conflicting definitions of "consent" as western American progressive identity fractures regional and national cohesion. Didion's *Run River* notes a mid-twentieth-century transformation of "consent" as the world faces World War II and the pioneer myth gives way to new iterations of speculation in the West. For the majority of *Run River*, Martha is dating Ryder Channing, a man from Tennessee who has moved to California in the hopes of striking it rich in the real estate business, which is now taking the place of gold and agriculture as California's boom business. Ryder eventually breaks his relationship off with Martha, who represents what is quickly becoming an irrelevant pioneer past, after he enters a spontaneous marriage with a San Francisco socialite and the daughter of a real estate mogul. A few weeks into his marriage, Ryder returns to the McClellan family home and sexually assaults Martha while she is there alone. The scene is quick and jarringly violent. "I'm trying to sleep," she tells him, and then, "Fifteen minutes later he had her down on the floor; she had refused to go near the couch. 'You want it,' he said. She had her legs crossed and her face turned away from him. 'I do not.' 'What difference do you think it makes now?' He pushed her skirt up around her waist. 'After I've screwed you maybe four, five times a week every week for the past five years.'"[34] Surprisingly, some critics read this scene as consensual. As Katherine Henderson describes this scene, "Ryder stops by the ranch, finds Martha alone, and seduces her without love or tenderness."[35] Seduction, whether it is loving or not, is not what happens here, and to say so is a failure to see into the silences Didion attempts to articulate. This scene clearly depicts an instance of rape. Martha "refuses" to go near the couch, her legs are "crossed," and her face is "turned away." Ryder forces Martha's clothes off and verbally assaults her by telling her nobody will believe she didn't consent after her relationship with him over the past five years. History is used as a sexual weapon in this scene, and the assault, taken within the context of Martha's and Ryder's near five-year relationship, is emblematic of Martha's prior consent being exercised against her.

As with all sexual assaults, Ryder's attack on Martha is one of power and domination, and in this case it represents California's changing social order. More precisely, the sexual assault against Martha is a meditation on western American women's manipulated consent to be governed by the nation's narratives, histories, and agendas in the name of "progress." While there is the obvious layer in which Martha's consent is violated by Ryder, the specific placement of this scene within the novel also suggests Martha has but superficial access to American liberal institutions. Once given, Martha's consent cannot be revoked, even after the terms of the relationship between her and Ryder have changed. As such, women's consent is but a formality, as the terms under which Martha consents can change and alter without her renewed agreement. Even Lily's marriage to Everett, another descendant of Sacramento's pioneer elite, is described as "[having] been, really, no decision at all: only an acquiescence."[36] In Lily's words, her marriage to Everett "seemed as inescapable as the ripening of the pears, as fated as the exile from Eden."[37] Therefore, Lily's consent is but an expectation and a way for her to act out a narrative that is as "fated as the exile from Eden."

As such, Didion's *Run River* is an acute revelation of how the debilitating consequences of founding a family identity and tradition on the national promise of western American progress and freedom becomes the genealogical burden of women. But the burden is greater than even Didion could imagine. Or perhaps she could imagine it and that is why she spent her sixty-year writing career working that burden out on the page. Either way, I argue that the burden is felt by a community of diverse western American women and that they experience this burden from unique locations within American sociopolitical infrastructures. I trace this burden from Ruiz de Burton in the 1870s to Rutland in the 1950s and 1960s to show how that burden evolves—how definitions of consent change—and how it impacts the women writers included here at different but always concurrent points of suffering.

INTERSECTIONAL WESTS

Didion offers me a starting point to unravel the intertwined and deeply ambivalent literary histories with which Ruiz de Burton, Jackson, Sui Sin Far, and Rutland contend as they compete with the California dream. I aim for a more microscopic reading of western American women writers to locate them within the interstices of national, regional, and individual histories and narratives. While Judith Fetterley and Marjorie Pryse have also argued for a rereading of women regionalists, they place emphasis on the ways regional women write from outside the nation and its urban—read "masculine"—sociopolitical concerns. As such, Fetterley and Pryse remain indebted to a feminism born out of critiquing the "separate spheres" ideology, an ideology important at one point but one that has increasingly been challenged by intersectional directions in contemporary feminist analysis. In contrast, *California Dreams and American Contradictions* participates in Krista Comer's call for a feminist critical regionalism by suggesting that western American women writers offer us a new vantage point from which we can evaluate the role regionalist writing plays in nation-building projects *and* in individual cultural and political self-representation. The western American women writers included in this book are not "separate," nor would they pretend to be so. Rather, they are at the very center of the pressing sociopolitical and geopolitical issues of their day, most of the time writing in dominant forms from urban rather than rural settings and brushing shoulders with prominent political and cultural figures. Jackson's *Ramona*, for example, borrows upon the success of Harriet Beecher Stowe's *Uncle Tom's Cabin* and centers the nation's move West at the end of Reconstruction in the American South, taking up the nation's most pressing political anxieties. Though these women writers do not always occupy privileged places in political debates—surely Jackson's original political treatise, *A Century of Dishonor*, was laughed off by senators to whom she personally delivered copies—their literary contributions *were* read *and* acknowledged by their regional and national societies. The reactions they received, even if condescending laughs, are important to our understanding of the tensions between dominant national and regional literatures and women's relationships to their national and individual cultural histories.

Scholars of western American literature such as Annette Kolodny, Jane Tompkins, Krista Comer, and Nina Baym have made important strides in recovering western American women writers in the face of a literary tradition that assumes masculinity, violence, and depravity. But as Victoria Lamont argues, "A newcomer to the field might be surprised, however, to find relatively few 'big books'" on western American women writers.[38] Lamont suggests rightly that the lack of such "big books" is due to the tedious and often unseen nature of recovery work and to the fact that scholars developed a western American women writers subfield that remains separate from larger western American literary structures and concerns. Lamont predicts a new era in western American women writers scholarship that, while it still works to recover women writers, also situates them within larger regional discussions. Extending Lamont's call, *California Dreams and American Contradictions* adds to the list of "big books" on western American women writers by placing regional women writers within even larger intra-regional cultural institutions. Cathryn Halverson argues that scholars need to focus less on identifying how western American women writers write to challenge a masculine literary tradition in the region and focus more on "contributing to the larger project of excavating a shared tradition among women writers in the West."[39] I agree and organize *California Dreams and American Contradictions* to consider the productive, if not always similar, ways western American women writers navigate the singularity of their role as women writers in the West. Halverson also notes that one point of relation among many western American women writers is that they often "felt themselves to be alone" in trying to write the West from a female orientation.[40] While the women writers I collect here must have felt themselves isolated at times, I also recognize that many western American women writers were trying to write the West not only from a female orientation but also from an intersectional orientation that accounted for the totality of their individuality, including their ethnicity, race, sexuality, gender, and cultural histories. As such, their literary products often relied on specific cultural knowledge that informed the modes and genres within which they were working and that they used to speak not just to dominant national audiences but also to other women, communities of color, and immigrants. Therefore, I agree with those who suggest that scholars working on western American women writers should not try to superimpose a generalized and universal "women's West" upon the western American geographic region (for this would be just as unproductive as the dominant narratives of the West we have now) but should also consider the different pathways, technologies, and communities through which women traveled to arrive west and to find their West.

I recognize these different pathways, technologies, and communities in *California Dreams and American Contradictions* to suggest that the writers included here do not necessarily revolutionize literary genres to bring attention to their histories and experiences. This is not a volume on resistance literature. Instead I argue that the women collected here regionalize the popular literary genres and modes of their era to uncover the ways these genres must always already contend with their identities, communities, and histories. Dominant nineteenth- and early twentieth-century literary genres and modes of writing have often been read as oppositional to literary regionalism, but as the western American women writers gathered here attest, dominant genres and modes found their way into regionalist writing, and in bringing these traditions together, western American women writers attempted to write a more holistic view of American cultural and political history. My argument builds off Benedict Anderson's work on the relationship between print-capitalism and nationalism. Anderson argues that in the seventeenth and eighteenth centuries the novel and the newspaper contributed to the "idea of 'homogenous, empty time,' in which simultaneity is, as it were, transverse, cross-time, marked not by prefiguring and fulfilment, but by temporal coincidence, and measured by clock and calendar."[41] The novel's rendering of multiple characters living multiple lives all within the same time but in separate geographies and the newspaper's tendency to be read ritualistically each day unite a community of readers in time and space, regardless of whether they will ever actually meet. Anderson recognizes that national consciousness developed out of this "new way of linking fraternity, power and time meaningfully together" and that these communities were largely established through "print-capitalism, which made it possible for rapidly growing numbers of people to think about themselves, and to relate themselves to others, in profoundly new ways."[42] Such a persuasive argument leads me to ask how print-capitalism's role in fostering national cohesion becomes more complex in the era of Manifest Destiny as national expansion stretches the nation's borders into territories that previously belonged to Spain, Mexico, and Indigenous populations. How does the nation reconcile what seem to be competing histories in its new regions? And how does the nation consolidate these histories into a singular, progressive national narrative?

In response to these questions, I would still answer as Anderson does: print-capitalism. However, I find that the story grows more complicated as we consider the late nineteenth and early twentieth centuries' shifting modes of literary production and the equally shifting scales of value placed on various literary genres and publications. If Anderson's argument is focused on the proliferation of daily newspapers and novels in vernacular "print-languages" in the eighteenth century as nationalisms are on the rise around the globe, then my argument recognizes that as the U.S. print industry moves into the mid-nineteenth century, new adaptations of these old forms are competing in and transforming the American literary marketplace and, therefore, American national narratives. In an American context, Anderson points out, the problem print-capitalism addressed wasn't so much uniting a national body of readers around a unified language, as it was in other parts of the world. Rather, print capitalism conquered language and forcibly indoctrinated diverse linguistic communities in an American idiom codified by white European settlers. While late nineteenth- and twentieth-century literary innovations, such as literary periodicals, and new literary modes, such as realism, have been seen as democratizing forces in national literary production, it is my contention that these innovations revived the literary establishment's aims to consolidate these physical and linguistic geographies into a homogenous national identity—a Didion "we," that is.

California Dreams and American Contradictions is indebted to Amy Kaplan, Stephanie Foote, Donna Campbell, and others who have drawn our attention to the importance of nineteenth- and twentieth-century serialized magazines such as *Atlantic Monthly*, *Harpers*, and *Century Magazine*. This scholarship points to the concurrent rise of literary magazines with new literary modes, including realism and regionalism. These new forms of literary distribution and the new modes of writing they featured appeared at a specific time in the nation's expansion. They helped draw eastern interest in the West while they also supported the incorporation of the West into American founding ideologies. As Stephanie Foote indicates, "Regional writing's dissemination in high cultural venues, its appearance in the late nineteenth century (a moment when the newly reunited states were becoming not just a powerful nation but also a powerful imperial force), and its substantive preoccupation with dialect as the formal corollary of something like ethnic self-expression combined to make it a genre uniquely suited to imagine a homogenous past for a heterogeneous nation."[43] Regionalism, a mode of writing that found its home and its largest readership in the literary magazines of its day, works to bring together the otherwise disparate geographies newly accumulated by the United States and to emphasize the continuity of these different regions through a historical discourse of Manifest Destiny. In addition, Donna Campbell draws our attention to how the rise in magazine culture and regional writing also corresponded with a rise in female authorship. Arguing for the ways literary modes like naturalism emerged to combat the success women writers garnered with their regionalist short stories and sketches, Campbell links the undervalued nature of regionalist writing to its "feminine" associations.[44]

Given the proliferation of magazine culture, regionalism, and female authorship in these later decades of the nineteenth century, it is no surprise that all the women writers included in this book wrote for magazines and that they contributed to a journalistic regionalism in some of the day's leading newspapers and periodicals. It would seem that if, as Anderson argues, newspapers and periodicals contributed to a national narrative and a sense of national cohesion, then the four women included here participated in codifying such a unity of national identity through their contributions. And yet in her autobiography, published in just such a national magazine, Sui Sin Far, the daughter of an English father and a Chinese mother, provocatively states, "I have no nationality and am not anxious to claim any. Individuality is more than nationality."[45] As with Didion, Sui Sin Far experiences how individual and national identities live in a mutually exclusive positionality to one another. To have national identity means to forfeit individual identity and to participate in the overriding narratives that subsume individual cultural and historical narratives. I consider such statements in relation to women writers' literary productions, and thereby I question whether *all* print culture contributed to a homogenous national identity and culture and to what extent all authors wanted to.

California Dreams and American Contradictions highlights a trend in western American women writers' works that uses emerging literary modes and genres to challenge national homogenization. Sui Sin Far's assertion of individuality over nationality, for instance, is at once an affirmation of American liberal ideology and a condemnation of the nation's tendencies toward a restrictive nationalism. Stephen Mexal expands Anderson's argument into the nineteenth century, when he argues that the West (and California in particular) became a cite for

American liberal performance as leading literary journals used a rhetoric of wilderness to act out a "homogenizing force, one that sustains its power precisely through the homogenization of difference."[46] More specifically, Mexal realizes the role western American magazines, such as *Overland Monthly*, played in negotiating the varied forms of liberal identification in the diverse western region. As such, Mexal argues that the writers included in the magazine "frame white liberal selfhood as a by-product of western wild spaces" and that "[in] yoking a set of narratives about freedom and the individual to a set of narratives about California and the West," these authors "made the magazine an instrument of liberal governmentality."[47]

I agree with Mexal's call to recognize the importance of the West in national negotiations of American liberalism, but I also expand the parameters of this discussion to consider how western American women writers asserted alternative definitions and narratives for liberal personhood through rearticulations of popular genres and literary modes. That is, the women writers considered here offer new ways of thinking about the "wilderness" and the "wild" West through their use of dominant literary genres. In many cases, the western American myths are rearticulated to expose the flaws in an American liberal ideology that situates the wilderness as a temporal and geographical precursor to American cultivation and liberal realization. For instance, Ruiz de Burton challenges the dichotomous relationship popular novels foster between the savage West and the civilized East. Her novels reassert Californio histories and domesticity as evidence of their qualifications for liberal personhood in face of national narratives that position Californios as either relics of the past or as a primitive population incapable of liberal behavior. In *The Intimacies of Four Continents*, Lisa Lowe evaluates an eighteenth-century global archive of liberal philosophy and history that knits together domestic interiority and global labor formations. She uses "the concept of intimacy as a heuristic, and a means to observe the historical division of the world processes into those that develop modern liberal subjects and modern spheres of social life, and those processes that are forgotten, cast as failed or irrelevant because they do not produce 'value' legible within modern classifications."[48] Lowe's argument pieces together a fragmented global archive to show the relationship among colonization, slavery, and classical liberalism. In so doing, Lowe rejects "a linear temporal progression from colonial abjection to liberal freedom" and instead shows how liberal subjects are formed "in relation to laboring lives in the colonized geographies or 'zones of exception' with which they coexist, however disavowed."[49] Lowe's framework helps me to resurrect the stultified histories of slavery and oppression that undergird American exceptionalism and American liberal democracy in the American West, a region that relies on geographical distance to remain largely disconnected from histories of American slavery. Lowe encourages us to revisit narratives of progress and to widen the purview through which we evaluate them as "progressive." Histories such as Manifest Destiny are just the kinds of histories Lowe would recommend we read for their global manifestations and consequences. Although it is not new to critique American Manifest Destiny and its rhetorical use of progress and civilization to justify its means, Lowe provides the framework for taking this critique further and to engage with the ways Manifest Destiny is "intimate" with other global and national histories and thereby to understand how such national discourses create "intimacies" with seemingly contradictory populations, ideas, and histories.

Ultimately *California Dreams and American Contradictions* draws attention to the fundamental problems in the American literary establishment's cooption of a "progressive" rhetoric to produce and disseminate literatures about the American West from the Manifest Destiny era through the American civil rights movement. I trace the ways western American women writers appropriate national genres to fill in the gaps in these "progressive" literary histories. As such, these writers also reveal the very real sociopolitical consequences of using literature and popular cultural products to establish national identity. The writers included in *California Dreams and American Contradictions* regionalize dominant national genres to challenge literature's role in creating (1) regional divisiveness, (2) conformist communities that support nationally sponsored images of gendered, ethnic, and immigrant others, and (3) liberal histories validated through a strategic vocabulary rooted in "freedom," "equality," and "progress." The women writers I consider are sensitive to the boundaries between their individualism and their place in regional and national sociopolitical collectivities. For some, such as Ruiz de Burton, regional identity is used to reinstantiate individual identity against invasive national stereotypes evident in national literatures. For others, such as Sui Sin Far, who declares "individuality is more than nationality," regional narratives are recognized as the generators of the ethnic and gendered oppression that the national literature uses to control individual identity and representation. And for others still, regional identity is also conflated with problematic forms of consent and with acceptance of oppressive national narratives, as I have demonstrated through the example of Didion. Thus *California Dreams and American Contradictions* is invested in an intersectional approach to the literary thread western American women draw through the long nineteenth century.

TRACKING THE GENEALOGY: CHAPTER SUMMARIES

The women writers included in this book come from diverse sociopolitical backgrounds and are themselves a survey of the diverse uses of progressive political and literary programs. As I have alluded throughout this introductory chapter, María Amparo Ruiz de Burton, Helen Hunt Jackson, Sui Sin Far, and Eva Rutland are complex personalities whose behaviors and beliefs do not always subscribe to the "good" politics we might want to read into them. But this is what allows us to read their literary texts as discursive artifacts of a western American literary history.

In the first two chapters of this volume I trace the ways sentimental narratives serve María Amparo Ruiz de Burton and Helen Hunt Jackson in reimagining the nation's liberal foundations. Brought together, Ruiz de Burton and Jackson help me to showcase the ways sentimental women writers responded to the sentimental limitations placed on late nineteenth-century women's writing. In chapter 1 I argue that Ruiz de Burton takes up the sentimental tradition to demand western American and Mexican American representative autonomy. While sentimentalism's foremost authors—Stowe, Catherine Maria Sedgwick, Helen Hunt Jackson—use the genre to draw national awareness to a number of regional issues as the nation expands, Ruiz de Burton's novels implicate these same dominant sentimental texts in the violent conquest of Mexican populations in the West. I consider Ruiz de Burton's two sentimental novels, *Who Would Have Thought It?* (1872) and *The Squatter and the Don* (1885), as they circulated within a mid-nineteenth-century American literary marketplace that thrived on romanticized depictions of the newly acquired western American territories. As a Mexican woman who chose to relocate to the United States and to marry a U.S. military general in the wake of the Treaty of Guadalupe Hidalgo, Ruiz de Burton foregrounds an antagonistic but conversational relationship to the United States' early imperialism, maturing capitalist economy, and the American West's up-and-coming literary scene. By evaluating her use of the popular sentimental romance novel, I recognize the nuances Ruiz de Burton applies to the genre's most important feature—the sentimental heroine. Pulling from Mary Louise Pratt, I argue that Ruiz de Burton deploys an autoethnographic version of the sentimental heroine alongside the genre's more conventional heroine to negotiate—rather than reject outright—the terms and conditions of liberal personhood and American citizenship. In so doing, Ruiz de Burton not only critiques the ways dominant literary representation proves detrimental for Californios' autonomy in the West, but she also highlights how the sentimental novel is a piece of the oppressive system wielded against white women as well. If Amy Kaplan has shown how middle-class white women located power in domesticating "foreign others" in the West, then chapter 1 of this volume acknowledges that the "foreign other" spoke against this domestication and, in the case of Ruiz de Burton, actively sought to reconstitute productive domestic identity.[50] My analysis works to show how Ruiz de Burton's complex network of female characters exposes the false promises the nation serves both women of color and white women through a rhetoric of domesticity as the growing nation further entrenches itself in exclusionary traditions to secure white male privilege.

I continue the discussion of sentimental liberalism in chapter 2 by considering Ruiz de Burton's contemporary Helen Hunt Jackson and her sentimental novel, *Ramona*. The chapter analyzes Jackson's genre move from her failed political treatise on Native American removal, *A Century of Dishonor* (1881), to the sentimentalized version of a similar story in *Ramona* as a means of applying pressure to progressive politics. Although there is no evidence to suggest that Jackson and Ruiz de Burton were aware of each other or read each other's works, this chapter posits that the relationship between Ruiz de Burton's hard-won readership and Jackson's commercial success in the literary marketplace reveals the imbalance in literary representation, as well as the liberal anxieties with which white literary progressives, such as Jackson, contended in crusading for their oppressed subjects. Despite scholarly conclusions that the parallels between Jackson's and Ruiz de Burton's novels "seem to have been purely coincidental as there is no evidence that Jackson knew of Ruiz de Burton nor that she read her work,"[51] there is evidence that Ruiz de Burton's and Jackson's San Diego associations overlapped, providing insight into the mechanisms through which Ruiz de Burton's novels were pushed to the fringes and Jackson's turned mainstream. Both Ruiz de Burton and Jackson were frequent correspondents of Ephraim W. Morse, one of the first and most prominent Anglo-American settlers in the San Diego region. Ruiz de Burton and Jackson wrote to Morse throughout the 1880s, suggesting at least one close connection between the two western American women writers. However, their experiences with Morse could not be more different, and their letters provide a telling story about the relationship between national literary production and the settler-colonial initiatives in the region.

Morse played a key role in San Diego's expansion, primarily in advocating for a railroad line to the city. According to the San Diego History Center, Morse "early learned the Spanish language and was regarded as a friend by the native population."[52] Given Morse's knowledge of the region and his supposed intimacy with native Californians, he proved invaluable to Jackson, who often solicited him for favors ranging from researching land titles to providing historical context to events such as the Temecula removal, which ended up featuring prominently in *Ramona*. It is ironic that at the same time Morse was helping Jackson raise awareness for the plight of the Native Americans in Southern California and to mythologize the Spanish-era history that Californios and their ranchos represented in the region, he was also ignoring Ruiz de Burton's letters and requests for help in securing ownership to her own land titles in California.[53] If, as Ruiz de Burton's novels show, the Mexican-American War stripped Californios of their economic and political power in the region, then figures like Morse and Jackson prematurely memorialized them by acknowledging their romantic history but denying their claims to the future.

Thus chapter 2 goes on to consider Jackson's colonial participation in literary manifestations of the western American region and her ambivalent approach to the nation's shifting notions of labor and domesticity in the post-emancipation era. By applying Jackson's archival materials to readings of her sentimental novel, I argue that the move from political treatise to sentimental novel reveals Jackson's and her larger society's anxiety over supposedly "progressive" changes in labor structures post-Reconstruction. Specifically the chapter utilizes Lauren Berlant's framework for reading sentimental texts and Lisa Lowe's *The Intimacy of Four Continents* to analyze a rather understudied character in the novel, the disenfranchised white southerner Aunt Ri, and her ignorant belief in American liberal democracy's ability to work for the oppressed. The chapter contributes to this volume's overall understanding of the dissociative powers of American liberal democracy as figures such as Aunt Ri and Jackson herself locate a liberal power in the continued oppression of people of color and immigrants.

By the time Sui Sin Far is writing three decades later, the American literary establishment has professionalized and uses this new specialized approach to writing to determine "good" from "bad" writing (also read "American" from "un-American" writing) along racial and gendered lines. Therefore chapters 3 and 4 move on to challenge dominant historical renderings of the Progressive and the civil rights eras, which have come to represent "progress" in the American cultural imagination. These chapters are critical of the rhetoric used to connote "progress," and they jointly argue that western American histories of Manifest Destiny and the pioneer spirit have corrupted "progress" for mid- and late-twentieth-century western Americans. In chapter 3 I consider progressive-era writer Sui Sin Far and her reaction to the white male writers who commandeered minority and regional literary representation in the name of democratizing American identity. To make the argument that Sui Sin Far's regional sketches manipulate realist tropes in order to reveal the colonizing impact American realism has on underrepresented populations (as opposed to the realist programs' claims to expanding American representation), I evaluate the role popular literature played in maintaining a rhetoric of American liberalism in a post-frontier American West. In an era when literary realism and its program of representing those previously underrepresented came to dominate national notions of "good" literature, Sui Sin Far continues to deride the genre, as Ruiz de Burton does sentimentalism, by making its liberal anxieties known. In this chapter I argue that Sui Sin Far's regional sketches intervene in the realist novel's program to democratize literature to show the ways it further entrenches popular culture in racist and sexist renderings of society's underrepresented populations. Through a consideration of Sui Sin Far's sketches, journalism, and autobiographical texts, I identify a pivotal moment in American literary history in which western American women writers combat the structures and systemic methods by which their societies extended them a compromised liberalism or a liberalism-with-limitations. Ultimately Sui Sin Far demonstrates the ways American liberal democracy, as expressed by realism, works against rather than for the nation's individuals.

Chapter 4 introduces Eva Rutland, a previously unstudied author from Sacramento, California. Born in 1917, Rutland grew up in Atlanta, Georgia, in a house her grandfather built after emancipation. The neighborhood was "a strange mixture of races and classes and creeds," and it was some distance from the all-Black neighborhood in which Rutland went to school and in which her family did most of their shopping and socializing.[54] Rutland graduated from Spelman College in 1937 before marrying Bill Rutland, who was just beginning his career as a civilian engineer for the Tuskegee Airmen. She describes her segregated apartment on the air force base as having "cement floors," over which she worried, "What if I should drop the baby?"[55] Once the air force integrated and decentralized, Rutland and her family were first relocated to Ohio and then to Sacramento, California, where they settled long term and enmeshed themselves in a thriving, middle-class Black community. Rutland started her writing career in the early 1950s, when her children were of school age. She was successful at getting a number of her fictional and nonfictional short stories published with women's magazines such as *Ladies Home Journal*, *Redbook*, and *Women's Day*. A few of these stories show up in altered forms in her maternal memoir, *When We Were Colored*, which was originally published by Abingdon, a Christian press, in 1964 under the title *The Trouble with Being a Mama*. The memoir was rather successful and remained in print up until the summer of 1972.

Throughout the late 1960s, as she dealt with an eye condition that caused her to go slowly blind, worked as a secretary for the California State Legislature, and helped her husband run for the school board, Rutland dedicated the majority of her writing efforts to a manuscript that was provisionally accepted for publication by Abingdon and titled "In Defense of Uncle Tom." The manuscript was ultimately declined by the press after it became apparent that the press and Rutland had different intentions for the project. In the late 1980s through the 1990s Rutland continued writing, but she turned to writing romance novels published by Harlequin Books. Although Rutland's agent once said she was "not a particularly prolific writer," Rutland published over twenty romance novels during this period and wrote two plays, one of which was selected to be performed at a Monterey, California, festival.[56] In 1999 Rutland contributed a novella, "Choices," to *Girlfriends*, a collection of stories by Black women published by Harper Paperbacks. *Girlfriends* was also a success and was nominated for the NAACP Image Award. In addition, Rutland received the Golden Pen Award for Lifetime Achievement in 2000, and in 2003 she published a 414-page semi-autobiographical novel, *No Crystal Stair*. Rutland continued to make appearances in Sacramento bookstores and on the local news up until her death in 2012.

As this brief biography indicates, Rutland was successful in publishing in several different genres and with a variety of publication platforms. She was a dynamic writer with a keen sense of audience and of the influence literature has to reach people of differing backgrounds and ideologies. However, Rutland remains unstudied in academic circles. Although the University of Oregon, Eugene, has housed Rutland's archive since the 1990s, as I am writing this, there has yet to be an academic publication on Rutland and her writing. Perhaps this is because

Rutland is a regional writer and, as Victoria Lamont suggests, the "study of women writers of the American West emerged from the margins of a marginal field" and often requires a great deal of archival and research work to locate out of print texts.[57] Or perhaps it is because Rutland's writing typically circulates within a maternal framework that narrates the everyday struggles of raising Black children and therefore is understood as trivial in comparison to the more assertive autobiographical writing of James Baldwin, Malcolm X, and Stokely Carmichael, also coming out of this era. Whatever the case, I introduce Rutland into the discussion of western American women writers and the literary identity of the West to emphasize the urgency with which women writers were responding to their male counterparts. Rutland's narrative may center the problems of mothers and the specific struggles of their children, but her deployment of Black motherhood in the West is a more complex documentation of the ways motherhood intersects with and is informed by Black womanhood, racial and class inequality, and the unyielding histories of race-based slavery and Jim Crow segregation.

Writing contemporaneously to Joan Didion—Sacramento's literary prodigy—Rutland describes her experiences moving from the Jim Crow South to the integrated American West and raising her Black children to navigate new forms of racism. Building on Black female theorists Patricia Hill Collins and Evelyn Brooks Higginbotham, the chapter locates Rutland within a tradition of Black women's autobiography, which finds political voice in motherhood. However, this chapter also takes a critical regionalist approach to Rutland's text by recognizing the adaptations Rutland makes to a Black woman's autobiographical tradition because of her specific situatedness in the geographic American West and within the West's color-blind sociopolitical climate while the rest of the nation battled over racial inequality. Rutland's experiential knowledge of the American South enables her to critique a mid-twentieth-century western American liberalism and progressivism by using her autobiographical platform to show how the region's claims to racial equality—supported by early integration initiatives and a color-blind approach to addressing racial injustice—are the consequences of rather than the exception to larger national histories of race-based slavery and segregation.

While Ruiz de Burton, Jackson, Sui Sin Far, and Rutland all met some degree of literary and political success (Ruiz de Burton posthumously won rights to her California land; Jackson's commercial success, *Ramona*, did have some effect on Native American policy after her death; Sui Sin Far prolifically contributed to regional and national magazines; and Rutland's memoir encouraged mid-twentieth-century white mothers across the nation to think differently about race), it is also always a compromised or limited success. As such, *California Dreams and American Contradictions* offers an archive of literary women's histories that deconstruct western American progressivism and reveal the nineteenth- and twentieth-century conflicts among liberal individualism, true equality, and national citizenship. But it also ends by highlighting the global reach western American regional narratives have well into our contemporary age.

As I began with Joan Didion, so too does this book end with Didion in the final chapter, which considers international iterations of the western frontier. Instead of offering a conclusion to this genealogical archive of western American women's literary history however, I offer Didion as a means of keeping these nineteenth- and early twentieth-century conversations open to avoid a premature foreclosure of the injustices and American contradictions they bring to light. In the conclusion I read Didion's 1967 nonfiction essay, "Slouching towards Bethlehem," alongside her 1977 novel, *A Book of Common Prayer*, to consider how even Didion's most globally minded fiction is influenced by a specifically western American brand of progressivism. "Slouching towards Bethlehem," Didion's first real literary success, is famous for its sharp critique of San Francisco, California's counterculture. In the essay Didion is concerned with the radicalization of America's youth and with what seems to her to be their undirected anger and "ignorant" understanding of the nation's problems. Didion's essay shows how western American progressivism has failed the nation, especially its youth, as well as the rest of the world. I argue that Didion's images of teenagers and children in "Slouching towards Bethlehem" preview the ways she represents American youth and global politics in *A Book of Common Prayer*, published ten years later. In the novel Didion explores the individual and global consequences of an American exceptionalism founded on western American progress. She acutely pinpoints new iterations of the frontier and the ways the United States has stretched western American narratives to encompass a new age of global expansion through capitalism and a military-industrial complex. But out of this reading, I posit that western American women have more to say and that this is a work-in-progress conversation that only becomes more urgent in our twenty-first-century moment as we contend with deep regional divisiveness and political extremism.

In the forward to Didion's latest publication, *South and West*, Nathaniel Rich situates Didion as "a warning unheeded."[58] Published in 2017, *South and West* is a collection of notes Didion wrote during her 1970s travels through the American South. It might seem strange that Didion's 1970s observations of the American South would find a publication outlet in 2017, but as Rich suggests, these notes predict much of the United States' twenty-first-century crises. The 1970s South Didion captures in these notes is, as Rich describes, "only reinforced by outside disapproval, particularly disapproval by the northern press. They have resisted with mockery, then rage, the collapse of the old identity categories" and "the premise that white skin should not be given special consideration. They have resisted new technology and scientific evidence of global ecological collapse."[59] These observations are familiar to a twenty-first-century United States that is now living out the consequences of this resistance. We are starting to see how the "force of this resistance has been strong enough to elect a president" and how it has fundamentally altered the nation's understanding of American liberal democracy.[60] In many ways Didion's *South and West* is a predecessor to Arlie Russell Hochschild's 2016 *New York Times* best seller, *Strangers in Their Own Land*. Like Didion, Hochschild leaves Berkeley, California, for the Gulf Coast out of alarm "at the increasingly hostile split in our nation."[61] She is in search of understanding about how an entire region of Americans could civicly act against their own interests. Hochschild names this "the great paradox," just as Didion names it the South's "contradictions." By bringing in Hochschild, I end *California Dreams and American Contradictions* by adding yet another western American woman's voice to the women's literary archive traced throughout the book. Hochschild's best-selling intellectual narrative of the South is the next iteration of western American despondency. *Strangers* moves beyond the liberal guilt expressed in much of Didion's speechlessness and seeks to find or generate, if need be, a common language that reconciles western American liberal idealism with the nation's illiberal histories. But as she seeks out this language, Hochschild must also reexamine her own role and thereby the West's role in "the great paradox." Hers is a lesson from which many of us could benefit and one that Ruiz de Burton, Jackson, Sui Sin Far, and Rutland all grapple with as they work to unravel the regional barriers to empathy that dominant narratives and literary programs help undergird.

1. "Autoethnographic" Heroines

María Amparo Ruiz de Burton's Sentimental Novels,
Who Would Have Thought It? *and* The Squatter and the Don

On August 14, 1895, the *New York Times* announced the death of Californio author María Amparo Ruiz de Burton in Chicago, Illinois. "Senora María de Burton, claimant to an immense estate in Mexico, which had been granted to her grandfather by the King of Spain for valiant services, died yesterday," the obituary begins. "For nearly a year she had lived in Chicago, carrying on negotiations for the sale of her heritage, which she valued at $5,000,000."[1] A late nineteenth-century reader of the *New York Times* would come to find from this obituary that in addition to her scandalous involvement in a legal battle over a Mexican estate, Ruiz de Burton was also the heroine of her very own romantic plot. During the Mexican-American War, the obituary continues, "General Henry S. Burton . . . captured Tedos [*sic*] Santos, the town in which she was living, fell in love with the heiress, and carried her away with the regiment. Six months later they were married."[2] In contrast to Ruiz de Burton, the fierce defender of her heritage, the obituary shifts to represent her as a romantic icon of the American West. She is a "beautiful Spanish girl" with "little knowledge of the English language" but who, after being "carried away" by Burton,

35

"entered a convent and gained a complete education" and "lived happily in New York City."[3] The sentimental language deployed here serves to romanticize the imperialistic violence also present in this telling of Ruiz de Burton's marriage. Although it is her obituary, the author makes Ruiz de Burton the passive subject—her husband "fell in love with [her]" (rather than "Ruiz de Burton fell in love with him"), and she was "carried away" to the East Coast, where, it is implied, she was made into a proper woman. The obituary ultimately delivers Ruiz de Burton to the reading public as a one-dimensional, if not fully objectified, sentimental heroine whose suffering terminated with her marriage to a prominent Anglo-American general.

It is conspicuous that the obituary does not mention Ruiz de Burton's literary ventures. Although she published two novels over the course of her life—*Who Would Have Thought It?* (1872) and *The Squatter and the Don* (1885)—the obituary forgoes mentioning these literary achievements. Instead she is remembered as a trophy of the Mexican-American War who, although she does complicate matters with her lawsuits, is heroically rescued by the American expansion west. This obituary is not in fact a eulogy for Ruiz de Burton's life but for the life of an American ideal. Written just two years after Frederick Jackson Turner declared the American frontier closed and consequently worried for the future of the American character, the obituary nostalgically remembers the opening of the frontier and reminds an anxious nation of its power. The writer features Ruiz de Burton as a sentimental device, much like Topsy in Harriet Beecher Stowe's *Uncle Tom's Cabin*, to propel the writer's actual mission—to reaffirm notions of American exceptionalism. Stowe deploys Topsy as a sentimental rendering of what Amy Kaplan refers to as the "process of domestication, which entails conquering and taming the wild, the natural, and the alien."[4] Eva, Stowe's sentimental heroine, effectively domesticates Topsy through her benevolent love rather than by physical violence. Even still, the novel remains problematically firm on the point that Topsy must be domesticated because her racialized identity is understood as "wild," "natural," and "alien," and therefore even Eva's benevolent love for Topsy is violent. Eva's domesticating force expands the nation to include Topsy only after Topsy has fully submitted to her designated role as a complacent and cooperative slave.

Topsy's outcome is not important to Stowe's novel. Rather, the novel places emphasis on Eva's modeling of sentimental domestication, which instructs the nation on how a post-slavery society might live up to the ideals of liberal democracy without sacrificing white privilege.

The *New York Times* writer of Ruiz de Burton's obituary tells a similar story of the recently closed frontier. In the obituary, Ruiz de Burton is important insofar as she is evidence of the nation's success in domesticating the diverse western American geographies and peoples. The writer presents a narrative that elides the violence in westward expansion by associating Ruiz de Burton's conquest with love. Out of love, General Burton removes Ruiz de Burton from the West and procures her a civilizing education in the East. The obituary is not interested in Ruiz de Burton's experiences from outside the nation, nor does it care to consider her literary attempts to represent a different side of the story. Just as Topsy is left to fade into the novel's background after Eva's heroic death, so too is Ruiz de Burton rendered an artifact from the past that will go on living in this recorded obituary as evidence of the nation's exemplary altruism. As such, the narrative is a commemoration of the nation's liberal triumphs as it has taken responsibility of, made room for, and educated an imperial subject.

The sentimental tradition has often been read as one concerned with social change. As other scholars have pointed out, the characteristic sentimental novel is written from the perspective of dominant culture on behalf of the nation's outcasts and its downtrodden. However, at the same time that the sentimental tradition looks to a more just future, it also looks to the past. As we see in Ruiz de Burton's obituary, sentimental language finds comfort in the future by memorializing what has passed. Therefore the sentimental novel found its popularity in antebellum America precisely because the nation mourned for its failure to realize the liberal democratic ideals it had assigned itself nearly a century before. Novels such as Stowe's are about abolition and the end of slavery, but underneath its cosmetic treatment of the issue is a deeper concern with the nation's struggles to live up to its founding ideologies. Stowe's novel memorializes a past promise of liberal achievement while it urges the nation toward a more liberal future. But this does not mean the novel is any less preoccupied with the tensions between the nation's liberal democratic aims and its obsession with social stratification and racial exclusivity. At the heart of the American sentimental tradition is a concern for keeping liberal democracy select. As I argue in this chapter, Ruiz de Burton's two novels deconstruct the ways dominant sentimental novels make liberal personhood exclusive. As meta-critiques of the popular genre, Ruiz de Burton's novels negotiate with the nation's democratic institutions and propose a restructuring of the nation's founding ideologies to account for a quickly globalizing world.

Many scholars are interested in the ways Ruiz de Burton makes room for Californios in the United States' preexisting racial hierarchies. The general consensus is that Ruiz de Burton uses the marriage plot—a premier sentimental trope—in order "to suture seemingly irreparable national, regional, ethnic, and even religious divides in order to posit an American future that includes the Californios."[5] Some scholars on Ruiz de Burton argue that because Ruiz de Burton stresses Californios' Spanish ancestry and therefore identifies Californios as white, she is not necessarily resisting American racism but using it to elevate Californio society within the nation. On the other side, there are also scholars who posit that "if [Ruiz de Burton] indicts American nationalism, she celebrates Mexican patriotism" and that Ruiz de Burton "is defending an economic order that originated among nineteenth-century Californios of Spanish/Mexican descent . . . that required little or no change to the social and gender hierarchy of pre-1848 Alta California."[6] This group of scholars finds Ruiz de Burton to be a sort of "Mexican patriot" who critiques American imperialism. And though there is indeed some truth to both claims, these arguments have largely been conceived out of frameworks that privilege nationalist renderings of belonging—to either "posit an American future that includes the Californios" or to staunchly support Mexican patriotism in face of American conquest. But Ruiz de Burton is not a nationalist in either the American or the Mexican sense. Her novels are less concerned with notions of national citizenship and more concerned with global iterations of liberal personhood and individual sovereignty as these notions are circulating worldwide and contending with global formations of race, gender, and labor. Recognizing the global rather than national implications of Ruiz de Burton's novels places American liberal discourse in relationship to the global renegotiations of liberal republicanism as the world confronted slavery and its contradictions at the same time that it implicates the acquisition of the American West in the nation's post-emancipation restructuring.

Ruiz de Burton wrote her two novels in the span of thirteen years, 1872 to 1885, during which time the United States was working to define its presence in the West and to reshape the American South. Both projects—westward expansion and southern reconstruction—applied pressure to American definitions of citizenship and civic inclusion. The nation now had to face a population of emancipated slaves previously denied their humanity at the same time it had to consider Mexican populations with their own complicated racial hierarchies in the West. The liberal notions upon which the nation was founded were revisited as the nation questioned how to manage these newly incorporated populations. U.S. requirements that an individual be white to qualify for citizenship became increasingly more important. The Fourteenth Amendment, ratified in 1866, was carefully written to account for Black individuals while also rhetorically leaving the possibility to restrict citizenship and naturalization to other ethnic groups. At the end of the Mexican-American War, certain communities of Mexicans—namely Californios—fell into a category of dispute. While the nation found some benefits to identifying Californios as white, there were also concerns that this would set a difficult precedent for future international acquisitions. For a nation hungry for global power, the concerns outweighed the benefits, and the 1848 Treaty of Guadalupe Hidalgo failed to identify Californios as white at the same time that it made promises to extend Californios' citizenship and protect their rights in the region. As Natalia Molina argues, the "failure to link whiteness to citizenship for Mexicans would become the Treaty's Achilles' heel, providing an opening for those who fought to make Mexicans ineligible for citizenship for decades to come."[7] It is at this important juncture, when the United States did a double take on Mexican American citizenship, that Ruiz de Burton's novels appear.

Ruiz de Burton's novels also appear amid the nation's gendered restructuring. At the same time the nation was reconceptualizing citizenship around race, it was also forming new sociopolitical ideologies around gender and family life. Thus the nation's incorporation of new and diverse identities through emancipation and expansion west also required a renegotiation of Anglo-American women's roles. Catherine Beecher's *Treatise on Domestic Economy* (1841) instructs nineteenth-century women on the "cult of domesticity," a program that encourages women to take a "subordinate" position to their husbands in order to ensure "the general good of all; so that each individual shall have his own interest, as well as the public benefit."[8] Beecher thus situates women's subordinated place in the nation as imperative to the nation's liberal mission. Beecher commends the nation for having "established, both by opinion and practice, that woman has an equal interest in all social and civil concerns" but assigns women the responsibility of protecting their interests through subordination.[9] She tells women that "in order to secure [them] the more firmly in all these privileges, it is decided, that, in the domestic relation, [they] take a subordinate station, and that, in civil and political concerns, [their] interests be . . . instrusted [sic] to the other sex, without [their] taking any part in voting, or in making and administering laws."[10] Women's liberal inclusion, according to Beecher, is predicated on their submission to their husbands and their devoted faith to the nation's male-dominated governing institutions. Beecher sustains this submission within a liberal framework by suggesting that subordination is a choice. She differentiates between a forced subordination—slavery—and Anglo-American women's subordination by explaining that "no woman is forced to obey any husband but the one she chooses for herself; nor is she obliged to take a husband, if she prefers to remain single."[11] Beecher maintains the façade of female choice and therefore protects notions of American liberalism by implying that women are not forced to submit but *choose* to do so in service of their best interest and the best interests of the "general good of all." But as Charlotte Perkins Gilman argues in *Women and Economics*, women's only chance of survival in the nation is to marry.[12] Therefore, a woman's choice is reduced to that of whom to marry, not whether she should marry at all. Likewise, marriage becomes synonymous with a woman's submission and her pressured consent to a "subordinated station."[13]

The women's culture Beecher outlines in her treatise became the central principle of the sentimental novel, which also rose to popularity during these decades of racial, ethnic, and gender restructuring. In many ways the sentimental novel is an instruction manual on women's conditional liberal existence because it privileges marriage, motherhood, and women's submission to national ideologies of race and gender. Women's suffering and emotional labor is featured as a means of celebrating the sentimental heroine's eventual choice to submit through marriage and motherhood by the end of the novel. Certainly the sentimental novel navigates nineteenth-century women's culture to find arenas in which Anglo-American women can exert their civic influence, as Jane Tompkins argues *Sensational Designs*. At the same time, however, the genre also sustains a version of femininity that stakes its claim to the nation through an attachment to white men. Ruiz de Burton's sentimental novels challenge American women's culture and pinpoint this culture's intimacy with the nation's paternalistic imperialism in the West.

Ruiz de Burton's first book, *Who Would Have Thought It?*, is an East Coast domestic novel set to the backdrop of the impending Civil War. Ruiz de Burton treats the East Coast drawing room as the domestic "contact zone" through which her heroine, Lola Medina, becomes articulated by her Yankee caregivers. The novel begins with Dr. Norval, a Yankee doctor, returning to his New England home after many years exploring and collecting rocks, plants, and other curiosities from the American West. With him he brings the dark-skinned Lola, a Mexican girl he helps rescue from the Native American Indian tribe that captured her and her mother during a raid on their Mexican village. Norval's family, rather ironically for a Protestant abolitionist family, meets the young Lola with racist disgust and refers to her as another of the doctor's "specimen[s]."[14] However, when Mrs. Norval discovers that her husband is also the guardian to Lola's large fortune, her attitude toward the girl changes. Soon after his return, Dr. Norval exiles himself to Africa because his criticism of the United States fighting against itself in a civil war is considered traitorous to the Union, and after his long absence, he is assumed dead. The rest of the novel traces Mrs. Norval's schemes to take hold of Lola's wealth; interfere in the romantic relationship forming between Lola and her son, Julian; and gain the romantic affections of her partner-in-crime, Reverend Hackwell. Meanwhile, Lola's skin begins to lighten as the reader learns that her skin was dyed by the Native American Indian chief to distract Anglo settlers from noticing and rescuing her and her mother.

While Ruiz de Burton's first novel critiques American imperialism's movement from east to west by reversing the novel's movement to that of west to east, her second novel, *The Squatter and the Don*, more explicitly features the American West and the land grab that occurred in the region in the latter decades of the nineteenth century. The novel's many twists and turns, didactic digressions, and literary mashups have particularly stumped scholars on how to understand the novel's many competing claims. As Rosaura Sánchez and Beatrice Pita point out, *Squatter* is separated into two paralleling plots: the historical, which traces Californio Don Mariano Alamar's litigious process of securing rights to his land, and the romantic, which follows the love affair between Mercedes, Don Mariano's younger daughter, and Clarence, William Darrell's son.[15] The novel begins with William Darrell and his family relocating to the Alamar rancho, which is understood to be a rejected land claim and available for Anglo-American settlement. The novel traces the many obstacles Don Alamar runs into in securing his land, including the loss of his property to squatters and the corrupt mismanagement of his affairs in the U.S. justice system. These obstacles, though part of the historical plot, are not completely separate from the romance plot between Clarence and Mercedes, whose relationship runs into corresponding obstacles that result in the delay of their marriage. *The Squatter and the Don* makes a point to be overtly political, didactic even, but it is also always under cover. It is immersed in an American cultural moment where descriptions of a largely untouched western American geography feed into descriptions of the native populations. It is a novel that directly responds to an Anglo-American literary establishment that portrays the West as romantically decayed, vulnerable, and primed for the taking.

Both novels are sentimental performances of American Manifest Destiny. However, unlike other sentimental narratives that deal in American westward expansion (Maria Susanna Cummins's *The Lamplighter*, Susan Warner's *The Wide, Wide World*), Ruiz de Burton's novels feature Californio heroines. While other sentimental novels feature Anglo-American heroines who assert their value to the nation against a series of underprivileged characters, Ruiz de Burton's heroines reframe mainstream sentimental narratives that claim conquered subjects need to be rescued or, in the very least, civilized. Ruiz de Burton's novels are autoethnographic manipulations of the popular sentimental novel and, as such, negotiate the terms dominant literary culture uses to represent conquered subjects and geographies. The American West is a "contact zone," to use Mary Louise Pratt's term, within which we see competing histories vying for legitimacy. However, the American West is not just the site of colonial struggle; it is also one of literary struggle. Ruiz de Burton's novels engage in this literary struggle to show how the late nineteenth-century American literary marketplace is another iteration of the "contact zone," one that transcends regional boundaries and brings the asymmetrical meetings, clashes, and grapplings to the American East as well.[16]

More specifically, I argue that Ruiz de Burton responds to the imperial impulses in dominant narratives of the West with autoethnographic sentimental heroines who reshape the genre's conventions and posit alternative western histories. Pratt refers to "autoethnographies" as "instances in which colonized subjects undertake to represent themselves in ways that *engage with* the colonizer's terms."[17] Pratt uses "autoethnography" and "autoethnographic expression" to address how the colonized subject is in "dialogue with those metropolitan representations" of a region and its populations.[18] When the autoethnographer's perspective is privileged over that of the European ethnographer, emphasis is placed on the colonized subjects' agency and competitive power rather than on their dependency and primitiveness. For an author such as Ruiz de Burton, who is both colonized and colonizer, Pratt's autoethnographic framework offers a new point of entry into Ruiz de Burton's novels and a way to make sense of their competing impulses.

Ruiz de Burton's Californio heroines reassert perspectives and histories that dominant genres ignore in their efforts to justify American imperialism and encourage westward expansion. As mentioned, Stowe's Eva is a conventional example of the sentimental heroine with whom readers "have always been able to identify with . . . even while they worship, or weep, at her shrine. She does not demand the respect we accord a competitor. She is not extraordinarily gifted, or at least she is young enough so that her talents have not had the chance to take on formidable proportions."[19] As a sentimental trope, Eva is both relatable but exalted, admired but unthreatening. Despite her hyper-religious character, "Little Eva doesn't actually convert anyone. Her sainthood is there to precipitate our nostalgia and our narcissism. We are meant to bestow on her that fondness we reserve for the contemplation of our own softer emotions."[20] The sentimental heroine reaches its pinnacle in Eva because she functions to turn the readers' gaze inside themselves rather than toward the public world. The Anglo-American female audience reading *Uncle Tom's Cabin* mourns for Eva and becomes inspired to silently suffer within the "softer emotions" of their own religiosity and good intentions. Ruiz de Burton's Lola Medina in *Who Would Have Thought It?* and Mercedes Alamar in *The Squatter and the Don* are thus unconventional from the very first pages of their respective novels because they are not relatable to the white, middle-class women reading sentimental fiction. Lola's and Mercedes's ethnic and Catholic identity, not to mention their origins in the West, set them apart and confuse the genre expectations, which would conventionally place them in the background as domestic servants or, at the very most, as the romanticized representatives of the western region's need for eastern American civilizing efforts and rescue. Rather than serving as the vehicles through which Anglo-American women assert their liberty, Lola and Mercedes challenge these more conventional sentimental heroines and resist their rescue and domestication.

As Ann Douglas indicates, the sentimental tradition has been critiqued as excessive. This argument suggests that the genre stimulates emotion to pacify a sense of liberal guilt but does little to incite real action or change in its audience. As a central principle of the sentimental novel, the heroine mourns for those less fortunate than her—usually a racial or ethnic other—but is bound to a strict social code that restricts her capability to act or sometimes even speak out beyond her mourning. As Elizabeth Maddock Dillon argues, the sentimental heroine's mourning "enables the *public* articulation" of what has been popularly theorized as the private sphere.[21] Through the sentimental novel's display of grief, which, since the novel is an openly circulating publication, is understood to be a public display of grief, the private sphere is constituted in tandem with the public sphere and is used to manage the distribution of liberal identity. Both Dillon and Lisa Lowe argue that the intimate realm of domestic life is an important prerequisite of liberal personhood. In *The Intimacy of Four Continents* Lowe traces how, when a society terminates legal slavery, there follows a reconstitution of personhood through domesticity. Those with access to interiority and privacy through domesticity are recognized as possessing a personhood capable of liberal behavior while those who do not have access to domesticity are understood as incapable of liberal behavior. New forms of race-based labor, such as migratory labor, and new definitions of domesticity, such as those described by Beecher, restrict access to heteronormative interiority, and therefore the nation finds ways of denying racial and ethnic communities liberal personhood.

It is important, then, that the sentimental heroine's mourning is not for herself but for another, whose inhumanity is registered against the sentimental heroine's excessive humanity. By placing her Californio heroines alongside a more conventional archetype, Ruiz de Burton performs the contradictions in an American liberal ideology that holds women as the gatekeepers to liberal personhood but that also fundamentally denies them a seat at the democratic table. Women's capacity to feel constitutes their personhood, but because women are understood to lack emotional restraint, they are also recognized to be dependent upon male reasoning and are therefore unsuited to make liberal decisions that account for the greater good. That is, rather than defying liberalism by behaving selfishly—as certain of the founding fathers worried—women were understood to behave unselfishly to the point that their behavior might inflict harm upon themselves to satisfy their mourning for an unfortunate other.[22] Women's emotional power is recognizably threatening to the privileged place of Anglo-Americans in the nation in the nineteenth century, and as a consequence, the cult of motherhood arises to justify the inclusion of women into Anglo-American society through their very exclusion from democratic identity. They are relegated to the governing of family matters that, though thought to indirectly influence public behavior, place restrictions on their influence nonetheless. Popular domestic doctrines such as "the cult of domesticity" functioned to reinforce an American individualism at the family level. In encouraging women to think about moral matters as they impacted their own families, these popular doctrines also dissuaded women from critically engaging with the consequences their moral teachings had on the world at large. Sentimental literatures also failed to register these potentially harmful consequences. For instance, Eva's martyred death in Stowe's novel still does not realize the abolition of slavery but instead changes the way the family treats the slaves it continues to control. Her power is restricted to what occurs within the family and has little impact on national institutions sanctioned by the pseudo-democratic process, regardless of what the popular domestic doctrines of the era might say. In fact, Eva's domestic advocacy for kinder treatment toward the family slaves only serves to support southern arguments that the majority of slave masters were benevolent and that Black slaves were happy with their enslavement.

Ruiz de Burton's cultural positioning as a colonized woman of color, entering American society through her marriage to a prominent Anglo-American general, positions her to see the slippages between the cult of domesticity and American liberal democracy. Originally from Baja California, Ruiz de Burton was one of the Baja Californians who took advantage of the U.S. government's offer to relocate them to the United States when it was determined that Baja California would remain part of Mexico. It was shortly after this relocation to Monterey, California, that Ruiz de Burton married Henry S. Burton, the military general who led the invasion of her Mexican village. The couple then moved east while Burton served in the Civil War, giving Ruiz de Burton the opportunity to enmesh herself with prominent politicians and leaders of both the Union and the Confederacy, including President Abraham Lincoln and Confederate president Jefferson Davis. After her husband's death in 1869, Ruiz de Burton returned to San Diego, California, where she wrote her novels and began litigation over her estates, a project that would remain unfinished at the time of her death. Through her social connections in the East and her litigious projects in the West, Ruiz de Burton became well versed in both American drawing-room etiquette and a political rhetoric maneuvered to protect an imperial nation. The sentimental novel is thus an ideal outlet for Ruiz de Burton to negotiate what she clearly came to see as the nation's competing loyalties and to liberate the western region from the era's nationalist discourses of Manifest Destiny and American exceptionalism.

In a review of Ruiz de Burton's first, anonymously published novel, *Who Would Have Thought It?*, Ruiz de Burton is once again discussed as a sentimental heroine. In "A Native, Californian, Authoress,—A Literary Incognito Lost in an Interview—A New Sensation for the Public," a reviewer from the San Francisco *Daily Alta California* writes of meeting Ruiz de Burton upon the steamer *California* while in the company of the Texas Pacific Railway party. The reviewer discusses with Ruiz de Burton the mysterious authorship of the novel, to which Ruiz de Burton is represented as coyly trying to dismiss. However, the reviewer traps Ruiz de Burton into outing herself as the author. When asked if she has read the book, Ruiz de Burton responds:

"'Read It?' No! Yes! Why, of course I have!"

The manner of the answer and a little attendant embarrassment caused the bachelor to look at the charming widow with some surprise and awakened a feeling of curiosity. "Excuse me for repeating your words, Mrs. Burton"; he cautiously ventured to remark; "'but of course I have' seems to imply that you have some particular interest in the work." He was rather rude in his scrutinizing way of looking and speaking. The ruse, however, succeeded. "Why! That's my book! No! Well, there, now, I didn't mean to tell you; but you know it now."[23]

The review plays out like a scene from a sentimental novel in which the heroine is seduced into confessing her love for the novel's hero. However, instead of confessing her love, Ruiz de Burton confesses her authorship. It is a moment of imperial violation in which the sentimental narrative, which situates Ruiz de Burton as "the charming widow" and the newspaper reviewer as "the bachelor," is conflated with a scene of conquest driven by the "[bachelor's] surprise and awakened feeling of curiosity" in Ruiz de Burton. Ruiz de Burton is forced to give up a part of herself—her authorship—at the behest of the reviewer, who then capitalizes off this conquest by publishing it in the newspaper.

Ruiz de Burton pleads with the reviewer to protect her secrecy. She expresses concern that "they [the public] know that English is not my native language, . . . and they would say that my expressions partake of the Spanish idiom and that my English is not good. . . . I only wrote this to see how I saw it in print."[24] For Sánchez and Pita, this dialogue reveals the reviewer's violent manipulation of Ruiz de Burton.[25] And so it does. However, this review also reveals Ruiz de Burton's acute awareness for the rhetorical tactics wielded against her and provides insight into how she responds.

Ruiz de Burton's plea should be critically read within the context of her documented interactions with dominant Anglo-American society. To think of Ruiz de Burton as having no agency in this moment is to oversimplify her position and to underestimate her fluency in nineteenth-century dominant American culture. We can surmise from reading Ruiz de Burton's letters that she had few problems or insecurities about writing in fluent English. Moreover, she was representing herself in court and writing up her own legal documents due to her inability to secure her lawyers' attention. Rather than expressing her language insecurity, this moment in the review draws the reviewer's—and, by extension, society's—attention to the incoherent arguments used to discredit Californio participation in dominant society. Ruiz de Burton rearticulates the common misconceptions Anglo-American readers have about Californios back to them to show the inaccuracies in their assumptions and the palpable racism and sexism they serve in institutionalizing their misconceptions and assumptions. Ruiz de Burton points out that an Anglo-American audience "would think" it sees errors in her English not because they are there but because that is what it expects to find, and therefore the documented interaction between Ruiz de Burton and her reviewer calls out how literary conventions and expectations are arbitrarily prescribed by mainstream society's misconceptions and assumptions. As such, Ruiz de Burton redirects the stereotype to say more about her Anglo-American reviewer than about herself.

Ruiz de Burton is aware of her society's expectation that as a Californio woman, she is to be the exploited subject, not the author, of sentimental novels. But as this review of her first novel suggests, Ruiz de Burton manipulates these expectations and takes advantage of the dominant culture's consumption of popular literary forms to translate them back to this audience in new terms and from new perspectives. Anticipating the representational license this review would take, Ruiz de Burton performs the sentimental heroine in her conversations with the reviewer as a means to take control over her representative power. She feigns a feminine embarrassment and confusion at being asked if she has read the novel, stumbling: "No! Yes! Why, of course I have" and "Why! That's my book! No! Well, there, now, I didn't mean to tell you." The sentimental tradition is already one built on powerfully subversive characteristics. Jane Tompkins argues that the women of the sentimental tradition "make submission 'their boast' not because they enjoyed it, but because it gave them another ground on which to stand, a position that, while it fulfilled the social demands placed upon them, gave them a place from which to launch a counterstrategy against their worldly masters that would finally give them the upper hand."[26] Submission is a powerful tool in this respect. Women's "subordinated position" can serve the sentimental woman writer and the sentimental heroines she writes into being as a means of gaining "the upper hand" and exerting a degree of power in an otherwise oppressive situation. In choosing to submit to the role society prescribes her, the sentimental woman writer and her sentimental heroines reassert a representative authority. To submit to a subordinated role is to also avoid the unknown consequences and possible representational violence that society uses to force women back into their sanctioned space. Submission may be a small choice, but it *is* a choice women are at liberty to make nonetheless. As we see in the review of her first novel, Ruiz de Burton chooses to make submission her "boast." As much as the reviewer is exploiting Ruiz de Burton for his own benefit, Ruiz de Burton is also exploiting this reviewer and his misconceptions about women and Californios to generate talk around her novel. As it turns out, the anonymity under which Ruiz de Burton published was not intended to remain anonymous at all but was meant to reveal itself as her submissive "boast" against nineteenth-century literary practices that relegated her to the shadows of their narratives and plot structures. In this sense, choosing to be the sentimental heroine, however one-dimensional and excessive that role might be, provides Ruiz de Burton with a stage upon which she can act out.

But for an ethnic woman in American society, submitting to society's expectations is more complicated than for her Anglo-American counterparts and requires more literary finesse. There are more demands placed on Ruiz de Burton's identity, and she must consider what roles she is to play as a woman, as an ethnic woman, and as an imperial subject. But often, to Ruiz de Burton's noted frustration, these roles contradict one another or compete for dominance.[27] If Ruiz de Burton submits to society's expectations of middle-class womanhood, for instance, such a submission directly defies society's expectations of her ethnic identity. This is why the San Francisco reviewer finds it particularly newsworthy that Ruiz de Burton authored *Who Would Have Thought It?* It isn't so interesting that this sentimental text is authored by a woman. That, according to gender roles, was very likely. However, as Ruiz de Burton articulates in her feigned fears of being thought incompetent in English, it is shocking to this nineteenth-century society that a *Californio* woman could write such a novel or that an imperial subject could so fluently tap into an American literary tradition. Ruiz de Burton's novels thus make submission their "boast," but they also speak back to the inconsistencies and polarities with which she must contend as a Californio woman in American society.

Likewise, Ruiz de Burton's two sentimental novels feature Californio heroines who, recognizing the submissive "boast" of their more conventional counterparts, "boast" back to draw attention to the genre's incongruencies. As autoethnographic translations of the conventional sentimental heroine, Lola and Mercedes interact with conventional plots and character archetypes from different access points and perspectives than dominant readers might expect. As reflections of more conventional heroines, Lola and Mercedes reveal dominant society's fears and anxieties, as Ruiz de Burton does in her encounter with the San Francisco reviewer. Ruiz de Ruiz de Burton's sentimental heroines function in much the same way conventional heroines do; they draw upon the sympathies of the reader to pose questions about social institutions and to mourn for an unreconciled past. Ruiz de Burton draws upon "the colonizer's own terms" to reach a dominant audience, but in their unrelatability, Lola and Mercedes also force the white female readers' gaze away from their own emotional fulfillment and redirect that gaze to the outside world. As readers find themselves sympathizing with Lola and Mercedes, Ruiz de Burton translates tropological sentimental scenarios into scenes of global violence that leave the reader little room to emotionally cope and ascertain closure.

In the first few pages of *Who Would Have Thought It?*, Ruiz de Burton deploys her characters and settings in strategic ways that encourage readers to read from multiple, competing perspectives at once. For instance, the reader's first glimpse of the Norval family is from outside and through the front window of their humble New England home. From the perspective of a nosy neighbor, the reader spots the two Norval daughters, Mattie and Ruth, waiting at the window for their father's arrival after four years of traveling in the western territories. Mattie, the younger and less refined of the two, has her face "flattened against the window-pane so that it had lost all human shape," while the socialite Ruth is "rocking herself in a chair, reading a fashion magazine" in a most disinterested way.[28] In a stylistic move that reverses the perspective of the scene, Ruiz de Burton then ushers us into the house, where we listen to the two girls poke fun at the same nosy neighbor with whom they were just standing outside. As Mattie and Ruth trade puns on this neighbor's unfortunate name, Mrs. Cackle, we are introduced to the novel's Californio heroine, Lola Medina. Again we first glimpse Lola through a window, but this time it is we, the readers, who are on the inside and Lola who is on the outside of the Norval house. Alongside Mrs. Norval and her daughters, we watch Dr. Norval and a "mysterious figure in [a] bright-red shawl" descend from a wagon and "proceed towards the gate, the doctor again tenderly throwing his arm around the female in the shawl,—for it was a female: this fact Mrs. Norval had discovered plainly enough."[29]

This scene is at once an appropriation of a common sentimental trope and a translation of it. Kaplan argues that "many domestic novels open at physical thresholds—such as windows or doorways—to problematize the relation between interiors and exteriors."[30] Kaplan goes on to argue that these thresholds are important to sentimental plots as they "are propelled in part by the effort to reconstitute the domestic sphere, both by enlarging its domain beyond the narrow definition of familial bloodlines and by purging it of the foreign bodies this expansion incorporates."[31] Through these permeable door and window spaces the outside and the inside meet. They are, as Pratt would call them, "contact zones" within which cultural exchanges occur and power relations are asserted. The typical sentimental novel, through the "private sphere of female subjectivity" reasserts "narratives of nation and empire" and places the Anglo-American heroine in a position of power over the "foreign" other.[32] Ruiz de Burton, though she does recognize this threshold as an initial site of struggle, confuses "narratives of nation" and thereby leaves the reader unsure of who holds more power over whom. There is no closure in this scene, and power relations are left undefined as they never would be in the more mainstream sentimental novels circulating in the literary market. Ruiz de Burton deploys the threshold trope in a way that forces us to ask exactly who is "domestic," or "inside," and who is "foreign," on the "outside." By first placing the reader on the outside, viewing the "insiders" critically for their unladylike behavior and their superficial obsession with fashion magazines, Ruiz de Burton complicates what it means that the reader then joins the "insiders" to view Lola in the "outside." Ruiz de Burton incorporates the reader into the scene as a spectator character and leaves us unsure who benefits from this domestic expansion and who needs to be "purged" from it. As readers, we don't know with whom we are supposed to align and sympathize—is it the misbehaved Norval daughters, or is it the dark and "mysterious figure in the bright red shawl"? It begs the question: if from out there we, the readers, were critically watching the Norval girls, then isn't it also likely that Lola is viewing them, and now us, just as critically? Ruiz de Burton begins the novel at this window threshold to destabilize what the reader knows about dominant literary tropes and to deny readers the safety they find in sentimental conventions. By placing readers at once on the "inside" and the "outside," Ruiz de Burton also complicates what they think about the American social hierarchy at the time of imperial expansion. As such, Ruiz de Burton guides her readers into themselves as they explore the sentimental portrayals of gendered and racial politics.

In Ruiz de Burton's novels, readers still confront the expected sentimental narratives, but they do so from unexpected perspectives that create an uncomfortable intimacy between readers and the "othered" characters typically deployed as plot devices or as local color background. For instance, the threshold scene places Lola in competition with Mrs. Norval, the novel's more conventional sentimental heroine, and reorients women's subordination as an act of liberal renunciation. Ruiz de Burton situates the white Norval women in conversation with Lola to enact a dialogue around notions of female piety, virtuosity, and maternalism and to reflect back to white women the ways these notions restrict their democratic participation rather than expand it. Mrs. Norval is described as having "high principles," including a pious frugality, and stands in as the novel's "great abolitionist" who "doesn't mind negroes."[33] Like other conventional sentimental heroines, Mrs. Norval is rescued from a modest family history by an educated, hardworking man. Mrs. Norval "lived on a small farm," where she "put up pickles, and made butter and apple-sauce" until her "twentieth year, when one morning,—a Saturday morning,—as she was counting the eggs to send to market, a young man, dressed as a college boy" made her acquaintance and "fell heels over head in love" with her.[34] Mrs. Norval's history acts out a prominent sentimental fantasy in which the devout and self-sacrificing maiden is rewarded with an upwardly mobile future through an equally charming, though lonely, young man. She is rescued from her provinciality, taken to the city, and exalted to the privileged role of mother, where, supposedly, her greatest purpose is served. With Mrs. Norval's character, Ruiz de Burton iterates a popular sentimental heroine trope in which Mrs. Norval's commendable patience and suffering ultimately end when she submits to marriage and is thereby inducted into an appropriate public space from which she can more effectively perform her maternalism and religious devotion.

The novel's nuance is in how Ruiz de Burton places Mrs. Norval's history in contrast to Lola's history. At the start of the novel, when Dr. Norval brings Lola home to his wife and daughters, he promises that Lola "is only ten years old; but her history is already more romantic than that of half of the heroines of your trashy novels."[35] Lola stands in contrast to the conventional heroines in the "trashy novels" the Norval women read, but Ruiz de Burton also positions Lola against the Norval women, who, in reading those novels, place value on the sentimental histories associated with them and contribute to a women's culture steeped in nationalist violence. With Lola, Ruiz de Burton rearticulates the sentimental novel's romance plot—what we might call the sentimental heroine's origin story—and instigates a conversation about popular representations of women's culture. In addition to rescuing his wife from her small family farm, Dr. Norval also rescues Lola from Native American captivity. The contrast draws attention to the rhetorical differences that racialize the otherwise similar rescue narratives. While dominant notions of the sentimental genre situate Mrs. Norval's rescue from rural existence as a reward for her piety and as a sign of her moral superiority, Lola's rescue from the West is shrouded in dominant society's assumptions that she is inferior and primitive. The Norval women greet Lola as if she is another "specimen" Dr. Norval has collected on his travels West.[36] Mrs. Norval, exasperated at her husband's "idiosyncrasy . . . for collecting all sorts of rocks," surmises that he has "exhausted the mineral kingdom, [and] is about to begin with the animal, and this [Lola] is our first specimen."[37] The Norval women understand Lola as an artifact of the American West and consider her relocation from the West to the East a consequence of Dr. Norval's eccentric obsession with what they understand to be the uncivilized geography. And even Dr. Norval—who appears to defend Lola and "evidently had bestowed great care" toward her[38]—shores up the imperial violence in this scene by telling Reverend Hackwell that "I,—a good-for-nothing Democrat, who don't believe in Sambo, but believe in Christian charity and human mercy,—I feel pity for the little thing."[39] Dr. Norval rescues Lola out of pity. But pity, like love, is a self-interested emotion that can be used to justify imperial behavior.

The "pity" Dr. Norval expresses for Lola distorts the love he expressed for his young bride and unearths new realities about the sentimental romance plot that otherwise goes unnoticed. In rescuing Lola, Dr. Norval satisfies his "good-for-nothing" democratic spirit, pays into his "Christian charity," and alleviates his "pity for the little thing." Lola, on the other hand, is thrust into an East Coast domestic space, a space supposedly more civilized than the West but one that proves just as hostile as Native American captivity. Mrs. Norval, rescued to satisfy the "inconsolable" bachelor's loneliness, is also installed in the

New England domestic space and indoctrinated in a number of "civilizing" social patterns.[40] Dr. Norval's rescue of both heroines is about his own needs (his charity and his loneliness), and the emotions he uses to motivate his rescue of each heroine (pity and love) are undergirded by a white savior complex that wishes to see each heroine in a more "civilized" setting over which he ultimately has control.

Lola's placement in the plot alongside Mrs. Norval certainly expresses a colonized perspective on dominant genre tropes, but she also serves to reflect back to a dominant audience the ways such genre conventions also dictate Anglo-American femininity. If nineteenth-century women's culture extends middle-class Anglo-American women a degree of influence through their imagined moral superiority to men, then that moral superiority is only imagined as it complies with Anglo-male notions of propriety. Mrs. Norval, the quaint farm girl, is only extended such influence after she is established in the New England home and perched to manage the household affairs, including household budgets, children, and the family's religious devotion. Ultimately these mandates on her identity lead to her madness as they stifle her human impulses and conflict with her womanly desires. The process by which Mrs. Norval becomes a respectable woman in society is, as Kaplan suggests in "Manifest Domesticity," the very definition of domestication, and thus Ruiz de Burton flips the script on dominant gender roles to show how women only superficially hold power within their roles as household matrons and mothers. Women's liberty is but a farce, conjured through a sentimental language that the nation deploys to recruit women in their own submission.

At the same time, Lola's rescue reframes the white savior narrative to show how dominant understandings of suffering, violence, and civilizing are imbricated in nationalist histories of Anglo-American domination. Recall that sentimental novels are always about their Anglo-American protagonists. The emotional labor sentimental protagonists exert for suffering characters (slaves, immigrants, the working class) is explored in the conventional sentimental novel for what it offers white society, not for how it ultimately impacts the subjects of that emotional work. That is, it is not important to the dominant sentimental novel how "othered" characters experience Anglo-American sentiment, only that, in expressing their emotional capacity to suffer for another unlike themselves, Anglo-American protagonists *feel* themselves changed. In the case of Ruiz de Burton's novel, she shows how the sentimental novel is also always about Anglo men, even while it features female characters and is often written by a female author. Dr. Norval *feels* his change by rescuing Lola. His pity for her reassures his sense of having done good. But Ruiz de Burton elevates Lola to a second heroine of the novel in order to translate Dr. Norval's pity into the violence that it is. As the cult of domesticity dictates, now that Lola has been delivered to the East Coast domestic space, the onerous task to see to Lola's civilizing falls upon Mrs. Norval, the household's mistress. Ultimately Mrs. Norval attempts to "regulate" Lola's presence in her home by sending Lola to sleep in the servants' quarters with her Irish cook and chambermaid. Despite Lola's having spent the first ten years of her life in Native American captivity in the West, the New England servants' quarters prove too violent for her to remain. She "refused to share the bed of either of the two servants," watches in horror as the two Irish women shed their clothes for the night, and cringes as she is offered only a "blackened pillow" to make her sleep on the floor more comfortable."[41] Lola ends up fleeing the loud snores of the two Irish women and spends the night curled up on a rug outside Mrs. Norval's bedroom with the family dog.

No doubt this scene is evidence of Ruiz de Burton's indoctrination in American racism. Her depictions of Irish servants reflect dominant society's prejudices and problematically undergird the white superiority with which Ruiz de Burton writes Lola's character. But the scene also questions the ways dominant Anglo-American society defines civilized behavior versus barbarous behavior. At the center of this New England household, Lola faces a barbarism she did not face in the West. Her suffering in the servants' quarters is so intense that it impels her to flee, flight that neither she nor her mother attempted in Native American captivity. Simultaneously to Lola's encounter with the Irish servants, Dr. Norval is upstairs in his bedroom relating the story of Lola's discovery to his wife. While Lola "groped her way along the hall" in search of a place to sleep—"anywhere, only as far from the Irish-women as possible"[42]—Dr. Norval tells Mrs. Norval that regardless of her captivity, Lola's own mother kept the most pristine domestic space. Lola's mother's "surroundings were cheerless enough to kill any civilized woman," Dr. Norval says, "but the bedclothes, I noticed, were as white as snow, and everything about her was clean and tidy."[43] By placing this scene in temporal simultaneity with Lola's encounter in the servants' quarters, Ruiz de Burton questions whether Lola was truly saved. She places the white savior's story—one that articulates Lola's mother's qualifications for rescue through a New England sense of domestic propriety—in conversation with Lola's experience of that rescue. In consequence, notions of safety and vulnerability and "civilized" and "barbarous" collapse in the novel to emphasize dominant society's misunderstandings about the West and its native populations. Rather than upholding a nationalist timeline that places the conquered West in the primitive past and the American East in the progressive future, Lola's history suggests that Anglo-American culture has degraded rather than progressed as a consequence of its moves west. At the same moment the Irish servant hands Lola a "blackened pillow," Dr. Norval explains to Mrs. Norval that Lola is accustomed to sleeping on clean bed linens, "white as snow." While Dr. Norval tells Mrs. Norval that Indian captivity was "cheerless enough to kill any civilized woman," Lola cries for her deceased mother and is "almost frantic with terror and desolation, and almost stifling with the foulness of the air."[44] From Lola's perspective, Ruiz de Burton redeploys an Anglo-American rhetoric of the West to describe the New England home as terrifying, desolate, and foul. Lola may have been rescued from Native American captivity, but it is clear that her new situation in New England society is not any better.

Anne Goldman reads *Who Would Have Thought It?* as a "revision of the captivity narrative," in which the native, Lola, in this case, is captured by East Coast society.[45] Indeed, as Goldman suggests, Lola moves from Native American captivity in the West to a drawing room captivity in the East. Her life is defined by captivity, and her sentimental rendering is encrypted in her experiences with both the supposedly untamed western geography and the hyper-civilized New England home. But rather than a revision, I argue that Ruiz de Burton's novel is a translation. Ruiz de Burton does not change sentimental tropes and expectations. Rather, she works within these conventions to negotiate the limitations of an American women's culture that deploys a sentimental language to affirm women's liberty and value to the nation's democratic structures. The distinctions in Ruiz de Burton's sentimental novels are noted in the ways she places unconventional heroines—which I call autoethnographic heroines—within these conventional plots and has them interact with conventional sentimental heroines. This is not a revision. Even her autoethnographic heroines do not change or even resist dominant tropes. Rather, Ruiz de Burton's autoethnographic heroines perform dominant gender roles to make visible the gaps in the gendered ideologies of American liberalism. In fact, Lola is sidelined for much of the novel, shifting the focus to Ruiz de Burton's other, Anglo-American, heroines. This is not to say that Lola is unimportant to the narrative but that her purpose is in how her experiences in the novel reflect upon those of her Anglo-American counterparts. While Lola's misery in New England captivity draws attention to the misconceptions American society has about the West, her misery also reveals Mrs. Norval's suffering as a New England matron. Amy Kaplan has shown how middle-class Anglo-American Protestant woman have served as civilizing forces in the American home. A discourse of domesticity, disseminated through the sentimental novel, instructs Anglo women in how to "contract and expand" both the domestic home and the domestic nation to fortify national borders in an increasingly global world.[46] With Lola, Ruiz de Burton provides the other side of this story, but in so doing, she also shows how the role Anglo-American women imagine for themselves; the role of domesticator—or, as Mrs. Norval calls it, "regulator"—is meant to contain them as much as it is meant to contain racial, ethnic, and cultural others.

Women represent a dangerous counter to the nation's official histories because while necessary to those histories, Anglo-American women's conditional inclusion in the nation creates a vulnerability in the national fabric. Anglo-American women at once uphold the nation's histories and justify the nation's imperial projects and stand as clear contradictions to the liberal foundations upon which the nation stands. Ruiz de Burton emphasizes American women's culture as a border culture—situated in the contact zone between nationalist narratives of conquest and the oppressive histories lived out by the conquered. She identifies the ways American women participate in imperial projects, but she also points out the potential that American women have to disarm those projects. The sentimental romance plot proves a valuable resource for Ruiz de Burton to translate to her white readers their own imbalanced relation to the nation and to render insufficient the sacrifices women make to be a part of dominant national narratives.

By articulating the sentimental romance plot alongside and, at times, even through a seduction plot, Ruiz de Burton furthers her translation project by showing how the sentimental heroine is always situated in a precarious position to the nation. In conventional sentimental novels, the seduction plot serves one of two purposes. It either tests the heroine or it serves to differentiate between the worthy and the unworthy female characters in the novel. If the seduction plot is deployed to test the novel's heroine, the sentimental hero typically rescues the heroine just in time and marries her to redeem her close encounter with ruin. In other iterations, the seduction plot is used to warn women against sexual temptation and measures the sentimental heroine's worth against the seduced fallen woman. In both cases, seduction and marriage are mutually exclusive plot lines. However, Ruiz de Burton plays with these plot structures to show the close relationship between the romance plot and the seduction plot, both of which usually end in a redemptive marriage.

Marriage, therefore, is just another form of seduction in Ruiz de Burton's novels. While the sentimental heroine's submission to the romance plot renders her valuable and worthy of protection, Ruiz de Burton's seduction plot reminds women readers that submission of any kind leaves them vulnerable and unable to ensure their own protection against men and, by extension, imbalanced democratic systems. While the romance plot provides Lola with a sentimental origin story that introduces her into New England society (the heart of American identity), the seduction plot threatens to ruin her, foreclosing the notion that once saved, the sentimental heroine is forever safe. The novel emphasizes that both Lola and her mother were untouched by their Native American kidnappers and that, if anything, the Native Americans worshiped them. Dr. Norval explains to his wife that Lola's mother "was carried off by the Apache Indians, and then sold to the Mohave Indians" and that Lola was born into captivity.[47] He then answers the unspoken question that he assumes his wife has about Lola's heritage and that, no doubt, so too does Ruiz de Burton's white audience. He relates that "Lolita was born five months after her [mother's] capture. So you see how Lolita's blood is pure Spanish blood, her mother being of pure Spanish descent and her father the same, though an Austrian by birth, he having been born in Vienna."[48] The math is irrefutable and effectively dismisses the possibility that Lola is Native American. At the same time Dr. Norval also assures his wife that Lola is of a European lineage and implies that this is the reason the Native Americans took good care of Lola and her mother. Dr. Norval tells his wife that Lola's mother was able to amass a fortune because "the Indians brought her emeralds and rubies, seeing that she liked pretty pebbles."[49] He thus offers further proof that Lola and her mother were relatively unharmed by their Native American captivity. In fact, Lola emerges a wealthy woman. Aside from being "carried off by the Apache Indians"—a language that is ironically similar to the ways the *New York Times* obituary described Ruiz de Burton's marriage to General Burton—Lola and her mother were treated rather well by their Native American captors.

The emeralds and rubies the Native Americans showered upon Lola and her mother are placed in dialogue with Lola's sexual vulnerability in New England society. Out of lust for both Lola's beauty and wealth, Reverend Hackwell devises a plan to trick Lola into marrying him. Hackwell tells Lola that her father is looking for her and that she must accompany him to a lawyer's office to be reunited with her father. But "as *only married* ladies go to such places," Lola is told she must pretend to be Hackwell's wife.[50] Though this makes the demure Lola uncomfortable, she agrees if it means that she will get to meet her father. Hackwell takes Lola to an office in which "three gentlemen [are] in the room" who, feigning an interest in her family background, coax her into speaking aloud that she is married to Reverend Hackwell.[51] Ironically Lola's speech renders the marriage legal, and Lola becomes "tied" to Hackwell, who then threatens to "detain [Lola] by force" if she tries to leave.[52] Regarded as an idol in Native American captivity upon whom riches were lavished, Lola is treated as a commodity to be exploited in New England captivity. And while Hackwell does implore Lola to let him try to win her love, he also defends his actions by using the adage "All is fair in love." Although he leaves off the "and war" in this popular saying, the connection is clear, and Ruiz de Burton indicates that Hackwell's intentions are to forcibly conquer, not honestly win, Lola's affections. Lola's reluctant submission to Hackwell is predicated on her understanding that he has her best interests at heart. Since Beecher instructs women to not only submit to their husbands in marriage but also to submit their civic voice and their vote to men who better understand women's needs and interests, Lola's submission to Hackwell, which in actuality is a coerced consent, falls in line with dominant gendered behavior. However, Ruiz de Burton asks readers to question male notions of women's best interests when Lola is led to ruin and her small claim to liberty is revoked.

In addition to once again dismissing the notion that the East Coast is more civilized than the West, Lola's seduction also serves to show the ways marriage can be manipulated by the nation into an act of "force" that contains women rather than secures their liberty. In the sentimental tradition, a heroine's marriage is her final escape from suffering and a way to transcend earthly and moral struggles. It is also a way for the heroine to exert a new power through a public display of maternalism and religiosity. As we saw with Mrs. Norval's marriage to Mr. Norval, part of the heroine's rescue is from an entirely private space of female maturing to that of a public space in which the heroine can act out her fully fledged womanhood through pious, moral influence. But Lola's choice to marry—the only semblance of choice women in nineteenth-century American society have—is fraudulently taken from her, and the impropriety of the marriage forces her further into the recesses of the private sphere. Her suffering does not end but multiplies as she must confess her predicament to Julian and solicit his help in enacting an equally dubious plot to get out of her commitments to Hackwell. The seduction plot emphasizes Lola's vulnerability in respectable New England society and draws attention to the many threats lurking behind seemingly civilized façades. But the seduction plot is all the more telling because Ruiz de Burton once again imbricates Mrs. Norval in Lola's suffering. Hackwell's first plan to exploit Lola's wealth is to seduce

Mrs. Norval, who, thinking her husband dead, is overcome by a lustful passion for Reverend Hackwell. Mrs. Norval falls in love with Hackwell because she believes he "was worthy of the old Covenanters, . . . and of course was a model of Christian virtues."[53] She becomes "absurdly silly" as a woman in love, and after Hackwell secretly marries her, Mrs. Norval unknowingly agrees to be employed in his plot to seduce Lola. Hackwell tells Mrs. Norval, as Lola's guardian, to "advise Lola to be guided by him."[54] Mrs. Norval listens and tells Lola "to obey [Hackwell] implicitly," which Lola does.[55] Mrs. Norval does not know that his plan is to trick Lola into marriage, but because she aids him nonetheless, her own marriage to Hackwell is thrown into controversy and scandal. Her marriage to Hackwell is both insincere—a gross misuse of the marriage vow to gain access to Lola's wealth through her guardian—and questionable, as Hackwell uses his clandestine marriage to Mrs. Norval as an instrument to secretly marry another as well. Thus Mrs. Norval's submission to marriage is reframed as another seduction but one with consequences that fall on Lola as well.

Mrs. Norval's marriage to Hackwell and her subsequent role in Lola's seduction clearly place her in a precarious position to the nation. As the assumed widow of a national traitor, Mrs. Norval's only choice is to submit herself once again to a worthy man. Her choice to marry a religious leader speaks to her Puritanical values, and in any conventional sentimental novel, such a choice would raise her character in even higher regard. However, like Lola, Mrs. Norval submits her well-being and interests to Hackwell and is duped. Mrs. Norval performs all the right duties and makes all the right choices according to nineteenth-century women's culture and sentimental doctrine, but she is ruined all the same. Together Mrs. Norval and Lola face the consequences of their feminine vulnerability and are sacrificed to Anglo-male greed.

While they began the novel in a face-off over the threshold of New England society, Mrs. Norval and Lola end the novel in shared ruin. Mrs. Norval's second marriage is described as an unfortunate consequence of her loss of self-control. Her passion is likened to "imps" that, "powerless when thus ignominiously imprisoned and ganged together like galley convicts," are "so anxious . . . to be at liberty, and so impatient of restraint, that it was next to impossible to try to let any one free without the whole gang rushing out."⁵⁶ Mrs. Norval's "imps" are, as others have suggested, a commentary on Puritan repression. Furthermore, this language also realizes the ways sentimental heroines, as models for femininity, are "imprisoned and ganged together" by a patriarchal order that aims to control those feminine passions "so anxious" for "liberty." Rather than recognizing women as liberal persons in a democratic society, Ruiz de Burton demonstrates how Anglo-American women are made "powerless" by the doctrines of nineteenth-century American femininity. Women's "imps," or potential for power, are harnessed by sentimental tropes and models of womanhood to "do good service to the master" at the expense of women's liberty.⁵⁷ And so Ruiz de Burton's narrator asks her readers to "let us be charitable with [Mrs. Norval] . . . for we also may find how difficult it is to maintain such *diapason*."⁵⁸ Ruiz de Burton recognizes Mrs. Norval to be as much a victim to the genre's structures as the ethnic, racial, and impoverished "others" it attempts to rescue. She intimately draws together Mrs. Norval's and Lola's seductions and positions Anglo-American women as the sacrificial front line in imperial projects in the West. If Lola is "a great acquisition," as Dr. Norval says, then Mrs. Norval is simply the means by which Dr. Norval manages this acquisition and by which Hackwell exploits this acquisition for power and wealth.⁵⁹ Ruiz de Burton reorients the sentimental novel to depict marriage as another form of seduction and to thereby emphasize not only white women's lack of liberty but also the role they play in securing Anglo-male liberty and further oppressing communities of color.

Of course the liberties Anglo men take in the novel are deployed in violent plots to pillage women for their wealth, their beauty, and their charitable devotion. Before *Who Would Have Thought It?* begins, Lavinia, Mrs. Norval's spinster sister, is jilted after becoming engaged to Hackwell, and by the time the novel begins, she has reconciled herself to her loneliness and dependence on her sister's family. But being single— which Beecher indicated was a choice women were at liberty to make—is not a choice for Lavinia, and it only makes her more vulnerable than both Mrs. Norval and Lola. In addition to feeling her rejection, Lavinia is sexually assaulted in her own home. Hackwell, catching Lavinia as she faints, "put his hand to feel Lavvy's heart's pulsations."⁶⁰ Feeling no beat, the narrator explains, the "reverend gentleman smiled.... He smiled because he remembered having heard Mrs. Hackwell and Mrs. Hammerhard observe that Lavinia had a very handsome bust now, when, previous to the sudden prosperity of the Norval's, she was as flat as a pancake."[61] Hackwell decides to "experiment on Lavvy," and thinking "she will never know it," he "applied his lips to those of the fainting Lavvy."[62] Lavinia remains unconscious while Hackwell continues to take advantage of her. He "tried another kiss, and then another," and he stops only when Lola walks into the room and witnesses his assault on Lavinia.[63] In this rather explicit scene for a nineteenth-century sentimental novel, Ruiz de Burton captures Lavinia's vulnerability as a woman unattached to a husband. Although Hackwell rejects her as his wife, he still desires to dominant her body and to know its intimacy through his "experiment" upon her. And in an assumption that alludes to the rhetoric modern-day sexual predators use, Hackwell thinks that "if she is pretending [to have fainted], she expects it."[64] Not only does this twist the sentimental language of pity and love to justify violence against women, but it also suggests that Hackwell believes his assault on Lavinia is her own fault. In failing to secure a husband, Lavinia is understood to be unworthy of protection, and therefore Hackwell is at liberty to violate her body. Thus in breaking off his engagement with Lavinia, Hackwell participates in Lavinia's exclusion from the cult of domesticity and proper womanhood. Hackwell then uses this exclusion to justify his own violent impulses.

Hackwell's assault on Lavinia emphasizes the lack of choice women have and the ways their consent is disregarded, even within the most intimate spaces of family and domestic life. Ruiz de Burton then moves on to show how the violence women withstand appears in the nation's larger sociopolitical institutions. Just three chapters after Lavinia is assaulted by Hackwell, in a section titled "Lavinia's Experiences in Washington," Ruiz de Burton implies that Lavinia is once against sexually assaulted. This time Lavinia goes to Washington to solicit the federal government to find her brother, who is being held as a prisoner of war in the Confederacy, and to serve as a nurse in a Union hospital. Having no domestic duties herself, Lavinia "wanted nothing better than plenty of employment for her exuberant moral energies and redundant force of will."⁶⁵ And so she projects her untapped womanly energy onto a patriotism that allows her to submit to the nation rather than to a husband. Upon arriving in Washington, Lavinia goes to the War Department, where she plans on asking the secretary of war to help her in her search for her brother. She is forced to wait for an extended period, and when she is finally able to see the secretary, the narrator informs the reader that "what passed between the Secretary and Lavvy no one shall ever know, for neither of them ever told it. All that is known of that episode is what the driver was able to tell; and that was not much, for he only saw Lavvy come out crying convulsively, and that is a common occurrence with the sex; and he heard her talking to herself, and that is a common occurrence with old maids, and Lavvy was past thirty-two!"⁶⁶

Though more implicit than Hackwell's violence against Lavinia, this scene is another example of the vulnerability women face in American society. We "shall never know" the brunt of it, but Lavinia's pain is clearly marked in her convulsive crying and her incoherent "talking to herself." Once she returns to the hospital for which she volunteers, Lavinia "felt more sick at heart than any of the patients at her hospital, and the wounds in her spirit were deeper and bled more profusely than any of those she had bandaged so tenderly."⁶⁷ But the narrator tells us, "If the flesh was weak, the spirit was yet undaunted."⁶⁸ Lavinia's pain is one of the "flesh," suggesting the sexual nature of her violation. This passage also indicates that Lavinia's sexual violation is "deeper" and "bled more profusely" than the injuries men incur during war. While Lavinia tends to male soldiers' battle wounds and eventually nurses them back to health so that they can go on to be viable members of democratic society, Lavinia cannot heal her wounds, for the violation is systemic, compounding, and built into the nation's democratic structures.

Furthermore, the passage once again decries a violent rhetoric that dismisses Lavinia's violation by assigning that blame back onto women, among whom it "is a common occurrence" to cry and mumble to oneself. But unlike the scene of Hackwell's sexual assault, this scene more directly links women's sexual vulnerability to their lack of liberty, for in this scene Ruiz de Burton captures Lavinia's sexual assault in the nation's capital. Despite "sitting up at night, toiling, and tending disgusting sickness, and dressing loathsome wounds, all for the love of our dear country," Lavinia is once again rejected, this time by the nation itself.[69] Her submission to the nation goes unrewarded, and Lavinia is violated rather than extended liberal validation. She "was intimidated by her experience at the War Office," and she leaves the nation's capital with a fear of the nation's leaders rather than a belief in their protection.[70]

Ruiz de Burton's marriage plot, seduction plot, and assault plot work in an intimate network of violence to condemn a women's culture that falsely promises women liberty in exchange for their subordination. Although many of Ruiz de Burton's novels end with the marriages of her heroines, these marriages are imbricated in women's violation and in the desperation that comes with having no other choice. It is typical for sentimental novels to end in marriages or in the triumph of heterosexual love in the face of outstanding obstacles. But marriage, as Ruiz de Burton emphasizes in her novels, is a false ending and prematurely cuts off the narrative to distract its audience from what Lauren Berlant calls the "unfinished business" of the sentimental novel.[71] Love and pity only provide a *sense* of ending for the reader, who at least *feels* justified in a marriage plot or the restoration of a heroine challenged by seduction.

In her first novel Ruiz de Burton refers to love as a "*diapason*" that unsettles a woman's senses and confuses her impulses.[72] But in her second novel, *The Squatter and the Don*, Ruiz de Burton's narrator says, "Love is woman's special province—she has, or has had, or will have, power there."[73] But this still frames love as a "province" in a precarious state. Does the heroine have, had, or will have power? The wording suggests a coy antagonism to sentimental romance plots that promise women power but that fail to ever actualize that power. The narrator goes on to say, "Man might take, and absolutely appropriate, monopolize and exclude her from money-making, from politics and from many other pursuits, made difficult to her by man's tyranny, man's hindrances, man's objections—but in the realms of love he is not the absolute dictator, not the master."[74] Superficially these words might suggest that Ruiz de Burton locates feminine power in the sentimental romance plot and taps into that power to reassert her Californio heroines. However, in a letter to her financial adviser, Ephraim W. Morse, Ruiz de Burton expresses that she "did not write for glory" and thus considers her sentimental novels to be "money-making" ventures that intervene in national politics surrounding westward expansion and settler colonialism.[75] It is unlikely then that these lines from her novel concede the "money-making" and political pursuits in which Ruiz de Burton actively engaged while writing the novel. Instead I read these lines for their subtle rebuke of the "special province" of love to which Anglo-American women cling as a condition of their liberal survival in the nation.

The Squatter and the Don sustains this claim through its own East Coast seduction plot. Doña Josefa, the Alamar family matriarch, sends her youngest daughter, Mercedes, east in the hopes of deterring her romantic affections for the squatter Clarence Darrell. In another reversal of the east-west travel narrative, Mercedes accompanies her newly married sister east only to be tricked on trains, cornered at beach picnics, and ogled by men at dinner parties. Two of these men, Arthur Selden and Bob Gunther, follow Mercedes across the country, hoping to secure her affections. Selden, the more determined of the two, recognizes his hopeless attempts toward Mercedes, but her unattainability and mythic western American identity is part of her allure for him. Selden "closed his eyes to the future and let himself float down this stream of sweet pleasures, knowing that they were but a dream, and yet for that reason more determined to drink the last drop of that nectar so intoxicating, and enjoying being near her, within the sound of her voice, within the magic circle of her personality."[76] Mercedes sustains a myth of the "endless frontier" and provides the terrain upon which eastern Americans exercise their liberty. Selden, who is described as "a millionaire and considered 'a catch'" with many other women vying for his attention,[77] is of an indulgent class of New England Anglo Americans who can "close his eyes to the future" and pursue what he knows to be "but a dream." He intends to drain the "dream" of Mercedes dry, "determined to drink the last drop of that nectar so intoxicating," in order that his competition—Gunther and Clarence—are left with nothing. Not only is this language violent in that it considers Mercedes as something to be consumed, as if an intoxicating nectar, but it also suggests Selden's love is nothing more than an exertion of dominant masculinity, a competitive exercise in conquest against his fellow Anglo-American men. Ruiz de Burton critiques burgeoning notions of Anglo masculinity that position the West as a playground upon which Anglo men can validate their "virile qualities" and live out a fantastic dream.[78]

In the novel Ruiz de Burton makes a point to dispel dominant notions about women's culture by showing that Anglo men, such as Selden, wield love against women rather than the other way around. Like the leading Anglo-American sentimental heroines, Mercedes makes submission her "boast" and "amiably [takes] part in all their games and other amusements."[79] She attempts to manipulate the various men vying for her attention against one another and finds that "both young gentlemen were a most excellent protection against one another, as neither one was ever willing to go leaving her alone with the other."[80] But in submitting to both men's "games," Mercedes creates new problems, "ardent loving looks" from both.[81] She only becomes a more challenging catch, and Selden's and Gunther's stalking only becomes more "ardent." Mercedes "knew that the best way of eluding them was by having recourse to her little trick of dropping her gaze, as if she must look down for something missing near by. That little trick came to her from her timidity and bashfulness long ago."[82] Ruiz de Burton exposes the "tricks" sentimental heroines use to make love their "special province," but rather than placing Mercedes in control, her "bashfulness" and "timidity" only make her more desirable to these men and increase their daring when it comes to securing intimate moments with her. But the biggest danger Selden and Gunther pose to Mercedes is that their interest in her is unstable. Ruiz de Burton declares love is but a fad, a "special province" that gives women fleeting glimpses of power; "she has, or has had, or will have, power there," but never shall she keep that power. As one New England matron suggests, Mercedes "will be the rage next winter."[83] As the object of men's lust, Mercedes's power is brief at best. She is described as the season's "rage" and as "an epidemic" sweeping New England society. But Ruiz de Burton acknowledges that epidemics end and that Mercedes will soon be stopped "from spreading any further."[84] Whatever amount of power she does derive from her sexual vulnerability is limited and has little permanent ground to stand upon.

However, both novels end in marriages that redeem their heroines after a series of close encounters with sexual and economic ruin. These marriages, as I mentioned at the start of this chapter, are inter-ethnic and are often pointed to as Ruiz de Burton's call for cross-national and cross-ethnic "unification."[85] However, I argue that Ruiz de Burton ends her novels in marriages that leave their couples in unreconciled relationships to the nation and that refuse to conclude in a "happily-ever-after" trope that prematurely forecloses the wounds each novel opens. By the end of each novel, both of the Anglo-American men to which Ruiz de Burton marries her Californio heroines are disgruntled with the federal government and are positioned as anti-patriots, clearly on the outs with their nation. While Julian in *Who Would Have Thought It?* speaks out against the U.S. president, declaring, "I have fought, thinking myself a free man fighting for freedom; and I awake from my dream to find that I do not have even the privilege granted to thieves and cutthroats,"[86] Clarence in *Squatter* is positioned as a young capitalist with a conscious. Clarence, who is the one character who ends Ruiz de Burton's second novel in better shape than when it started, uses his accumulated capital to invest in the Texas Pacific Railroad, a venture that "should bring through San Diego the commerce between Asian and the Atlantic seaboard, between China and Europe" but that both U.S. business and Congress block.[87] While Ruiz de Burton critiques American capitalism in *Squatter*, she does so only because it is used to further nationalize American presence in the world rather than globalize it. Ruiz de Burton is an advocate of capitalism as an equalizing force. Her archive is full of details pertaining to her own capitalist ventures in San Diego, including letters to advisers that speak about her literary ventures as capitalist endeavors.[88] Furthermore, Ruiz de Burton understands the western American region as crucial to American capitalism's expansion globally. However, Ruiz de Burton condemns corrupt capitalists who effectively terminate projects such as the Texas Pacific Railroad because these threaten to engage in global exchange "between Asian and the Atlantic" and "between China and Europe." She charges American capitalists with prematurely killing San Diego and the West's potential on the global stage, and she recognizes the intense American nationalism breeding in the nation's unwillingness to foster global networks. *Squatter*'s narrator states that "San Diego lived her short hour of hope and prosperity, and smiled and went to sleep on the brink of her own grave, the grave that Mr. C. P. Huntington had already begun to excavate, to dig as he stealthily went about the halls of our National Capitol 'offering bribes.'"[89] Ruiz de Burton is not critiquing capitalism, nor is she critiquing American imperial takeover in this scene. Rather, she is frustrated by the "short hour of hope and prosperity" the nation offered San Diego as a global hub and the efforts of American capitalists, obsessed with their own power in "the halls of our National Capitol," to cut the region off from the rest of the world as a means of securing its plentiful resources for themselves.

The novel ends in mourning, not only for the death of Don Mariano Alamar, the Californio patriarch, but also for what Ruiz de Burton recognizes as the western American region's unfulfilled potential. Clarence's and Mercedes's marriage is finally realized at the end of the novel, but rather than offering a neat conclusion to the West's problems, their marriage refuses to ignore its losses and mourns for its past and for its uncertain future. In fact, Clarence's and Mercedes's union is offset by the destruction of Mercedes's parents' marriage in the wake of her father's death. Doña Josefa, Mercedes's mother and Don Mariano's widow, is the last character to speak in the novel. In a conversation with Clarence, Doña Josefa says: "Let the guilty rejoice and go unpunished, and the innocent suffer ruin and desolation. I slander no one, but shall speak the truth."[90] Doña Josefa asserts that she will not allow her "truth" to be covered up by a whitewashed history that celebrates the "guilty." Rather than allowing the reader to feel justified in the punishment of one or two perpetrators, Ruiz de Burton refuses her audience this emotional fulfillment and forces her readers to face the "unpunished" and the "innocent" who continue to suffer even after heterosexual love is secured. The marriage plot—or in this case the widow's mourning—is twisted to "speak the truth" and to continue speaking this truth even after the novel has concluded. As such, the last chapter in *Squatter* occurs after the narrative has ended. It is a chapter entirely dedicated to expanding upon the fate of the "guilty" rather than healing the wounds of the "innocent." The didactic narrator deviates from the sentimental ending and its focus on the married heroine to inform the reader that "those pampered millionaires" continue their work to steal San Diego's "widow's mite to swell the volume of their riches!"[91] The novel ends without resolving the central issue—Californios' dispossession and their manipulated exclusion from the nation—and the reader is left to wonder about Mercedes's and Clarence's fate instead of being reassured of their happiness and salvation in marriage.

Likewise *Who Would Have Thought It?* ends with Lola's marriage to Julian, but this marriage, which arises from the ashes of her farcical marriage to Hackwell, also carries the parental burden of loss. Shortly after their marriage vows are uttered, Julian is forced to return to his duties in the U.S. military. Despite the nation's attempts to defame him because of his relation to his father—a traitor to the Union—Julian bitterly returns to his regiment to fulfill his requirements to the nation. After his departure, "Lola sobbed and moaned all night. Her sad father sat by her and tried to soothe her, whilst he thought how much he would have loved to have found his child before she had so entirely given her heart away."[92] Though Julian eventually returns and Lola's happiness is restored, Lola is never happily reunited with her father. Lola's father feels this loss, wishing he had been given a chance to love his daughter before she had "given her heart away." But Lola seems detached from her father and never finds the fulfillment she anticipates in their meeting, despite the novel's buildup to this moment. In conventional sentimental novels with an orphaned heroine, the heroine's reunion with one or both of her parents coincides with her happy marriage to an eligible bachelor. Or if the parents have died, the orphaned heroine finds solace in having known and loved them, and this guides the heroine toward a healing romance that ends in marriage and the replacement of a missing father with an honorable husband. With Lola, Ruiz de Burton defies both tropes. Born into Native American captivity, Lola was never given a chance to know her father, and her reunion with him only emphasizes the irreparable damage done to her fractured identity. According to the novel's timeline, Lola was born in 1848, the same year the United States and Mexico signed the Treaty of Guadalupe Hidalgo. Thus Lola was born at the important juncture that ended Mexican control over the western region and initiated American global domination. Her national identity is uncertain, and her marriage to Julian—a marriage that is as much an escape from Hackwell as it is a fulfillment of romantic love—fails to reconcile her nebulous histories. The very opposite of a marriage of unification, Lola's and Julian's marriage is a marriage in crisis. Lola does not represent Californios, as her clear disassociation from her Californio father indicates, nor does she represent Mexico since she was born in the American West in Native American captivity. Similarly Julian, on the outs with his nation, does not represent an elite class of Americans, at least not a patriotic one. Rather, each of them mourns separately for their national divisions, and when they come together, their marriage represents the irrevocable melancholia in which their investment in nationalist identities, even unrealized ones, results.

And these are not the only marriages with which Ruiz de Burton ends her novels. In each novel Anglo-American women are also married to heterosexual partners who reaffirm Ruiz de Burton's arguments that the traditional sentimental heroine and the femininity she represents are unsustainable in the wake of the United States' emergence as a global power. Mrs. Norval's fate is dire. After she learns that her first husband, Dr. Norval, is not in fact dead but is returning home, she devolves into "a violent brain-fever, which might deprive her of reason, if not life."[93] Though the reader is told "she might possibly recover," the novel resists the sentimental impulse to redeem her through her reunion with Dr. Norval, her right and proper husband.[94] Likewise, Mrs. Norval's two daughters—Mattie and Ruth—find marriageable partners but for all the wrong reasons, and by the end of the novel's concluding chapter, women have entirely disappeared from the narrative to be replaced by white male political soliloquies. Ruiz de Burton thus suggests that American women's culture has been overrun by a nationalist rhetoric that sedates them with mansions, possessions, and public displays of wealth. Ruth is seduced into marriage by being told she would not have to "give up [her] handsome carriages, *nor* [her] rich dresses, *nor* [her] fine house," and she rises to become "the leader of . . . all the well-dressed women who have a perfect right to be stupid, because their husbands have brains; who have a perfect right to be silly and trifling, because their husbands conduct the mighty affairs of the nation."[95] Ruiz de Burton concludes her first novel with a critique of the commodity culture prescribed by sentimental novels and their heroines, a culture that has reduced American women's culture to something "stupid," "silly," and "trifling." While Ruth represents American women's wasted future, her mother, Mrs. Norval, is represented as a relic, much like Helen Hunt Jackson will represent Californios in the next chapter. Mrs. Norval is the last of her kind, and her devolution into madness signals American women's culture's failure to adapt to the changing world. Neither Mrs. Norval nor Ruth is capable of liberal behavior. Mrs. Norval is stunted by her devout commitment to Puritanical beliefs that stifle progress, and Ruth's obsession with wealth and possessions places her in collaboration with the land-grabbing squatters in the West who base their inclusion in the nation off of land and possessions rather than a moral code of human rights and freedom.

While *Squatter* is about the United States' failure to uphold the Treaty of Guadalupe Hidalgo and its dispossession of Californio families, it is also a critique of American hyper-individualism. Ruiz de Burton's concern in *Squatter* is not necessarily with American settlement in the region or with American capitalism, as Ruiz de Burton's positive support of the Texas Pacific Railroad suggests. Rather, she critiques the individualism that undergirds these American ideologies and that stifles liberalism's service to the greater good. In the decades Ruiz de Burton wrote her two novels, notions of liberalism were circulating worldwide. Ruiz de Burton first addresses liberalism in *Who Would Have Thought It?* in the context of the French occupation of Mexico City. Don Luis, Lola's father and a member of Mexico's Liberal Party, is serving in the Liberal army to defeat French occupation and Mexican conservatism. However, Don Luis, who is of Austrian birth himself, finds it "difficult to make up [his] mind to fight against an Austrian prince" if Archduke Maximilian should accept Napoleon's offer of the Mexican throne.[96] Don Luis agrees with his father-in-law, Don Felipe, that the "Mexicans did not want a republic; they wanted a good and just prince" and "that a republican form of government is not suited to the Mexicans."[97] Together Don Luis and Don Felipe blame the United States and its "despotic sway over the minds of the leading men of the Hispano-American republics" for the "*fatal* influence,—*which will eventually destroy us.*"⁹⁸ However, Ruiz de Burton's narrator condemns Don Luis's torn allegiance to liberalism, and instead of agreeing with him about the United States' "*fatal* influence," the narrator ends the chapter by castigating Mexico. The narrator suggests that "if Mexico were well governed, if her frontiers were well protected, the fate of Doña Theresa [Lola's mother] would have been next to an impossibility. . . . Does a plea of economy counterbalance an appeal for life?"⁹⁹ The narrator emphasizes life over economy, the greater good over individual or even national economic prosperity, and goes on to say that "a nation can, with a good government, avoid the majority of those misfortunes which we now call '*unavoidable* human sorrows.'"¹⁰⁰ In this chapter from her first novel, Ruiz de Burton takes an opportunity to speak not to dominant Anglo-American readers but to her Californio community. As Pratt explains, "Autoethnographic texts are typically heterogeneous. . . . That is, they are usually addressed both to metropolitan readers and to literate sectors of the speaker's own social group."¹⁰¹ This heterogeneous quality in Ruiz de Burton's novel facilitates cross-cultural negotiations that recognize the benefits and shortcomings in both American and Californio societies. Ruiz de Burton's narrator implies that Mexico's greatest problem is its inconsistent loyalties, which result in weak borders and which make Mexico vulnerable to attack. Mexico's lawmakers are tasked with a "fearful responsibility," and according to Ruiz de Burton's narrator, they are failing to place the "life" of their people—the greater good of the nation—above individual "economy."

By the time Ruiz de Burton writes *Squatter*, she is equally unconvinced that the United States is a model for liberal democracy. The United States' "despotic" and "fatal" influence to which she refers in *Who Would Have Though It?* is elaborated upon in *Squatter* as the novel concerns itself with the ways the United States incorporates and represents the western region to the rest of the nation. While both novels find the tenets of American liberalism to be commendable, they also cite both the United States' and Mexico's failure to protect liberal democracy against the extreme individualism breeding in American capitalism and the nation's imperial projects worldwide. The West is recommended to a class of Anglo-American citizens as the great equalizer. The Homestead Acts make it possible for the underprivileged and landless to stake a claim for themselves and pursue freedom and opportunity. However, as *Squatter* documents, this freedom is predicated on the dispossession of Californios and other native populations in the region and thus contradicts a liberalism that encourages mutual benefit and that does not sacrifice the masses for the benefit of a privileged few. While American femininity and the cult of domesticity are seen as a safeguard to the rampant greed of men, Ruiz de Burton's Anglo-American heroines in *Squatter* indicate that as the nation grows and expands its global influence, women are becoming less and less influential over the nation's liberal identity.

The Anglo-American heroines in *Squatter* are less controversial and more pathetic than those in *Who Would Have Thought It?* as their domestic kingdoms fail to come to fruition in the West. *Squatter* starts in the East by introducing the squatter William Darrell as he courts his soon to be wife, Mary. A devout Catholic, Mary resists Darrell because of his "strong trait of character," which she perceives as "more apt to be uncontrollable."[102] Regardless, Mary "felt as if being carried away in spite of herself, by the torrent of his impetuosity. She was afraid of him, but she liked him and she liked to be loved in that passionate, rebellious way of his."[103] She finally submits to marriage and spends the rest of her life cautioning Darrell against his attempts to settle western American homesteads. By the time Darrell lands in San Diego, Mary pleads with her son, Clarence, to secretly purchase the land from the Californio owners to ensure their domestic right to the land and to allow her to set up a more stable home. In this narrative Ruiz de Burton demonstrates how notions of women's domestic power are sacrificed to a cutthroat settler colonialism in the West. While Anglo-American squatters make Californio livelihoods uncertain, Anglo-American domesticity is made equally uncertain by the vague laws about how to establish and protect a homestead. As such, Ruiz de Burton raises concerns for the region's sustainability. At the center of Californio and squatter tensions is a fundamental disagreement about the best way to use and manage the land. While Californios have been successful in raising free-range cattle and planting orchards and vineyards, the Anglo-American squatters want to grow wheat, which, as Don Mariano Alamar tries to warn them, is not efficient in the dry region. The Californios' cattle are attracted to the squatters' wheat, and the squatters ruthlessly shoot and kill the cattle to protect their crops. Instead of mutual benefit and opportunity for all, the West is destructive to all—and only because the nation encourages fierce competition rather than fostering a workable community in which all, including the land, benefit.

Encouraged by a hyper-masculine and hyper-individualistic rhetoric of Manifest Destiny and an American pioneer spirit, the squatters are resistant to accepting compromises or to striking cooperative deals with Don Mariano. And Clarence, the last Anglo man to value and be swayed by the influence of women, is unable to persuade them otherwise. The squatters "did not make any pretense to regard female opinion with any more respect than other men."[104] Women are excluded from all discussions of settlement in the West, including where and how to erect domestic dwellings, so Ruiz de Burton emphasizes the slippages in a western American rhetoric that promises the West as the culmination of American liberal democratic ideals but presents instead a West that is a harsh terrain of masculine individualism, competition, and survival of the fittest. Mary's secret plot to purchase the land from Don Mariano is her last attempt to assert her feminine authority, restore the moral backbone of her family, and assuage her liberal guilt. But this too fails. William Darrell learns of his wife's and son's agreement with the don, and in the novel's climactic scene, he accuses the don of using his daughters to seduce Clarence into paying for the land. Taking offense, the don engages William Darrell in a humiliating scene that ends with William Darrell being lassoed into defeat as both his wife and his daughter, Alice, look on. Mrs. Darrell approaches her husband and his fellow squatters as they plot against the don and confesses to having paid for the land out of recognition that "we have treated the conquered Spaniards most cruelly, and our law-givers have been most unjust to them."[105]

It is not surprising that Mrs. Darrell's impassioned speech has little impact on them. After she leaves, Gasbang, the most ill-behaved of the squatters, dismisses Mary's actions as female deviancy, "because women are bound to do mischief."[106] Mary and Alice are left to emotionally and physically decline over the remainder of the novel. Mary, humiliated by her husband, secludes herself in shame and marital exile while Alice's health fades despite the romantic attention she is paid by the don's son, Victoriano.

Mary and Alice, like Mrs. Norval and her daughters, are vestiges of an old American feminine identity that is quickly becoming unsustainable as the United States expands and nationalizes. But ultimately Ruiz de Burton cautions the United States from misappropriating the West. Just as the squatters insist on growing wheat and thereby destroying the West's usable land, so too does Ruiz de Burton criticize the nation for mishandling the West's incorporation into the nation, and she cites this mismanagement as unsustainable to American liberal democracy. The nation advertises the West as a rugged geography in which there is plenty of opportunity for those willing to work for it. The region is heralded as the nation's last chance to realize its liberal potential and to correct the social inequalities plaguing the East. However, it is also represented as a tabula rasa that not only invites Anglo-American settlement in the region but also incites a masculinist rhetoric of rescue and taming of the region. Ruiz de Burton's sentimental novels translate back to dominant American society the contradictions in these two representations of the West and show how the West does not in fact need American rescue or taming, domestication or civilizing, but rather needs liberation from the hyper-masculine and hyper-individualistic rhetoric used to represent the region to the rest of the nation.

It is ironic that Ruiz de Burton's *New York Times* obituary works against everything Ruiz de Burton stood for in her sentimental novels. As I argued at the start of this chapter, Ruiz de Burton is reduced to a sentimental icon of the American West. Her novels, her lawsuits, and her clear dissatisfaction with the West's incorporation into the nation are asides the writer treats lightly, if at all. Instead the obituary illustrates a liberal fantasy in which Ruiz de Burton is rescued and loved by the nation. Her marriage to an American general and her assumed upward mobility in the wake of the United States' defeat of Mexico is championed as the nation's greatest liberal achievement. But this less-than-accurate representation of Ruiz de Burton only degrades American liberalism by encouraging a version of the West that is fundamentally illiberal. Helen Hunt Jackson's sentimental novel, *Ramona*, capitalizes on the images Ruiz de Burton's *New York Times* obituary establishes and deploys romanticized notions of a bygone Spanish California to fuel her ambivalent Native American advocacy.

2. The Liberal Fantasy

Helen Hunt Jackson's Sentimental Advocacy in Ramona

In a pivotal scene from Helen Hunt Jackson's 1884 sentimental novel *Ramona*, Jackson's two protagonists are caught in a snowstorm. After their San Diego home is taken over by Anglo-American squatters, the half-white, half–Native American Ramona and her Native American husband, Alessandro, flee with their infant daughter to a remote Native American village in the Southern California mountains. Nearly there, they are overtaken by a blizzard, and Ramona falls unconscious while still holding her baby tightly to her chest. In what Jackson's narrator calls "a marvellous [*sic*] rescue," Ramona is "shaken and beaten" back to consciousness by a poor white southern man, Jeff Hyer, who carries Ramona to the safety of a sheep corral before he takes Ramona's child and "[puts] the crying babe into his wife's arms."[1] Assuming Ramona and Alessandro are Mexican and sensing their ignorance of English, Jeff tells his wife, Aunt Ri, "Ef I'd knowed 't wuz Mexicans, Ri, I wouldn't ev'gone out ter 'um."[2] In response to her husband, Aunt Ri says: "Naow, Jeff, yer know yer wouldn't let enny-thin' in shape ev a human creetur go perishin' past aour fire sech wether's this."[3] But as she takes the baby from her husband, Aunt Ri notes the baby's "pooty, blue-eyed" complexion and concludes, "I bet thet baby's father wuz white, then."⁴ The baby's blue eyes imply that she is more than just the "shape ev a human creetur" and that she might actually possess a humanity not afforded Mexicans in this scene. The blue-eyed baby shifts the terms of the rescue mission as Aunt Ri and Jeff Hyer struggle to categorize Ramona and Alessandro's elusive racial identity and question their family structure. The "marvellous rescue" becomes an imperial foray into the western American landscape when the Hyers end the scene in possession of the blue-eyed baby.

In chapter 1 I argued that Californio author Ruiz de Burton translated the popular sentimental novel into an autoethnography, allowing her to negotiate the terms and limitations of American liberal personhood. Through the deployment of autoethnographic sentimental heroines, Ruiz de Burton explored the late nineteenth century's complicated notions of citizenship and national belonging as the nation was acquiring new and diverse territories and populations. In this chapter I recognize that Helen Hunt Jackson is part of that dominant literary society to whom Ruiz de Burton's autoethnographic sentimental novels speak. But Jackson is also typically understood to be a progressive figure, writing in advocacy of Native American rights and protections. It is my contention, however, that Jackson's progressivism has been all too superficially dealt with and needs more critical attention. Therefore I treat Jackson's Native American advocacy as a foundational case study for the beginnings of a western American progressive ethos that, as this book argues as a whole, has been ambivalent in regard to true democratic progress and inclusion.

As Mary Louise Pratt helped me to understand the autoethnographic strain in Ruiz de Burton's writing, so too does Pratt help me to situate Jackson's writing as partaking in an anti-conquest tradition. Pratt uses the term "anti-conquest" to refer to "the strategies of representation whereby European bourgeois subjects seek to secure their innocence in the same moment as they assert European hegemony."⁵ Pratt describes the author of the "anti-conquest" text as "'the seeing man,' . . . he whose imperial eyes passively look out and possess."⁶ With "anti-conquest" Pratt refers to the seemingly "innocent" or well-intentioned white European author of travel narratives whose mission for knowledge and understanding about a geography and peoples becomes imperialistic in its attempts to possess the subject through naming it and its particulars. Pratt's framework for understanding the white European travel writer is also helpful for recognizing the progressive fantasy in Jackson's *Ramona* and the imperialist foundations of a mainstream western American progressive political identity.

Ramona is situated in the Southern California region after Mexico's defeat in the Mexican-American War and traces the romantic relationship between Ramona and Alessandro, whom the novel describes as an "exceptional" Native American man.[7] Raised by her adopted Californio family, Ramona's stepmother, Señora Moreno, refuses to allow Ramona to marry Alessandro because he is Native American. As a result, Ramona and Alessandro are forced to run away from the utopian but declining Moreno rancho and marry in a small Catholic church in San Diego. They live a few happy years in an idyllic Indian village nearby before the encroachment of Anglo-American settlers in the region again forces them to pack up their young child and move to a more remote village in the Southern California mountains. The second half of the novel, initiated by Ramona's and Alessandro's encounter with the Hyers, veers into a tragedy as their infant daughter dies as a result of an Indian agent's neglect; Alessandro goes mad and is murdered after accidently stealing a white man's horse; and Ramona must be saved by her Californio stepbrother Felipe, who then marries her and takes her back to Mexico, the site of a final "untried future."[8]

While the novel has largely been read as an "Indian reform novel,"[9] my reading of *Ramona* sides with scholarship that understands that Jackson's "writing about Indians was not first and foremost about collectivity; rather, it was about validating oneself as an author, a citizen, and a person."[10] I recognize that Jackson's sentimental portrayal of the Native American plight in Southern California is a negotiation of the era's changing racial, gendered, and labor relations. Just as the "marvellous rescue" scene was a racial negotiation between the Hyers and the new, diverse identities of the West, so too does Jackson use her novel as a way to explore the sociopolitical anxieties that late nineteenth-century Anglo-American society had about the changing terms of American liberal personhood.

The anti-conquest impulse in Jackson's *Ramona* stems from yet another oversight in Jackson scholarship: the novel's straddling of regions. *Ramona* is often discussed as a western American text that chronicles a particularly western American problem with Native American displacement and that centers western American debates surrounding the incorporation of Indigenous and Mexican populations into the national imaginary. However, as the Hyer family represents, Jackson's treatment of these seemingly western American topics is influenced by the South's failed Reconstruction era and the beginnings of the nadir in American race relations. The Hyers meet Ramona and Alessandro as they too flee their home. Rather than fleeing Anglo-American squatters (which is indeed a particularly western American problem, though one initiated by federal policies determined in the East), the Hyers are fleeing the post-Reconstruction South's overly saturated labor market. In a last-ditch effort to cure their son, Jos, of his "hemorrhage after hemorrhage," the Hyers "sold their little place for half it was worth, traded cattle for a pair of horses and a covered wagon, and set off, half beggared, with their sick boy on a bed in the bottom of the wagon."[11] Jos's hemorrhaging is representative of the hemorrhaging social position that the poor white southerners face as recently emancipated slaves become competition for land, wages, and civic voice. In response to this competition, the Hyers go West in search of new economic opportunities but also to reaffirm their imagined superiority as white citizens.

That Jackson introduces us to the Hyers as Ramona's and Alessandro's saviors positions the white family—even one as poor and "half beggared" as the Hyers—in a privileged place above the mixed-race and Indigenous Ramona and Alessandro. The "marvellous rescue" is also a rescue of the Hyers' place in American sociopolitical identity. It is about rescuing what was lost in the South—a race-based labor system in which all racialized actors have clearly defined roles—in the newly acquired American West. The West's promise for the Hyers is not that it will offer them something new but that it will restore something that has been lost or, in the very least, something that they think has been lost. A sentimental nostalgia for the old South permeates the novel's telling of Native American removal and competes with Jackson's aims to advocate for Native American rights. As I argue in this chapter, the Hyers and Jackson herself are anti-conquerors who deploy their progressive interest in Ramona and Alessandro as a means of securing a more stable and privileged relation to the nation just as that nation is rapidly changing the terms of citizenship, individual rights, and labor. I read Jackson's progressivism as an ambivalent fantasy because while it is concerned with the displacement of Native American populations, it is also preoccupied by the consequences of that vein of progressive politics—namely, the dissolution of old power structures that privilege white Americans.

Ramona is Jackson's sentimental adaptation of her failed political treatise, *A Century of Dishonor*. Published in 1881, just three years before *Ramona*, *A Century of Dishonor* documents the U.S. government's mistreatment of Native American tribes across the United States. Jackson was inspired to write *A Century of Dishonor* after attending Chief Standing Bear's lecture in Boston, and she famously became "[what she] said a thousand times was the most odious thing in life,—a woman with a hobby."[12] But in writing *A Century of Dishonor*, Jackson vows that she "shall not write *one word* as a sentimentalist! Statistical Records—verbatim reports officially authenticated, are what I wish to get before the American people:—& are all which are needed, to rouse public sentiment."[13] In fact, in 1879 Jackson proudly writes to her second husband, William Sharpless Jackson, about "the praise [she is] getting for the manly method in which [she has] stated things—the quiet tone—the repression" she has in speaking about the Native American plight.[14] A "manly method" of literary production—a method that is not only "quiet" but also repressed and that relies on "Statistical Records" and "verbatim reports" rather than emotional experience—is, in Jackson's perspective here, more effective in rousing "public sentiment" than the sentimental (feminine) genres. Thus Jackson begins *A Century of Dishonor* by situating her authorial voice "between the theory of some sentimentalists that the Indians were the real owners of the soil, and the theory of some politicians that they had no right of ownership whatsoever in it."[15] However, despite the fact that she personally delivered copies of the treatise to each member of Congress, *A Century of Dishonor* was a political and a literary failure.

Whether it was because the political treatise associated Jackson, a woman, with "what is technically known as 'lobbying,'" as her frequent correspondent, Senator Henry Dawes, feared, or because the book was too burdensome for a popular audience, *A Century of Dishonor* never became the popular best-seller that many of Jackson's previous short fictions and poems were.[16]

Just a few short years later, as Jackson begins work on *Ramona*, she famously writes in a letter that she hopes her novel will "do one hundredth part for the Indians that Mrs. Stowe did for the Negro."[17] Between the publication of *A Century of Dishonor* in 1881 and this January 1, 1884, letter, Jackson's steadfast desire to avoid sentimentalism softens to the point that she hopes her work-in-progress novel will compare favorably to the gold standard of sentimental writing, *Uncle Tom's Cabin*. The question is then: what changed Jackson's mind? What influenced her to leave behind the "manly method" and return to a sentimental tradition built on what Lauren Berlant calls "the Uncle Tom genealogy?"[18]

No doubt Jackson quickly pivots her literary agenda to meet the expectations of her established readership. But the ferocity with which she adapted her failed book into a sentimental retake also indicates Jackson's insecurities as both a female author and a member of dominant society. In the sentimental adaptation of her Native American advocacy, Jackson's progressive cause must share space with her dominant readers' anxieties. That is, while *A Century of Dishonor* is a well-researched treatise on Native American suffering, it takes place within a sociopolitical vacuum. In *Ramona*, on the other hand, Jackson must contend with Native American suffering as it interacts not just with federal treaties and legislation but also with ordinary Anglo-American individuals. As I discussed in chapter 1, a cornerstone of the sentimental tradition is that regardless of who the novel appears to be about, it is always also about the Anglo-American reader. Berlant points out that the Anglo-American female audience is "at the center of the *story* of what counts as life, regardless of what lives women actually live."[19] The sentimental novel is successful only insofar as it is able to make its reader feel something, and in order to do this, it must persuade its reader not that a particular political or social issue matters necessarily but that the reader herself will receive "her own value back not only in the labor of recognition she performs but in the sensual spectacle of its impacts."[20] The sentimental novel is a transactional genre in which Anglo-American women give their emotional labor to a suffering "other" in exchange for recognition as members of the national imaginary, something their voiceless subjects are fundamentally denied. Therefore, when Jackson claims that she hopes *Ramona* does "one hundredth part for the Indians" that Stowe's *Uncle Tom's Cabin* did for African Americans, we must also acknowledge the "value" Jackson and her Anglo-American female readership derive from this success as well.

The sentimental novel is always bifurcated. It is a reflection on the competing impulses of a benevolent women's culture that finds its own value in the suffering of inferior "others." But as Jackson's *Ramona* attests, the sentimental novel is also a meditation on the era's increasingly distorted boundaries among laboring bodies. A novel such as Stowe's *Uncle Tom's Cabin*, for instance, manipulates notions of a Puritan work ethic to find value in certain Black bodies to prove their humanity, even though this value system contradicts the novel's progressive advocacy for abolition. Stowe's treatment of labor serves to distinguish between Black and white bodies even while attempting a case for their shared humanity. This is part of the "critical" but "ambivalent" nature of sentimental writing that Berlant recognizes as the "unfinished business of sentimentality."[21] A novel like Jackson's *Ramona* remains "unfinished" because a full execution of its politics would sacrifice the privileged place from which Jackson is able to speak and would break transactional contract with the sentimental tradition. If *Ramona* is Jackson's political expression and access point into American civic identity, then that political expression and identity are predicated on Native American oppression and exclusion from the democratic process. The sentimental female author must not appear to be using her voice for herself but for another, thus requiring the silencing of another to elevate the democratic voices of Anglo-American women.

Jackson navigates this sentimental paradox by recouping her value in western American labor structures primed for the re-entrenchment of the American slave economy recently defeated in the South. Joseph Fichtelberg identifies a relationship between sentimental language and fluctuations in the nineteenth-century American economy. He argues that the sentimental novel "provided the imagery through which Americans sought to explain and shape the market" and that this work was largely executed by women sentimentalists.[22] In this chapter, I shift Fichtelberg's analysis of the sentimental novel to explore more precisely how sentimental language and women's emotional labor served the post-emancipation decades in reshaping the labor economy. To do so, I read *Ramona* as a text at the crossroads of American regional histories. With *Ramona* Jackson draws into relation the nation's rhetoric of emancipation and liberal democracy—an American political discourse that enters into new negotiations at the end of the Civil War—with that of Manifest Destiny and the nation's positioning as a global power. Furthermore, Jackson also finds a platform in *Ramona* to consider what these national credos mean for ordinary, everyday Anglo-American individuals like the Hyers. The novel traces the competing and often contradictory inclinations that certain national programs such as Manifest Destiny and American liberal democracy instill in everyday Anglo-American citizens as they struggle to reassert their civic voice and worth amid transforming regimes of power.

The abolition of slavery in the South does not immediately indicate more equitable forms of labor, as the United States' contemporary labor issues attest. Rather, Lisa Lowe helps to show how the abolition of slavery is followed by global patterns of migrant labor, which rephrase the rhetoric of the enslaved from "free" (meaning unpaid) labor to that of mobile "free" (not enslaved) labor.[23] This manipulation serves to protect the exclusivity of liberal personhood and erects new divisions between laboring bodies, even while tearing old ones down. Jackson's *Ramona* captures these rhetorical manipulations as they pervade dominate culture and consequently normalize racialized notions of labor in the West. African slave labor is substituted in the novel with a Native American migratory wage-labor system constructed out of the nation's residual histories of racism and is used to differentiate between Anglo-American skilled labor and Native American unskilled labor. These new forms of labor—both of which are paid in wages—are defined against one another through their respective access points to domestic intimacy. While the novel sentimentalizes Ramona's and

Alessandro's repeated displacement from their homes, it also cannot imagine any other course of action. Anglo-American families such as the Hyers, also displaced by the South's failed Reconstruction project, require the removal of Native American villages in order to reestablish their own, stable forms of white domestic interiority in the West. As domestic interiority is the prerequisite to liberal personhood, Jackson's novel rehearses the exclusion of Native Americans from liberal personhood, and therefore civic identity, by assigning them to migratory labor, which separates the domestic family or, in the very least, demands their constant movement across the region.[24] At multiple points in the novel Jackson provides images of Native American dwellings and settlements inhabited by disenfranchised Anglo-American squatters who, as we saw in chapter 1, capitalize on the U.S. government's Homestead Acts to realize their citizenship and liberal personhood through land ownership. While Jackson does represent many of these Anglo-American squatters negatively, I situate these representations in light of the regional histories from which the Anglo-American squatters are themselves fleeing. I pay closer attention than previous scholarship to what exactly influences Jackson's vulgar depictions of the Anglo-American characters in the novel, and I uncover Jackson's sentimental slippages, which position the Anglo-American family as the novel's true sentimental-political subjects. Ultimately I argue in this chapter that Jackson's *Ramona* initiates a mainstream western American progressivism that is politically undecided about its own initiatives and that fears more for the vulnerability of the everyday white American than it does for Indigenous communities in the West.

Despite her Native American advocacy, Jackson was not a particularly progressive individual. She was never associated with the era's women's suffrage movement, nor did she seem to take a real interest in abolition, a stance that makes her comment about Stowe's *Uncle Tom's Cabin* all the more suspicious. In fact, evidence in Jackson's archive suggests that she not only personally benefited from slavery but that she also supported the institution for the very fact that it bolstered white supremacy. While living in Washington DC with her first husband—a man who disapproved of slavery because it "allowed a black population to grow up in America"[25]—Jackson hired a slave woman, Lucy, from her master. In a letter to a friend, Jackson writes of Lucy: "I have grown very stylish and keep my servant! . . . She is a slave, and all that her master asks for her is $5.00 a month: she takes care of the rooms—sets the table—helps me dress—*puts away* everything that I leave out of place—in short, makes a fine lady of me—all in the quietest pleasantest way around."[26] Jackson describes Lucy as a "stylish" commodity that transforms her into "a fine lady." Lucy is valuable because she assumes Jackson's feminine labors—setting tables, dressing, housekeeping—and therefore elevates Jackson to a class of Anglo-Americans whose only work is in keeping up with appearances and elite social networks. While this is violent in and of itself, Jackson also celebrates the fact that Lucy completes these labors "in the quietest pleasantest way around," indicating that Lucy is unthreatening and possibly even acquiescent in her role as slave. In this praise Jackson ignores that Lucy is forced labor, that the five dollars a month Jackson pays (and that she finds to be a fair price) is not going to Lucy but to her master, and that Lucy's docility and dedication are not by choice or by nature but are governed by a system that would otherwise invoke physical harm to her body. In fact, Jackson goes on to consider Lucy "one of the illustrations of the *bright* sides of slavery."[27] Jackson celebrates the institution of slavery for reducing Lucy to nothing more than a quiet, pleasant laboring body. Jackson finds it "bright" that slavery has stifled Lucy's ability to speak out in order to free Jackson to speak up in her own writing. In this letter Jackson seems both aware of and enthused by an institution that dismantles an individual's humanity and stifles that individual's agency. Although she will go on to write *A Century of Dishonor* twenty-eight years later, Jackson defends slavery and justifies Lucy's forced labor with the paternalistic rhetoric that Lucy is quiet and pleasant and therefore must be happy. Jackson perceives slavery as a transactional win-win for both herself and Lucy rather than seeing Lucy's deficit as her personal gain.

This quick moment from Jackson's archive has significant implications for the ways we read and understand Jackson's Native American advocacy. That Jackson identifies "*bright* sides of slavery" at all and that she fails to think about Lucy's humanity—we are left to wonder about Lucy's family, of the possibility that she was torn away from a parent, a spouse, or children in order to provide this labor to Jackson—presses us to reexamine the progressive intentions Jackson had toward Native American populations in the West. Jackson spent only the last six years of her life involved in the Native American cause, and during this time she remained aloof from organized, women-led advocacy groups such as the Women's National Indian Association (WNIA). While she wrote frequently to WNIA's co-founder, Amelia Stone Quinton, and although Quinton capitalized off Jackson's literary success in the wake of her death, Jackson opposed the WNIA's most fundamental goals. The WNIA was a predominantly Protestant organization that emphasized Christian education, assimilation, and eventual citizenship for Native Americans. Its approach sought to break up tribal lands and instruct Native Americans in heteronormative family structures and labor. Jackson, on the other hand, admired the old Franciscan order and advocated for a reservation system that protected Native American lifeways. In some ways, Jackson's approach may appear more progressive than that of WNIA. Jackson's aims were to protect Native American lands and tribal culture rather than break them up and assimilate them into dominant institutions. However, Jackson ignores the violence imbedded in the Franciscan order's approach. Like much of the era's literature, Jackson's works romanticize Spanish California and position the United States as its heir.

In her 1878 travel memoir, *Bits of Travel at Home*, Jackson revises the discourse of American Manifest Destiny to account for the United States' inheritance of a bygone Spanish California:

> Does anybody believe that, if the Pilgrims had landed where Father Junipero Serra's missionaries did, witches would have been burnt in the San Joaquin Valley? Or that if gold strewed the ground to-day from Cape Cod to Berkshire, a Massachusetts man would ever spend it like a Californian? This is the key-note to much which the expectation and prophecy about California seem to me to overlook. I believe that the lasting power, the true culture, the best, most roundest result—physical, moral, mental—of our national future will not spring on the Western Shore, any more than on the Eastern. It lies to-day like a royal heir, hidden in secret,

crowned with jewels, dowered with gold and silver, nurtured on strengths of the upper airs of the Sierras, biding the day when two peoples, meeting midway on the continent, shall establish the true centre and the complete life.[28]

In this scene from her first travels west, Jackson borrows on the ideas and rhetoric of Manifest Destiny, but she also critiques it. While she does relate expansion to the "lasting power, the true culture" and the "physical, moral, [and] mental" health of "our national future," she does not accept the "prophecy about California." Rather, she finds that the national future "lies to-day like a royal heir" in "meeting midway on the continent," in establishing "the true centre and the complete life" of the nation. This rhetoric of uniting the East and West in the center harkens back to early claims that U.S. progress would bring "the Empires of the Atlantic and Pacific . . . together into one,"[29] yet Jackson expresses skepticism toward the "prophecy" and "expectations" of California and indicates a "meeting" of the two coasts rather than a takeover of one by the other. She is aware that California already has its own history, and she ties temporality to geography, history to region, when she suggests that California is inseparable from Father Junipero Serra and his missionary history, just as the East is inseparable from a Pilgrim history descended from European colonists. Even as she erases the history of Indigenous populations living in the region before the Spanish missionaries arrived, Jackson rejects Anglo-America's "expectation and prophecy about California" precisely because she recognizes and values the history of Spanish-era California. Rather than forgetting or erasing Spanish and Indigenous histories of California, as dominant discourses of Manifest Destiny do, Jackson advocates for their inheritance and suggests that part of annexing the western territories is the annexing of these histories as well. In fact, the "royal heir" suggests a union of histories rather than the erasure of one by the other, while it also articulates positioning Spanish-era Californian history and culture as a natural precursor to American Manifest Destiny.

As such, Jackson does not agree with the WNIA's push to extend U.S. citizenship to Native Americans. Rather, Jackson embraces the Spanish mission system and realizes the American reservation system as its close relative. "To administer complete citizenship of a sudden, all round, to all Indians," Jackson argues toward the end of *A Century of Dishonor*, "would be as grotesque a blunder as to dose them all round with any one medicine, irrespective of the symptoms and needs of their diseases. It would kill more than it would cure."[30] In part Jackson resists generalizing Native American identity and culture. She makes a case for treating Native Americans as individuals rather than assigning one single "cure" to all. But this language also stems from the same paternalistic language used to justify African slavery and the plantation system in the South. It assumes that Native Americans do not know what is best for themselves and suggests it is the responsibility of Anglo-American society to determine what is. In the first of a series of California articles Jackson wrote for *Century Magazine* in the 1880s, she asserts that the best way of "dealing" with Native Americans in the West is not to assimilate them as U.S. citizens but to collect them onto reservations.[31] Jackson spends a great deal of the article admiring the Spanish mission system and praising the Franciscans on their ability to bring order to the California wilderness. She writes: "That [Native Americans] looked so kindly as they did to the ways and restraints of the new life, is the strongest possible proof that the methods of the friars in dealing with them must have been both wise and humane."[32] Unlike citizenship, which Jackson thinks would be a "grotesque blunder" and would "kill more than it would cure," she paints the Franciscan mission system as "both wise and humane." Echoing her earlier description of the slave woman Lucy's quiet and pleasant complacence with slavery, Jackson dismisses the Spanish mission system's violence—just as she ignores the agency citizenship might bring to Native Americans—by emphasizing the "kindly" Native American response. In neither of these instances is Jackson concerned with the methods by which each oppressive system manages people. She makes her assessments based on whether or not Lucy and the mission Indians make *her* feel uncomfortable. Since neither Lucy nor the mission Indians offend Jackson or indicate through their interactions with her that they are dissatisfied with their "restraints," Jackson ignorantly and selfishly allows herself to assume that both slavery and the mission system are "wise and humane."

Jackson draws an enthusiastic comparison between the plantation system and the reservation system and charges each with producing a source of docile and pleasant labor. This comparison becomes the basis for the ways Jackson treats the often competing motivations she has toward Native American labor and autonomy in *Ramona*. Jackson's novel treats Californios as a romantic and fading artifact of the pre-American West. Señora Moreno, the novel's Californio matriarch, is described as both a "tremendous force" and "a sad, spiritual-minded old lady, amiable and indolent, like her race."[33] Like Ruiz de Burton's *New York Times* obituary writer, Jackson is careful to celebrate the elite Californio lifeway but also to render it something of the past, something to be admired and inherited by a new American regime. Jackson deploys popular stereotypes of Mexican and Californio populations to account for what she and dominant Americans view as their failures. "Through wars, insurrections, revolutions, downfalls, Spanish, Mexican, civil, ecclesiastical," the novel narrates, Señora Moreno's "standpoint, her poise, remained the same. She simply grew more and more proudly, passionately, a Spaniard and a Moreno; more and more stanchly and fierily a Catholic, and a lover of the Franciscans."[34] Like the Spanish history she represents, Señora Moreno is described as stuck in what *Ramona*'s readers would recognize as a bygone and backward civilization. Her pride and passion for her Spanish heritage, her once-powerful family estate, and her fiery dedication to Catholicism are what make her romantic and admirable but also what render her vulnerable and pathetic. Her refusal to submit to Anglo-American culture and to assimilate into U.S. institutions makes her a threat to the nation, but her worship of a history and a lifeway that, aesthetically beautiful as it may be, has been so thoroughly conquered by American expansion and capitalism renders her threat benign.

Like the squatters in Ruiz de Burton's *The Squatter and the Don*, Jackson believes Californios do not use the land to its fullest potential and uses this to make room for an American takeover of the region. In particular Jackson views Native American labor as another resource of the land and traces what she recognizes to be the Californios' increasing mismanagement of it. At the start of the novel Señora Moreno expresses her concern with the lack of Native American labor to help her rancho with the annual sheep shearing. Señora Moreno "did not realize how time was going; there would be no shearers to be hired presently, since the Señora was determined to have none but Indians."[35] The problem, as Jackson quickly identifies it, is not that the Moreno rancho refuses Mexican labor in favor of Native American labor; it is that the elite Californio families such as Señora Moreno's have allowed the Franciscan mission system to crumble. As a result, Native American labor is scattered across the region instead of collected in centralized locations under the control of elite Spanish society. The Morenos are left to hope that Native American laborers "will wait until we are ready for them" and that they find the terms of their employment satisfactory enough.[36] This degree of Native American autonomy—small though it may be—disrupts the Californio economy and threatens the elite social order. In addition, Jackson's novel assumes that Native Americans are not fit to govern their new autonomy. The novel implies that such autonomy leaves Native Americans "in confusion and ill humor . . . with nothing to do, and still worse with not much of anything to eat."[37] In clear contrast to the "kindly" Native Americans Jackson surveyed in the *Century Magazine* articles, Alessandro and the Native American laborers under his charge are depicted as "cold and distant."[38] As if they were cattle, crops, or some other form of property, Jackson's sentimental introduction of Alessandro as a suffering but noble Native American suggests that Californios neglected their duty to Native Americans and dismantled the centuries-long work of the Franciscans.

Thus Jackson represents Californios in the novel as incapable masters and incompetent land managers in need of Anglo-American bailout, and she introduces a sentimental white rescue mission, as depicted in the Hyers' rescue of Ramona and Alessandro, to recoup Californio losses in the western region. In a conversation Alessandro has with Father Salvierderra—a once influential leader of the Franciscan order who is now forced to travel by foot from rancho to rancho to deliver mass in front of a dwindling audience—Alessandro worries over his Native American village's land grant. The land grant, granted to Alessandro's grandfather by a Californio elite, serves as a kind of pseudo-mission, providing Native Americans with a place to live and ensures their close proximity and indebtedness to Californio ranchos. But with American settlers arriving in the region, Alessandro worries that the village is not safe. Father Salvierderra tries to reassure Alessandro, telling him that "there has to be some such paper, as I understand the laws . . . some notice, before any steps can be taken to remove Indians from an estate."[39] When Alessandro asks how it could be legal to take the land on which someone else has built a home and that was granted to the Native American community by Señor Valdez, Father Salvierderra asks Alessandro if Señor Valdez gave him "any paper, any writing to show it."[40] Of course Alessandro replies no, they were not given a paper—referring to a deed—but that "it is marked in red lines on the map."[41] This leaves both Father Salvierderra and Alessandro pessimistic about the village's future and all but secures the land's legal encroachment by Anglo-American squatters. While Jackson does criticize Anglo-Americans who take advantage of poorly written legislation to occupy another's home (she expresses a lack of "faith in the honesty of the Americans" through Father Salvierderra),[42] she does so at the same time that she blames Californios for not establishing a paper trail that could protect Native American lands in an American court. This situates Californios as an entirely historical cultural infrastructure, unprepared to lead the modern world.

The novel makes provocative comparisons between Californio California and a pre–Civil War American South. But rather than suggesting these lifeways were inhumane for their enslavement of a forced population of laborers, Jackson participates in a melancholic nostalgia for the past and what she understands to be the lost potential of the these regions. For instance, when Señora Moreno sees the small gathering of Native American laborers in her estate's chapel to hear Father Salvierderra's mass before the sheep shearing, she is left to reminisce over the "old times . . . as if [the Native Americans] belonged to the house, as they used to."[43] Señora Moreno's failure to properly maintain her labor source and her subsequent obsession with the "old times" renders her "of the past" and positions her disadvantageously for the future.[44] While Jackson maintains sympathy for Señora Moreno, she also recognizes her as the source of the labor problem in the West. As mentioned above, Señora Moreno is described as unadaptable, but Jackson is critical of the "tremendous force" she represents as well.[45]

After Señor Moreno's death in the Mexican-American War, Jackson's narrator explains that it was not the Moreno son, Felipe, who inherited power over the rancho but Señora Moreno. "In truth," the narrator says, "it was not Felipe, but the Señora, who really decided all questions from greatest to least, and managed everything on the place, from the sheep-pastures to the artichoke-patch."[46] It is not surprising, considering Jackson's well-known disapproval of early feminism, that the narrative tone undermines Señora Moreno's influence rather than celebrates it as a feminist achievement. The sinister treatment Jackson gives Señora Moreno is a consequence of her disapproval not of Señora Moreno's Californio culture per se but of her deviance from Victorian gender roles. Jackson's "In truth" statement rescues Felipe from taking the blame for the failed Moreno rancho and places it instead on his mother, whose overstepping in the rancho's business affairs leaves it without sufficient labor and influence. Señora Moreno's power is further described as "never to appear as a factor in the situation, to be able to wield other men, as instruments, with the same direct and implicit response to will that one gets from a hand or a foot,—this is to triumph, indeed: to be as nearly controller and conqueror of Fates as fate permits."[47] Señora Moreno "wield[s]" men "as instruments" and interferes with the "Fates." Hence Señora Moreno's power is dangerous, according to Jackson, because her "power is an instinct and not an attainment; a passion rather than a purpose."[48] Señora Moreno's inclination toward a feminine sentimentality—which we see in her nostalgia for the "old times" and her inability to adapt to the future—renders her incapable of exercising such power productively. Her power is primitive, "instinct" and "passion," instead of a power restrained by "attainment" and "purpose." In effect Jackson cautions against a women's power untethered from Victorian gender roles and identifies it as a threat to the western American ideal.

Aunt Ri, the Hyer family matriarch with whom I began this chapter, demonstrates Jackson's recommendation for a more appropriate female role in the American West. Though she is not a conventional sentimental heroine, Aunt Ri does provide Jackson's Anglo-American women readers with a character to whom they can relate in contrast to the unrelatable Ramona and Señora Moreno. Traveling with her family from Tennessee to California in hopes of curing her son, Jos, Aunt Ri is shocked to learn that Ramona and Alessandro are Native American. "'Injuns!' ejaculated Jos's mother. 'Lord save us, Jos! Have we reelly took in Injuns? What on airth.'"[49] Although Aunt Ri scolded her husband for his prejudicial remarks when he though Ramona and Alessandro were Mexican, her mixed reaction to finding out they are in fact Native American is a reflection of the era's popular dramatization of Native American identity, history, and culture and of the power popular literature has to sway public opinion. Aunt Ri explains: "I've always hed a reel mean feelin' about 'em [Native Americans]; I didn't want ter come nigh 'em, nor ter hev 'em come nigh me." This estimation, Jackson's narrator goes on to explicate, is derived from the era's popular literatures.[50] "Her ideas about Indians," the narrator says, "had been drawn from newspapers, and from a book or two of narratives of massacres, and from an occasional sight of vagabond bands or families they had encountered in their journey across the plains."[51] Like many of Jackson's Anglo-American women readers, Aunt Ri is portrayed as a misinformed victim of the American literary market. In contrast to *A Century of Dishonor*, which might have been too heavy-handed in blaming Anglo-American society for the mistreatment of Native Americans, Jackson gives her readers a way of identifying their prejudice as not their fault but as the fault of a literary industry that wields too much influence over the minds of otherwise well-intentioned Americans. Like Little Eva in Stowe's *Uncle Tom's Cabin*, Aunt Ri instructs readers on a more benevolent maternalism. As she sits with Ramona and her infant daughter in the sheep corral, protected from the raging snowstorm outside, Aunt Ri is impressed by Ramona's maternal affection for her baby. Aunt Ri says to her son: "Well, well, she's fond uv her baby's enny white woman! I kin see thet";[52] and to her husband, Aunt Ri admires the fact that "I dunno's ever I see a white man think so much uv a woman."[53] Because Ramona and Alessandro are able to love their child and one another in heteronormative ways identifiable to Aunt Ri, she admits to having had "a lesson 'n the subjeck uv Injuns."[54] Ramona and Alessandro do not match up with the barbaric, untamed images of Native Americans in the popular newspaper and penny dreadful stories Aunt Ri likely encountered. Rather, although Aunt Ri notes that Alessandro is "real dark; dark's any n—— in Tennessee," she "found herself sitting side by side in friendly intercourse with an Indian man and Indian woman, whose appearance and behavior were attractive; towards whom she felt herself singularly drawn."[55] With Aunt Ri Jackson demonstrates a separation between reality and literature. She encourages readers to form their own opinions based on experiences they have actually had rather than ones they have read about in magazines and cheap novels.

But even as Aunt Ri feels herself "singularly drawn" to Ramona, she maintains her superiority over Ramona at all points in the novel. As mentioned at the start of this chapter, it is important that Jackson introduces the Hyers into the novel as Ramona and Alessandro's rescuers. Although Alessandro, a native of the West, should have more insight into the region's climate, the Hyers, newcomers to Southern California, are the ones who demonstrate a more thorough preparedness to navigate and even protect others from the California wilderness. This is an illustration of an American exceptionalism and an instance that permeates the novel's celebration of Anglo-American settlement of the western American region. In addition, this scene allows Jackson to at once soften popular depictions of Native Americans without relinquishing Anglo-American superiority over them. Discourses of Manifest Destiny argued that it was the divine fate of the United States to occupy the continent from east to west because the American nation was the most equipped to tame the wilderness. In John O'Sullivan's 1845 essay, "Annexation," in which he first coins the term "Manifest Destiny" in defense of the annexation of Texas, O'Sullivan claims that the annexation is the "fault of Mexico herself, and Mexico alone."[56] He goes on to suggest that the California region is the same. "Imbecile and distracted, Mexico never can exert any real governmental authority over such a country. The impotence of the one [Mexico] and the distance of the other [California], must make the relation one of virtual independence; unless, by stunting the province of all natural growth, and forbidding that immigration which can alone develop its capabilities and fulfill the purposes of its creation, tyranny may retain a military dominion, which is no government in the legitimate sense of the term."[57]

O'Sullivan claims that Mexico's "impotence" in managing the western American territories is "stunting the province of all natural growth," and he cites the distance between Mexico's governing center and California as a justification for American conquest of the region. O'Sullivan claims that unlike the United States, which has proved itself capable of taming the vast wilderness time and time again, Mexico has proven "imbecile and distracted" and has failed to populate the region with a governing class of European descent. In many ways Jackson borrows upon this language to criticize Californios' mismanagement of the region's resources, as I have discussed above. By "forbidding that immigration which can alone develop its capabilities and fulfill the purposes of its creation," O'Sullivan implies that the Native American populations that do occupy the region are left to "no government in the legitimate sense of the term." O'Sullivan brandishes an American exceptionalism in taking what others cannot manage efficiently and transforming the land and the peoples into productive and dedicated national resources, introducing a rhetoric that will go on to become the basis of American expansion from the mid-nineteenth century to our contemporary time.

The Hyers' rescue of Ramona and Alessandro performs this benevolent exceptionalism, effectively modeling for Jackson's readers an imperialistic paternalism. By rescuing Ramona, Alessandro, and their infant child from the snowstorm, the Hyers exhibit their exceptional ability to weather the storm and to protect those who can't protect themselves. Rather than condemning American imperialism, as some scholars have argued, Jackson creates a necessity for Anglo-American settlement in the region.[58] Aunt Ri does in fact dismantle the popular literature's characterization of Native Americans, but she does so to reassure Anglo-Americans of their dominance in the "Wild West." While stories of scalpings and Native American ambushes plagued the Wild West narratives of Buffalo Bill Cody and pioneer travelogues, Jackson offers an alternative version that paints Native Americans as gentle and understanding of their inferior and dependent positionality to incoming Anglo-Americans. This is not necessarily to make Native Americans more human but to ease the fears of a largely vulnerable class of Anglo-Americans (like the Hyers) and to promote their settlement in the region. In making sense of Ramona's story, Aunt Ri says to Jos:

"[Ramona's] father wuz white, she sez, but she don't call herself nothin' but an Injun, the same's [Alessandro] is."[59] Reflective of an American "one-drop" rule, which identified an individual as Black if there was any evidence of miscegenation, Aunt Ri admires Ramona's humility in assigning herself what Aunt Ri believes to be an inferior racial identity when she could have passed as white. Indeed miscegenation is Aunt Ri's obsession here: she is skeptical of Ramona's self-proclaimed heritage. The "she sez" Aunt Ri inserts into the middle of her comment syntactically echoes the split Aunt Ri perceives between the part of Ramona that is white and the part of her that disowns this whiteness and clings to her Native Americanness. "She sez" functions in this way to reject both mixed identities and any notions of equality between Aunt Ri and Ramona. But it is Ramona's quiet and pleasant compliance with Anglo-American racial hierarchies that opens the West up to Anglo-American settlement and with which Jackson is able to redeem Native Americans from the violent images circulating in dominant culture.

Aunt Ri is often discussed as Jackson's "woman-centered critique" of western American expansion.[60] Such arguments read Aunt Ri's benevolence toward Ramona and Alessandro as a model for how Jackson wishes popular society to treat Native American communities. However, Aunt Ri's benevolence is still inappropriate given her intrusion upon Native American lands, and when *Ramona* is read as a cross-regional account of American labor anxiety in the post-Reconstruction era, Aunt Ri's character serves as Jackson's vision for an imperial maternalism. Jackson first suggests this vision when, after Aunt Ri's husband hands her Ramona's infant daughter, "the baby, which recognized the motherly hand at its first touch, . . . ceased crying."[61] Holding the baby, Aunt Ri declares: "Think o' sech a mite's this bein' aout'n this weather. I'll jest warm up some milk for it this minnit."[62] It is implied that Ramona and Alessandro, unfit to navigate the storm, are also unfit parents. The love Aunt Ri witnesses between Ramona and Alessandro is enough to soften the images Aunt Ri has of Native Americans, but it is not enough to protect their baby from the elements. Aunt Ri, however, has the "motherly hand" Ramona doesn't and is able, unlike Ramona, to comfort the baby into quiet. Aunt Ri can't think what would bring "sech a mite's this" out into the storm—failing to see Ramona's and Alessandro's travels as their only chance at survival in the American-conquered West—and immediately offers a solution to the problem, warm milk, which Ramona neither has nor thinks to ask for.

When the baby falls ill a few months into the Hyers' acquaintance with Ramona and Alessandro, Aunt Ri offers the only pathway of survival for the child. She convinces Alessandro to take his daughter to the Indian agent and to solicit the help of the government doctor. But when the agent's help comes with the contingency that Alessandro sign his name in the government ledger, Alessandro becomes distraught and asks Aunt Ri not to "let him write, till I know what he puts my name in his book for!"[63] Jackson's narrator describes how the agent, "with a look of suppressed impatience, yet trying to speak kindly," explains to Aunt Ri, "There's no making these Indians understand anything. They seem to think if I have their names in my book, it gives me some power over them."[64] Instead of understanding Alessandro's concerns about the implications of this power, Aunt Ri asks the agent, "Wall, don't it? . . . If yer hain't got it over them, who have yer got it over? What yer goin' to do for 'em?"[65] Aunt Ri's response is a demonstration of how the U.S. government manipulates liberal ideals to entrench the masses in an ignorant compliance with government malfeasance. Aunt Ri accepts government power as an altruistic mechanism to care for those who cannot care for themselves—a sacrifice of individual autonomy for the greater good. She believes that in signing his name in the ledger, Alessandro is giving his consent to be governed and thereby to be protected. No doubt this consent is a liberal exchange of autonomy for government protection, and Aunt Ri appears to have no problem with this arrangement. In fact, she locates her patriotic pride in such an exchange. Aunt Ri perceives that while Alessandro's consent provides him with the care that he needs, the governing body, having received Alessandro's consent, is able to better surveil and monitor the pulse of the nation's citizenry. In her blissful ignorance Aunt Ri overlooks that Alessandro isn't a citizen, and even if he was, his consent has been solicited through coercion and the threat of death. In Aunt Ri's character, Jackson misses the point that the tradeoff is not equal and that Aunt Ri's own consent, granted with the understanding that the government has her best interests at heart, is recruited under false pretenses. As such, the novel unwittingly positions Aunt Ri as an unknowing imperial actor and performs the surveillance Alessandro fears.

Aunt Ri's response to the agent puts pressure on the U.S. government to increase its paternalism rather than promote Native American autonomy and inclusion. With the acceptance of the government's power and her and Alessandro's submissive relation to it, Aunt Ri's role is to influence government men—much like the Victorian doctrines of Republican Motherhood instruct—to execute their promises to protect Native Americans and perform their duties as their paternal rescuers. In addition, Aunt Ri persuades Alessandro that the agent's demands are harmless, and she encourages him to consent to government surveillance. Aunt Ri acts as the conduit through which the government and Native Americans communicate and ultimately through which the government contains and exterminates Native Americans in the western region. With the same frustration she treats the Californios' failure to secure their land with a paper trail, Jackson represents Alessandro's fear of signing his name in the agent's ledger as immature and further evidence of his dependence upon Anglo-Americans. Aunt Ri's job is that of mediator, ensuring Alessandro that his fears are irrational at the same time that she demands the agent fulfill his end of the contract. Aunt Ri tells Alessandro not to "be a fool" and that "hevin' his name 'n' they book" is "only so the Agent kin know what Injuns wants help, 'n' where they air."[66] Her reassurance is that of a mother soothing a child with irrational fears. But even after Alessandro submits to Aunt Ri and signs his name, the government doctor "could hardly keep from laughing when it was made clear to him" that Alessandro wanted him "to ride thirty miles to prescribe for an ailing Indian baby."[67] Instead, without even seeing the patient, the doctor gives Alessandro medicine to administer to the child himself. Of course the "medicine did the baby no good. In fact, it did her harm. She was too feeble for violent remedies."[68] Just as Jackson relates the extension of Native Americans citizenship to negligent medicine at the end of *A Century of Dishonor*, dosing the baby "all round with any one medicine" results in the child's death, rather than in her assimilation into American society, and effectively ends Alessandro's lineage.[69] But Jackson does not hold the Indian agent entirely responsible. The agent deflects blame and explains to Aunt Ri: "That's just the trouble with this Agency. It is very different from what it would be if I had all my Indians on a reservation."[70] The agent indicates that because Native Americans are scattered across the region, it is difficult to reach them and to foster trusting relationships with them. Instead of providing critical commentary on the violent policies that drive Native Americans from their homes, Jackson takes this moment to advocate for reservations and to suggest that the federal government do more to centralize the location of Native American individuals. The fact that Alessandro's sick child cannot be helped may in part be associated with the doctor's neglect, but the doctor's neglect is the symptom of what Jackson identifies as a larger problem: the failure of the federal government to provide lands for Native American reservations.

In *Ramona* Jackson wrongly identifies the problem Native Americans face in the West. Instead of recognizing Anglo-American conquest and Indigenous displacement as the issue, Jackson accuses Anglo-American settler colonialism of insufficiently managing the displaced Native American population and suggests that Native Americans need more of an Anglo-American presence instead of more autonomy. As such, Jackson's Alessandro is a character fraught with irreconcilable intentions. When the Indian agent uses the possessive "my Indians" in his conversation with Aunt Ri, Alessandro's fear of signing his name in the ledger increases, and he pleads with Aunt Ri and Jos to let him leave. To this the agent responds: "That's all the use there is trying to do anything with them! Let him go, then, if he doesn't want any help from the Government!"[71] But Aunt Ri steps in, calms the agent's frustrations, and asks him to "jest explain it to Jos, an' he'll make [Alessandro] understand."[72] The solution, Aunt Ri believes, is in assuring Alessandro of the nation's good intentions and ability to provide him welfare. But Aunt Ri is herself a member of the dispossessed and does not realize the deeply violent mechanism in play, even when her attempts to reassure Alessandro appear as an ultimatum in which she tells him that if he does not comply with the Indian agent's demands, then "he can't hev the Agency doctor," and his child will surely die.[73] This gets Alessandro's attention, and as mentioned, Alessandro gives in. Aunt Ri's negotiations are considered a success, despite the fact that Alessandro is coerced and the child dies anyway.

In fact, although it could be argued that Aunt Ri's ignorant faith in the government's intentions is what ultimately kills Alessandro and Ramona's child, the novel finds a way to blame the child's death on the child's mother, Ramona. As she waits at home with her dying child, Ramona's sense of powerlessness to save her leads her to steal the baby Jesus figurine from the Madonna altar. She hides the figurine and tells the Virgin Mary that "she could not have him any more till she gave me back the baby well and strong."[74] When the medicine fails and the child breathes her last breath, Ramona's maternal loss is translated into self-chastisement. She wails, "I have killed her! I have killed her," and the novel does little to dismiss Ramona's guilt.[75] It is in this moment of grief that Ramona finally agrees to go with Alessandro to an even more remote Native American village, allowing readers to assume Ramona is punished for superstitiously stealing the baby Jesus and for losing faith in the American system.

Ramona and Alessandro are once again depicted as incapable of caring for their own child and unable to autonomously determine their own best interests. Alessandro wastes time in fretting over signing his name in the government ledger while Ramona, always skeptical of the agency doctor, resorts to Catholic idolatry—which Jackson's mainstream readers would have recognized as primitive superstition—to save her child. Jackson uses these moments in the novel to further suggest that the U.S. government does a disservice to Native American populations by failing to enact a proper reservation system in the West that could save Native Americans from themselves.

But there is more to Jackson's calls for Native American reservations. Jackson identifies a link between Native American containment on reservations and an expanded civic role for Anglo-American women. In the nineteenth century Anglo-American women subscribed to the ideas of Republican Motherhood, which positioned white, Protestant, middle-class women as the nation's moral guides. Women came to rule their households and thereby found influence over government and civic life through the civilizing force they had over their husbands and male children. Amy Kaplan has noted the impact Republican

Motherhood had on women's sentimental fiction and has shown how Anglo-American women expanded their influence over the home to cover the domestic nation as well. Anglo-American women sentimentalists and their female characters asserted a civic identity through the imperial mission of civilizing foreign others—both foreign to the home (African American slaves and servants) and foreign to the nation (the imperial conquests such as those of Native Americans and Mexicans).[76] But with the end of slavery and the ratification of the Thirteenth and Fourteenth Amendments, demand for women's civilizing force was greatly diminished. In many ways the success of Stowe's *Uncle Tom's Cabin* helped bring an end not only to slavery but also to a literary tradition that extended Anglo-American women sentimentalists the power to influence dominant society.

Jackson, a woman who established a lucrative career selling sentimental fiction to the nation's prominent literary magazines, sensed the shift away from sentimental, women-centered fictions in the late nineteenth century. Above I quoted Jackson's intentions not to "write *one word* as a sentimentalist" and instead to use *A Century of Dishonor* to raise public sentiment for the Native American cause through authenticated government documents.[77] While sentimental fiction might still draw a paying audience, Jackson implies here that it certainly hasn't maintained its power over public opinion. Rather, the genre is diminished to the excessive display of pathos that later critics—including Henry James, William Dean Howells, and Frank Norris—will use against sentimentalism to raise literary realism and naturalism to the nation's esteemed literary modes. However, *A Century of Dishonor* failed, indicating to Jackson that with the end of the sentimental novel's political edge also came the end to women's civic power. Women writers were not taken seriously in any other politically inflected genre—as Jackson's experience with *A Century of Dishonor* clearly demonstrates—and therefore Jackson returned to sentimentalism in *Ramona*. But even *Ramona*, which was a commercial success that initiated a profitable travel industry in California that lasts to this day, did not have the influence Jackson had hoped for. In a number of letters she wrote to friends in the months following *Ramona*'s publication, Jackson worried over reviews of the novel, which seemed more preoccupied by the picturesque quality of the novel than its Native American advocacy. She writes that *Ramona* was her "last weapon" and that if it did not influence the nation, "I know nothing more to do."[78] Jackson fears "the story has been too interesting, as a story—: so few of the critics seem to have been impressed by anything in it, so much as by its literary excellence, etc. etc."[79] Jackson grows frustrated over the fact that the literary form takes precedent over the novel's content. In the letters she wrote during this period, she clings to her "hobby" and desperately reaches for what she might do next.[80] Although she writes that she knows "nothing more to do," she also contemplates writing a children's story of Ramona, claiming that "children have more heart than grown up people."[81] As her letters approach the date of her death, her disappointment in *Ramona*'s public reception grows, and so too does her desperation to have someone, anyone, hear her. Just days before her death, Jackson sends a letter to President Grover Cleveland in which she asks him "to read [her] Century of Dishonor" so that she might die "happier for the belief I have that it is your hand that is destined to strike the first steady blow towards lifting this burden of infamy from our country, and right the wrongs of the Indian race."[82] That Jackson returns to *A Century of Dishonor* in the final days of her life indicates that she not only felt *Ramona* a failure despite its commercial success, but she also felt her own power in the literary market to be fading.

Jackson's frustration is twofold. In part she is frustrated by the fact that reviewers and the public miss *Ramona*'s Native American advocacy completely. In addition, Jackson is angered by her lack of influence as a woman writer in a shifting literary market. In a February 1885 letter to Charles Dudley Warner, Jackson complains about *The Nation*'s review of *Ramona*. She says that she would "give a good deal to know who wrote it," and she condemns the reviewer's careless reading of the novel.[83] She defends her ill treatment of the reviewer: "Nothing is more absurd of course than to ascribe hostile criticism to personal animus—but I cannot help the feeling that in this case there must be some such thing."[84] Jackson senses that the reviewer harbors a personal vendetta against her and that since Warner and Thomas Baily Aldrich have praised the novel, it can be the reviewer's only reason for writing as he did. Jackson goes on to say, "If Howells or James or Bishop wrote book-notices for the Nation, I should understand it!—of course I appear to them to deserve *tomahawking*."[85] Jackson documents a riff in the literary market as figures such as Howells and James rise to literary prominence and commandeer public opinion of literary texts. She dismisses James's, Howells's, and Bishop's unfavorable judgments of her as understandable because of their literary philosophies, but she is not quite convinced that their influence should be powerful enough to shape the industry as a whole. Therefore Jackson provides an important look into the shift from Victorian sentimentalism to early American literary realism and the consequences this shift had for women writers specifically. But Jackson sensed this shift even as she was writing *Ramona*, and it may be, as I have suggested, one of the reasons she returned to the sentimental tradition after *A Century of Dishonor* failed.

But Aunt Ri appears in *Ramona* as Jackson's meditation on the diminishing power and containment of Anglo-American women's civic voice. With her sentimental retelling of Native American removal in the West, Jackson draws together her frustrations with the literary shift away from sentimentalism and the nation's move toward a wage labor economy. She finds a parallel in women writers facing a reading public increasingly unenthused by sentimental fiction and everyday Anglo-American women who were stripped of their authority as subscribers to a Republican motherhood in the post-slavery era. Post-slavery, when wages are attached to hourly work outside the home, women who perform domestic upkeep and operate household processes are left undervalued and unrewarded (both monetarily and civically). Jackson's novel represents the consequences of this labor transition when Aunt Ri is forced to sell her Tennessee home in the wake of a failed Reconstruction era, thus sacrificing her domestic influence, in order to travel with her husband and sick son from Tennessee to California on a doctor's recommendation for their health and stability. Though they are thoroughly disenfranchised and dispossessed of their home, the Hyers are nonetheless "cheery as if they were rich people on a pleasure-trip."[86] Here Jackson refers to the prominent health tourism industry that encouraged wealthy Anglo-American families to go west as a means of curing their ailments. This kind of health tourism, as Jennifer S. Tuttle explains, was usually practiced by members of the "urban, white, privileged-class [who were] at the forefront of American cultural and economic development" and who held professions that "overtaxed their nervous systems."[87] The illness most associated with health tourism to the West was neurasthenia, which was created out of a "nationalistic" discourse that "went hand in hand with the forces of Manifest Destiny."[88] It suggested that the brainwork of a newly emergent professional class—a class that supervised, managed, and directed the new wage-laborer class—debilitated the body's physicality, and the only cure was to experience the rugged terrain and warm climate of the West. But the Hyers invoke a different kind of health tourism, one tied to poverty and disenfranchisement, and one that links southern Reconstruction to western settler-colonialism in ways that have not been attributed to the novel before.

The Hyers are not on "a pleasure trip" and are certainly not the "rich people" they imagine themselves to be mimicking in their travels. They are "half beggared" in the covered wagon they bought with the profits from the sale of their modest home.[89] Jackson emphasizes the Hyers' true identity at the same time that she discourages their false sense of belonging and their "cheery" attitude. With the Hyers, and Aunt Ri in particular, Jackson raises concerns for the ways the changing nation manipulates a class of Anglo-American citizens into believing in their continued power in American democratic institutions. Above I suggested that Aunt Ri holds misguided faith in the nation's use of power. Now I extend that argument to posit that Aunt Ri's character invites readers to critique the passive submission and blind patriotism an uneducated class of white southerners invested into notions of nation and national identity. After Ramona tells Aunt Ri of her family's forced removal from their village and the home they built themselves, Aunt Ri responds in disbelief: "I don't bleeve the Guvvermunt knows anything about it. . . . Somebody ought ter be sent ter tell 'em 't Washington what's goin on hyar."[90] Aunt Ri's surprise registers her ignorance about American democratic systems. Indoctrinated as she is in the rhetoric of Manifest Destiny and the West's representation as a new frontier in American democratic opportunity, Aunt Ri cannot believe that the government that promotes her settlement of the region does so at the expense of another's. But when Ramona questions Aunt Ri's faith in her government and suggests, "It's the people in Washington that have done it. . . . Is it not in Washington all the laws are made?" Aunt Ri can only respond with: "I bleeve so!"[91] She then turns to her son for reassurance, asking him: "Ain't it, Jos? It's Congress ain't 't, makes the laws?"[92] But even Jos, a supposedly enfranchised Anglo-male citizen, is not confident in his answer. He responds: "I bleeve so. . . . They make some, at any rate. I dunno's they make 'em all."[93] "Cheery" though they may be, the Hyers are invested in a patriotism they neither understand nor feel the need to question. If Ruiz de Burton captures the malicious Anglo-American squatter who takes advantage of every loophole in the law in order to steal land from the Californios, then Jackson depicts her Anglo-American settlers as all too ignorant to be malicious. The Hyers, and by extension the other Anglo-American settlers in the novel, are not educated enough in the American legal system to be so calculating in their takeover. Jackson's white settlers are just as much victims of the American political system as the Native Americans on behalf of whom the novel originally sought to advocate. As Aunt Ri says, "We're Ummerikens! 'n' we wouldn't cheat nobody, not ef we knowed it, not out er a doller."[94] Jackson deflects the blame to national institutions that have pacified families such as the Hyers into a cheeriness for the idea that, as U.S. citizens, they are exceptional and have exceptional rights and privileges. But in reality, Jackson shows, Aunt Ri and the Anglo-American settlers she comes to represent unsuspectingly carry out the brunt of the nation's imperial project in the West.

Jackson is critical of a U.S. nationalism that recruits its base through the manipulation of a poor, uneducated class of white citizens. After listening to Ramona's and Alessandro's story, Aunt Ri "was not convinced" that her government could do such a thing as force a family out of their home.[95] But she *is* convinced that she's "an Ummeriken" and therefore has "got suthin' to say abaout the country I live in, 'n' the way things had oughter be; or at least, Jeff hez; 'n thet's the same thing."[96] Aunt Ri still believes herself a Republican Mother. She believes that through her husband, Jeff, she can have "suthin' to say abaout the country" in which she lives and influence what goes on in Washington. She tells her son: "I ain't goin' to rest, nor ter give yeou 'n' yer father no rest nuther, till yeou find aout what all this yere means she's been tellin' us."[97] Aunt Ri deploys her matriarchal power as the moral influencer of her home—even though she is without a home—to demand her husband and her grown son act upon the immoral behavior Ramona relates to them. But she still only asks her husband and son to "find aout what all this yere means," indicating that she still has faith in her government and cannot believe Ramona's story is the full truth. But Jackson renders Aunt Ri's "say" ineffectual or, at best, a mere formality. Throughout the novel's remaining chapters, as Aunt Ri comes to Ramona's and Alessandro's aid over and over, her "say" is tolerated but not regarded with any authority. For instance, Aunt Ri's interactions with the Indian agent on behalf of Ramona and Alessandro are not taken seriously. When Aunt Ri implores the Indian agent to use his power to help Alessandro, the "Agent laughed in spite of himself" and said, "Well, Aunt Ri . . . that's just the trouble with this Agency."[98] Aunt Ri is literally laughed off. The agent condescends to her with his answer, which implies "that's just how it is" and there is no need for her to trouble herself any further with the matter. When Alessandro fears that Aunt Ri is also being "deceived" by the Indian agent, what he really senses is the placating way the Indian agent treats Aunt Ri.[99] Toward the end of the novel, after Alessandro has been killed and Ramona is sick with heartbreak, Aunt Ri once again visits the Indian agent to vent her disapproval. But "she did not wish to seem to reflect on the Agent's usefulness, and so concluded her sentence very differently from her first impulse,—'I'm free ter say I shouldn't like ter stan in yer shoes.'"[100] Aunt Ri still harbors a deferential respect for government agencies and their representatives. She rejects "her first impulse" and censors herself to avoid offending the agent and his government duty. Her "say" is silenced, and as such, any civic voice she derived from her role as woman and mother is reduced to sentimental idealism. The novel ends with Aunt Ri's continued devotion to a government that has let down not only Ramona and Alessandro but Aunt Ri and her own family as well. Jackson thus draws together the government's corruption and lack of accountability in Native American agencies and the declining influence of Aunt Ri's steadfast Victorian womanhood. Ultimately Aunt Ri's "say" does not amount to much, and Jackson indicates that the novel's final tragedy is one shared by Ramona's exile to Mexico and Aunt Ri's continued disenfranchisement.

Jackson's concerns for Native American removal and her concerns for the disenfranchisement of Anglo-American women increasingly compete for the novel's central attention. While Ramona and Alessandro become more and more desperate to find a safe, stable location to call home, Aunt Ri struggles to validate her civic voice with the nation. At multiple points in the novel these competing impulses rub up against one another in ways that create tension between the novel's progressive intentions and its anxieties over the nation's transformation from a slave economy to a wage-labor economy. Recall that as a member of the rural working class, the Hyers' son is not on "a [western American] pleasure-trip" to calm his nerves so that he might return to the taxing job of building the nation's wealth and culture from behind a desk. Rather, Jos Hyer hopes to recover and "to git settled 'n some o' these towns where there's carpenterin' to be done."[101] His desire is part of a pioneer national narrative underwritten by the federal government and reserved for the disenfranchised white populations of the post-Reconstruction South and the industrial North. More than just conflating Jos's hemorrhaging with job competition in the South, Jackson shows that Jos and his family are fleeing the possibility that they will become dependents to a wage-labor economy that has been established in the American North and that is encroaching on the American South in the post–Civil War decades.[102] Jos is in search of work such as "carpenterin'," skilled labor that maintains his economic individualism, gives him access to property ownership, and separates him from the massive populations of freed Black laborers who work agricultural and factory jobs for wages in the North and South. In addition, Jos's ability to get a job as a carpenter differentiates him from transient Native American laborers, such as Alessandro, who travel up and down the Southern California coast seasonally laboring on Señora Moreno's and other Californios' ranchos.

Jos Hyer's mobility from South to West gives him purchase on a white identity connected to land ownership and control over his own labor, but for Alessandro and the rest of the Native American laborers in the novel, mobility emerges in the form of dependent migratory agricultural work that racializes them at the same time that it restricts their access to a stationary domesticity tied to citizenship. Alessandro is "free" in the sense that he is not enslaved. However, he is part of a Native American migrant labor force that serves to "obscure the boundary between enslavement and freedom" precisely because their role as laborers dehumanizes them and establishes them as dependents on Anglo-American paternalism.[103] Described as "contented laborers in the fields," Native Americans in the novel are understood to be "natural enough" laborers who have "born in them" an affinity for agricultural work.[104] As a member of a "race [that] was never meant for anything but servants," the liberally educated Alessandro is represented in the novel as an "exceptional instance," but it is suggested that even this "exceptional instance" labors because it is natural rather than a way to make money or as a pathway to property ownership and citizenship.[105] Alessandro is not "so exceptional, but that if you were to offer him, for instance, the same wages you pay Juan Can," the novel's Mexican property manager, "he would jump at the chance of staying on the place."[106] Alessandro himself says that "it was not for the wages" that he worked for the Moreno rancho but because "it would be a pleasure [for him] to be of help to [the Morenos]."[107] Just as Ramona is redeemed for choosing to identify as Native American rather than white, Alessandro is heralded as "exceptional" because he cowers to a migratory, laboring existence. Jackson's description of Alessandro reflects an oppressive mentality that understood ethnic individuals to be best suited for manual labor, a mentality that echoes Jackson's remarks about Lucy, the slave woman she hired from her master, and the seemingly contended mission Indians she wrote about in the *Century* articles. In the novel's post-Reconstruction moment, the stereotypes of Black laborers as naturally inclined to work and eager to serve at the pleasure of their white masters are proving unsustainable. Therefore Jackson offers a replacement narrative that assigns Native Americans a concurrent role as "noble savages," which introduces a new population of "free" wage laborers for white society to exploit.

Just as the plantation system exerted its control over Black laborers through a withholding of domestic sovereignty, so too does Jackson's novel target Native American domesticity. During the time Alessandro completes the sheep shearing on the Moreno rancho, his Native American village is ransacked by Anglo-American settlers, and he returns to find his home occupied by a white family. Through a crack in the window he sees a "table was set, in the middle of the floor, and there were sitting at it a man, woman, and two children. The youngest, little more than a baby, sat in its high chair, drumming with a spoon on the table, impatient for its supper."[108] Alessandro's claims to domestic intimacy are stolen while he is laboring for an economy that values him for his labor but that discredits his humanity. He is ousted out of liberal personhood, literally, and reduced to looking through a window at an almost parodic depiction of a doppelganger family whose sameness to his only emphasizes their difference: they are white and their healthy baby clamors for food. Though this is the consequence of the racist-imperialist program of Manifest Destiny, of which this Anglo-American family is a key player, this family, like the Hyers, is also displaced and dispossessed by the abrupt move from a slave economy to an industrialized society. Their move West is predicated on the understanding that the West offers an economic freedom indicative of national belonging that has been lost to them in the other regions of the changing nation.

Once again Jackson softens this white family's conquest by suggesting not that it was wrong necessarily but that because it was led by the "brute" force of men unleashed from the civilizing influence of Victorian womanhood, it was executed with more violence than was required. Alessandro takes careful assessment of the white family inside his home. He notices that the "woman looked weary and worn. Her face was a sensitive one, and her voice kindly; but the man had the countenance of a brute,—of a human brute."[109] Jackson's gender contrast cannot be ignored here. Not only does this sentimentalize the plight of Anglo-American women settlers, but it also emphasizes the humanity of Anglo-American male settlers even as it chastises their violence. The man is "a brute," but he is "a human brute." Jackson is careful to maintain the white man's humanity, and in so doing, she renders him as much a victim of the era as Alessandro and the white woman. The white man's character is broken down as a consequence of his family's domestic displacement. His wife anxiously questions when the wagon with their belongings will arrive so that she can "clear up" the house they have stolen from Alessandro and provide a home for her young child.[110] In response, the husband "growled" about a landslide that has obstructed the road and delayed their domestic possessions.[111] Jackson documents the difficulties in traveling West and empathizes with the settler family that feels its dislocation as much as Alessandro, still watching through the window, feels his. The shared dispossession of this moment is reflected, once again, in the fact that Anglo-American women have little "say" in this period of national transition. The white man castigates his wife's anxiety over the missing wagon and tells her that "all women are good for [is to] grumble."[112] The Victorian woman's moral influence is reduced to a dissatisfied "grumble." But unlike Aunt Ri, whose insecurity in her "say" leads her to censor her own impulses, this white woman "seemed unable to repress the speech" and verbally lashes out at her husband for taking the Native American "houses this way!"[113] But even this attempt at moral rebuke holds little sway with her husband, who, spotting Alessandro out the window, pulls out his shotgun and shoots at him as his wife pleads for him not to. Jackson uses this scene to victimize white settler women, but she also uses it to negotiate what undoubtedly must have been her own undecided feelings toward progressive politics. For this woman to establish a stable home for her young child, she must leave the insecurity of the South or the East and install herself in the dwelling of a conquered Native American family. Her security is attainable only through her participation in the dispossession of another.

After this scene in which Alessandro's home is taken by the Anglo-American settler family, he and Ramona find little domestic security. Jackson's solution is to advocate for reservations and the containment of Native American domestic existence onto designated, surveilled lands. As I have shown throughout this chapter, Jackson valued reservations over Native American autonomy and citizenship because of the power reservations afforded white society to maintain what she saw as an integral labor resource. Of course Jackson's advocacy for reservations in the novel is at odds with a progressivism that sought to democratize the nation as it expanded to include new and diverse peoples. We can most provocatively see the tension in Jackson's progressivism through her dithering descriptions of Alessandro, her "exceptional" Native

American figure.[114] Alessandro is Jackson's representative Native American, but the novel is also inconsistent in its representation of Alessandro, as if Jackson could not fully commit herself to the progressive Native American advocacy that undergirded her intentions for the sentimental novel. In her introduction of Alessandro, we are told that he is a "simple-minded, unlearned man" who is confused but dazzled by the beauty of sunrises because he "could not have been made to believe that the earth was moving. He thought the sun was coming up apace, and the earth was standing still."[115] Alessandro is mystified by the rising and setting of the sun, but this description also suggests that he "could not have been made to believe" in the science behind such a basic phenomenon, even with an education. Jackson paints a romanticized but ignorant portrait of Alessandro that is, just a few pages later, contradicted when we are told that Alessandro is the son of Chief Pablo, who, providing him an education in literature and music, "had not done his son any good by trying to make him like white men. . . . The Americans would not let an Indian do anything but plough and sow and herd cattle. A man need not read and write, to do that."[116] At odds with the "simple-minded, unlearned" description we first get of Alessandro, Jackson appears to critique an American system that defines individuals by race over intelligence and education. Here she seems to imply that a liberal education benefits Native Americans but that the U.S. government does not support such an education and therefore participates in holding back Native American assimilation. But then another few pages later, we are again reminded that Alessandro "was not a civilized man; he had to bring to bear on his present situation only simple, primitive, uneducated instincts and impulses."[117] In the span of seven pages, Jackson deploys Alessandro as a "simple, unlearned" man unfit for citizenship to a man whose "exceptional" education has made him an outcast in an American society that does not want Native Americans to be educated and back again to the "uncivilized man" incapable of understanding "his present situation" and who, like a child, must be taken in by a system that can protect him from his own "simple, primitive, uneducated instincts and impulses." As Jackson's authorship battles over who is more in need of the novel's sentimental treatment, Native Americans or Aunt Ri, so too does Jackson's progressivism lag under the consequences of advocating for Native American inclusion in American democratic institutions. To admit Native American personhood would mean she could no longer defend containing Native Americans on reservations, a project she directly links to the novel's other disenfranchised subjects, poor white southern Americans.

Jackson's progressive message is distorted by the confines of the sentimental genre. As her Native American advocacy comes into contact with a popular Anglo-American readership, her advocacy grows less sure of itself. As Jackson explains in an 1884 letter to an "intimate friend," *Ramona* was a novel she had hoped to write for a while but "knew [she] could not do it; knew [she] had no background,—no local color for it."[118] It isn't until she was appointed agent of Indian affairs by the U.S. government and commissioned to travel to various Southern California tribes that Jackson felt she had "the very perfection of coloring" for a "story that should 'tell' on the Indian question."[119] That Jackson felt the need for "coloring" the region in order that it "should 'tell' on the Indian question" expresses a sense of the text's exploitation of—or, in the very least, manipulation of—a subject to "tell" on itself. This is a larger problem of the late nineteenth- and early twentieth-century realists of which Sui Sin Far is critical as she reveals the suffering such literary practices create for their subjects. It is also an anti-conquest move that elevates Jackson's sentimental novel from telling an entertaining and well-intentioned tale about Native Americans in the West to trying to conquer the region and its peoples through naming, knowing, and categorizing. In this very same letter, written in February 1884, just months before the novel's publication, Jackson informs her friend, "The success of [*Ramona*]—if it succeeds—will be that I do not even suggest any Indian history,—till the interest is so aroused in the heroine—and hero—that people will not lay the book down. There is but one Indian in the story."[120] Indeed the novel does not introduce Native American removal until nearly three-quarters of the way through the novel. The structure of the novel's plot, as this letter suggests, covers up, or at least delays, the introduction of some of this violent history in order that Jackson's audience maintain interest in her characters.

What is curious about this letter is Jackson's claim that there is "but one Indian in the story." Who is the "one Indian"? If it is Alessandro, then it discounts Ramona's half-Indian heritage. If it is Ramona, the novel's titular character, then it makes an interesting move in forgetting Alessandro. In either case Jackson's comment to her friend ignores the many other Native American characters we encounter in the novel, whether they be Alessandro's relatives, fellow laborers, neighbors, or the tribe that takes Ramona in after her husband is shot to death by an Anglo-American settler. It is hard to believe that Jackson understood her own novel to have "but one Indian" in it, but the fact that she advertised it this way is evidence of one of the many moments where Jackson's progressive ideas regarding Native Americans clash with her privilege, where her need to find the right "coloring" for her audience intervenes in what the story actually "tells." While her travel writings and political treatise were undeniably about Native American culture and their removal by U.S. legislation, her retelling of this story in a sentimental novel form reshapes the narrative to be about Americans and their Manifest Destiny to expand westward, leaving Native Americans and their experiences in the novel a kind of subplot that functions to propel the story of Anglo-American opportunity and perseverance.

It is precisely this kind of forgetting that should draw our attention to the novel as a post-Reconstruction novel that is concerned with configurations of citizenship and labor. While Jackson's *Ramona*, by her own accord, attempts to narrate the violence Native Americans experienced in California as a consequence of Manifest Destiny, the use of the conventional sentimental novel only allows her to tell this story from the perspective of domestic womanhood and white nationalism. Regardless of her intentions, Jackson's form fundamentally changes the message with which she set out in *A Century of Dishonor*. Native Americans default to the local color background in the sentimental novel, and they serve it by providing the liberal fantasy by which Anglo-American women maintain their civic identity.

3. Sui Sin Far's Genre of Intervention
The Regional Sketch and the "Real" in Realism

In "The Inferior Woman," the second sketch to appear in Sui Sin Far's 1912 collection, *Mrs. Spring Fragrance*, Mrs. Spring Fragrance contemplates writing a book about Americans. "As she walked along," Sui Sin Far writes, "she meditated upon a book which she had some notion of writing. Many American women wrote books. Why should not a Chinese?"[1] Thus Sui Sin Far begins by questioning the imbalance in American literary representative power. Her seemingly simple question—"Why should not a Chinese?"—points to the deep-rooted prejudices that recognized minority Americans as subjects rather than authors of American literature. Mrs. Spring Fragrance determines her "first subject will be 'The Inferior Woman of America,'" a figure who represents the nineteenth-century's New Woman and through whom Mrs. Spring Fragrance hopes to unveil what makes Americans "so interesting and mysterious."[2] The act of writing is, as Mrs. Spring Fragrance understands from dominant examples, an act of exposure and of making sense out of the "mysterious."

"The Inferior Woman" is a story with overlapping layers. While the story points out the imbalanced relationships in representative power, it also critiques the ways dominant literatures portend to tell the "real" and "true" experiences of their subjects. To learn about the "mysterious" "Inferior Woman" and to collect material for her book, Mrs. Spring Fragrance secretly observes a conversation between the "Superior Woman" (a woman who represents the era's feminine ideal) and her mother about the "Inferior Woman." Observation—a literary strategy deployed by Sui Sin Far's realist and naturalist contemporaries—is reconfigured here to expose the exploitation and unwilling participation of their literary subjects. In the process of connecting seemingly disparate global intimacies of labor and mobility, Lisa Lowe explains that "intimacy as interiority," as opposed to the dominant meaning of intimacy as an individual's sexual experiences, "is elaborated in the philosophical tradition in which the liberal subject observes, examines, and comes to possess knowledge of self and others. Philosophy elaborates this subject with interiority, who apprehends and judges the field of people, land, and things, as the definition of the human being."[3] Observation and interpretation become the mark of "the human being," further suggesting that those who observe are not observed themselves and that, quite the opposite, those observed cannot be observers. Lowe challenges this foundational liberal philosophy to argue that "this sense of intimacy [is a] particular fiction that depends on . . . the circuits, connections, associations, and mixings of differentially laboring peoples, eclipsed by the operations that universalize the Anglo-American liberal individual."[4] Lowe's framework for evaluating intimacy helps us to see the complex "circuits, connections, associations, and mixings" between Sui Sin Far's Anglo-American and Chinese characters as they stand in opposition to the often one-dimensional and flattened characters in the era's realist and naturalist texts. By reading Sui Sin Far's sketches for their network of intimacies, we can better identify the overlapping histories and cultural knowledges that Sui Sin Far brings to light through her rejection of realism's and naturalism's observational, and supposedly objective, literary qualities.

It is important that Sui Sin Far shows how even a book that centers a social outlier like the "Inferior Woman" is filtered through the gaze of dominant, "respectable" society. Rather than observing the "Inferior Woman" directly, Mrs. Spring Fragrance listens in on a conversation between the "Superior Woman" and her mother. The two women contemplate the ways in which the "Inferior Woman" "does not compare" with the "Superior Woman."[5] What is supposed to be an objective, observational account of the "Inferior Woman" is actually an observational account of dominant society's prejudice toward her. Although the story starts off with Mrs. Spring Fragrance's determination to write a book in defense of the "Inferior Woman," this overheard conversation leads Mrs. Spring Fragrance to declare to her husband: "I love well the Inferior Woman; but, O Great Man, when we have a daughter, may Heaven ordain that she walk in the groove of the Superior Woman."[6] Even while defending the "Inferior Woman," Mrs. Spring Fragrance remains loyal to a patriarchal and colonial order that values women for their submission to what Lowe terms the "'political economy' of intimacies."[7] In this "'political economy' of intimacies," Lowe traces the "asymmetrical and unevenly legible 'intimacies,'" which translate into the uneven distribution of liberal identity and freedom.[8] In drawing out the complexities and competing varieties of intimacy, Lowe provides a methodology through which we can see the relational ways oppressive regimes differentiate between "inferior" and "superior" subjects via a network of intimacy. Sui Sin Far's "Superior Woman" draws her value from the "Inferior Woman's" hyper-visible interiority, and—even more important—Mrs. Spring Fragrance validates the "Superior Woman's" superiority even while making room for the "Inferior Woman's" inferiority. With this ending Sui Sin Far applies pressure to dominant American literature's internalized prejudices and oppressive attitudes even as they claim to expand literary representation and to provide an objective glimpse into American reality. The era's dominant literatures may appear to defend and even celebrate the "Inferior Woman" and other underrepresented communities, but this defense is a mechanism to further protect and valorize the "Superior Woman."

Sui Sin Far's sketches reveal the ways intimate knowledge—an individual's experiences in both the domestic home and in domestic national politics—is coopted by dominant American literatures to contain ethnic and gendered identities. As Mrs. Spring Fragrance recognizes, while dominant American society admires her Chinese immigrant "husband because he is what the Americans call 'a man who has made himself,'" they condemn the Anglo-American "Inferior Woman who is a woman who has made herself."[9] Here Sui Sin Far insightfully reveals the American notion of "the self-made man" as one that offers an invitation to diverse identities—such as that of Mr. Spring Fragrance—to join in the national community but that simultaneously excludes women. While Mr. Spring Fragrance is admired for being "self-made," women who aspire to being self-made raise suspicions about their sexuality and therefore their value to the nation. "The Inferior Woman" is a sketch primarily concerned with whether the "Inferior Woman" is an acceptable romantic partner for Will Carman, a well-respected Anglo-American college student with both democratic and reproductive potential. Thus Mrs. Spring Fragrance's Seattle society is weary of Will's romantic interest in the "Inferior Woman." This society is critical of the "Inferior Woman's" professional success and attributes it to the "friendship and influence of men far above her socially" and her ability to "win men over to be . . . [her] friends and lovers."[10] Her independence and ambition, qualities for which Mr. Spring Fragrance is praised, are considered evidence of her sexual deviancy, loose morals, and ability to manipulate the nation's most promising men. As such, Sui Sin Far demonstrates one way the nation's founding mythologies—in this case the myth that anyone can climb the social ladder by working hard enough—operate through a set of coded intimacies to render the nation at once an inclusive and exclusive entity.

But even as the myth of the American self-made man delivers Mr. Spring Fragrance a degree of social capital, Sui Sin Far captures how this myth also doubles as a tool of social control over the Chinese immigrant man. Mr. Spring Fragrance's hard work and business success result in praise and admiration, but Sui Sin Far exposes an operation of surveillance deployed to contain Chinese male identity, just as it did the "Inferior Woman." In "The Inferior Woman's" prequel sketch, "Mrs. Spring Fragrance," Mr. Spring Fragrance invites Will Carman to a party he is hosting while his wife is visiting friends in San Francisco. Will accepts the invitation but implores Mr. Spring Fragrance not to "invite any other white fellows. If you do not I shall be able to get in a scoop. You know, I'm a sort of honorary reporter for the *Gleaner*."[11] Just as Seattle society questions the "Inferior Woman's" professional identity, so too does white Seattle society intend to "get in a scoop" on Chinese cultural customs and on the intimate interactions that take place within Chinese immigrant households. That Will believes there is "a scoop" to get implies the underlying Anglo-American suspicions of Chinese immigrant men such as Mr. Spring Fragrance, even as he is praised for being self-made and business savvy.

In Sui Sin Far's nineteenth-century society, American literature is stuck in negotiations between a desire to diversify American identity and liberal-democratic personhood and its prejudiced anxieties about national homogeneity. In using "intimacy as a heuristic," Lowe focuses on the ways individuals who "are forgotten, cast as failed, or perceived as irrelevant because they do not produce 'value' legible within modern classifications" are dispossessed of their liberal personhood and rights to citizenship through a devaluing of their intimate cultural, social, and gendered knowledge.[12] Lowe "unsettles the meaning of intimacy as the privileged sign of liberal interiority or domesticity, by situating this more familiar meaning in relation to the global processes and colonial connections that are the conditions of its production."[13] Likewise Sui Sin Far unsettles the production of dominant forms of intimacy by questioning the double standards placed on women and ethnic immigrants, as well as by indicating that both the "Inferior Woman" and Mr. Spring Fragrance are denied their privacy as a condition of national acceptance. While the "Inferior Woman's" relationships to men, women, and her career are put on open display for the "Superior Woman" and her mother to examine and judge, Mr. Spring Fragrance's access to American society relies upon his willingness to open the most intimate spaces of his own life up to scrutiny. Both individuals' intimate lives—their romantic lives, their deepest interior desires, their failures and successes—are exposed and measured against differing and (as Mrs. Spring Fragrance passively points out) opposing standards of acceptance. While the "Inferior Woman" is ultimately accepted as the social anomaly from whom the "Superior Woman" derives her value, Mr. Spring Fragrance is accepted because his hard work makes him successful enough so that he is not a burden to society but not so successful that he becomes a threat to Anglo-American masculinity. Each act of intimate exposure occurs through writing. The "Inferior

Woman" becomes the subject of Mrs. Spring Fragrance's book project, and Mr. Spring Fragrance is Will Carman's entry point into an article about Chinese intimacies and domestic customs. Sui Sin Far points out a network of literary representative power that exploits the interiority of cultural and social outliers to emphasize difference and to sustain a homogenous identity for the nation.

The late nineteenth- and early twentieth-century shift from romanticism to literary realism is often recognized as a democratization of American literary production. The leading authors of this literary movement—William Dean Howells, Jack London, Frank Norris, and Theodore Dreiser—are heralded for portraying Americans who were underrepresented in the romantic literary traditions and for paying close attention to the quotidian. However, Sui Sin Far explores how realism's literary aesthetics, which celebrate a perception of the "real" through observation, new narrative techniques, and diverse subjects, are used to contain rather than expand American identity. In this chapter I argue that Sui Sin Far's sketches disrupt the dominant realist novels' literary structures and strategies to emphasize how ethnic and gendered individuals are stripped of their representative agency by a literary enterprise that emphasizes diversity. In so doing, I argue that realist tropes rely on the exploitation of intimate ethnic, gendered, and immigrant cultural knowledges to substantiate the privileged place of Anglo masculinity in western American identity and to control American identity rather than expand it.

In her sketches Sui Sin Far is sensitive to the ways realist fiction works alongside the nation's legislative imperial powers, such as the Chinese Exclusion Act and *Plessy vs. Ferguson*, to disseminate the fictitious stereotypes and the manufactured images of Americans of color and immigrants, on which Chinese exclusion and Jim Crow rely. Scholars praise Sui Sin Far for her "realistically drawn portraits of Chinese, Chinese Americans, and Caucasian American people" at a time when the American West was expressing its anti-Asian xenophobia through the 1875 Page Law and the 1882 Chinese Exclusion Act.[14] But scholars do not just claim that Sui Sin Far produces more realistic portraits of the Chinese in America than her contemporaries. They also insist that she is representing Chinese immigrants and Chinese Americans "truly" and "truthfully." She is attributed as "the first Chinese American writer to depict truly the Chinese in America with empathy,"[15] and as Vanessa Holford Diana argues, "Like Howells, Sui Sin Far demands in fiction a *truthful* depiction of Americans."[16] Not only does this language go beyond the self-declared task of literary realism, but it also misdirects scholarly attempts to place Sui Sin Far's sketches. By "truthful [representation]," these scholars imply that Sui Sin Far is exerting control over representative identity as do the contemporaries of whom she is critical. Rather, in her 1909 autobiographical essay, "Leaves from the Mental Portfolio of an Eurasian," Sui Sin Far declares that she loves "poetry, particularly heroic pieces. I also love fairy tales. *Stories of everyday life do not appeal to me*. I dream dreams of being great and noble."[17] The "real" of "everyday life" does not seem to be what motivates her, as contemporary scholars want to argue. Sui Sin Far is interested in something more romantic than the "real." She values "poetry," "heroic pieces," and "fairy tales," the genres in which she imagines she can become "great and noble" and interest her audience in alternative realities and truths. But unlike Frank Norris, who also makes room for the romantic in naturalist aesthetics as an interpretative device, these more fanciful genres serve Sui Sin Far in detecting where realism's democratic programs fail the ethnic, immigrant, and poor communities they intend to represent and instead reaffirm the nation's investment in a colonial patriarchy.[18]

As both Donna Campbell and Eric Carl Link have pointed out, American realism has a romantic influence. In his attempts to expand the way scholars define American literary naturalism and to better understand its overlap with and differentiations from literary realism, Link asserts that the "romance allowed authors like Norris, Crane, and London to incorporate into their fiction the often abstract and hidden forces that naturalist theory revealed operating in nature."[19] It is the romantic impulse in American literary naturalism, Link further suggests, "rather than the novel [that] provided the flexibility needed to aesthetically frame the contradictions, [and] the disorder" with which literary naturalism took up.[20] Link suggests that the vestiges of the literary romance that show up in the works of Norris, Crane, and London are what give the naturalist text its interpretive power and serve as "the instrument" for bringing the "unplumbed depths of the human heart" to the surface.[21] But Sui Sin Far remains skeptical of the ways realist and naturalist writers, such as Norris, Crane, and London, utilize romance. For Sui Sin Far the romantic strand in naturalist writing is where the truth comes out. It is in the "poetry" rather than observation, in the "fairy tales" rather than the objectivity, through which realist texts are able to reach the "unplumbed depths" of their diverse subjects. The problem, according to Sui Sin Far, is all the ways the romantic impulse is resisted by dominant realist texts, even while authors such as Norris defend romanticism's incorporation into realist and naturalist narratives.

In part Sui Sin Far's collection of regional sketches shows how the emphasis and value placed on the novel form (to the detriment of the short story or sketch) is one way in which this romantic impulse is wasted in realist writing. In an era where literary society is dominated by the debates among Howells, Norris, and James about the forms, intents, and purposes of "real" American literature, Sui Sin Far's writing is a crusade against the very foundations upon which their debates are founded. Her writing critiques any literary agenda that seeks to become the dominant representative machine for American identity, diversity, and culture, and she problematizes the East Coast writers who attempt to capture an official version of the western American region. I read Sui Sin Far's writing from a genre perspective and with a focus on how her use of the regional sketch intervenes in the late nineteenth-century realist novel's privileging of the quotidian lives of its subjects. Kristie Hamilton suggests that "it is plain that the sketch's association with privacy and with that phase of the artistic process preceding formal fixity" gave authors "license" to be freer in their expression than if they were to write novels.[22] As a form "preceding formal fixity," the sketch gives the writer the freedom, or the "privacy," to explore that which is left unresolved by novelistic time. Sui Sin Far's sketch does not have to worry about creating an imagined national community as the novel does.[23] Instead her sketch is able to show difference without having to worry about how her readers will interpret that difference in relation to themselves, their own communities, and their national belonging. As such, Sui Sin Far's sketches challenge the very structure of the patriarchal national literary hub and the realist tropes that allow for one thing to be any more "real" or "true" than another.

As Amy Kaplan and Donald Pease suggest, literary realism rose to prominence at the same time the United States was ramping up its imperial activity. Kaplan and Pease treat realist modes of writing as tools of national and global surveillance that help disseminate dominant notions of race, gender, and national identity.[24] Kaplan explains that "realism has become a fictional conceit, or deceit, packaging and naturalizing an official version of the ordinary."[25] But like in any other art form, Kaplan reminds us that "realists do more than passively record the world outside; they actively create and criticize the meanings, representations, and ideologies of their own changing culture."[26] With objective observation comes subjective interpretation, which appears in realist fiction as another mechanism used to dehumanize and exploit immigrants, women, and the urban and rural poor. As we see with "The Inferior Woman," Sui Sin Far responds by questioning the origins of the "real" and "truthful" by placing Mrs. Spring Fragrance, a Chinese immigrant woman, in the role of observer and interpreter and her Anglo-American characters in the role of the vulnerable, unknowingly observed. By deploying these characteristically realist genre tropes with slight nuances, Sui Sin Far rejects the "truth" authors such as Howells and Norris claim to generate out of their literary philosophies and, in so doing, complicates the role literature plays in the incorporation of the West into national identity. I argue that in an era in which American literature was working to consolidate American identity into an imagined national community, Sui Sin Far's sketches critique the limited imaginations of her contemporary Anglo-American writers and their middle-class, Anglo-American readers, who sought new subjects only to instantiate old stereotypes.

In a laudatory review of Eliza Orne White's now forgotten realist novel *Miss Brooks*, Howells congratulates White on the fact that "nothing happens; that is, nobody murders or debauches anybody else; there is no arson or pillage of any sort; there is not a ghost, or a ravening beast, or a hair-breadth escape, or a shipwreck, or a monster of self-sacrifice, or a lady five thousand years old in the whole course of the story."[27] Howells's praise of White is clearly intended to suggest that her novel does not rely on sentimental or romantic notions to tell her story. However, the language Howells uses in this review also normalizes—as "nothing happens"—the dominant literature's violent treatment of women, ethnic Americans, and immigrants, and this normalized violence is precisely what Sui Sin Far's sketches attempt to uncover. Howells's celebration of "nothing happening" overlooks the racial and gendered violence that goes on beneath the realist novel's treatment of everyday life. In fact everyday life is treated in the dominant realist novel from the perspective of white society and is out of touch with the everyday lives and experiences of ethnic, gendered, and immigrant subjects. I began this book by pointing out the ways the phrase "nothing happens" is used by book reviewers to discredit and normalize the violence against women with the example of Joan Didion's often ignored first novel, *Run River*. Sui Sin Far's fictional sketches evidence how a different kind of violence—that against ethnic Americans and immigrants—is also being normalized by the literary establishment's rhetoric, and her writing accounts for what lies underneath the perceptions of "nothing happens" in realist texts.

To challenge the "nothing happens" in realist fiction, Sui Sin Far critiques realist tropes as an oppressive social force with which her literary subjects must contend. If the dominant realist text explores the human condition as its subject confronts a range of sociopolitical obstacles, then Sui Sin Far's sketches name realist literary conventions as one of these sociopolitical obstacles. In so doing, she exposes the imperial and representational violence embedded in realist and naturalist literary strategies and shows how dominant literary texts distance readers from the literary subject rather than bringing them together in a sense of community. For example, in several of Sui Sin Far's stories, she explores gender through characters that cross-dress. In the two stories that do so most explicitly, "The Smuggling of Tie Co" and "Tian Shan's Kindred Spirit," the Chinese female protagonist dresses and presents herself as a man—in one story to a white man and in the other to a Chinese man—as a means to express romantic love and sexual desire. These sketches show how literary realism's use of third-person limited narration—that narration of observation and interpretation—is not sufficient to convey anything "real" or "true" about these characters or their real-life counterparts. As realism's and naturalism's most characteristic form of narration, third-person limited narration functions to observe and interpret through the filtered gaze of a character, using the scientific logic of "seeing is believing" to enforce what Henry James calls the "air of reality" and what Frank Norris calls "immediate life."[28] Sui Sin Far critiques the observational objectivity in James's and Norris's literary theories in her two cross-dressing sketches by reducing literary observation to the superficial and brief examination of what gendered clothing a character wears, an observation that cannot be relied upon to tell us the characters' sex, let alone the characters' "vivid sense of reality" and truth.[29]

In "The Smuggling of Tie Co," Tie Co passes as a man to secure economic freedom in Canada. She solicits an American smuggler, Jack Fabian, to take her to New York after learning that his smuggling business is in a precarious state. Tie Co is first described by the third-person limited narrator as "a nice-looking young Chinaman," and the reader remains unaware for most of the story that she is a woman and that her travels to New York are motivated by her romantic love for Fabian. Halfway through the narrative, when Tie Co tells Fabian, "I not have wife. . . . I not like woman, I like man," the reader is led to believe that Tie Co has queer feelings for Fabian, a plot move that structurally links the mysteriousness of Tie Co's subdued character to her queerness.[30] Readers are convinced that Tie Co is a man based only on the observation of her clothing and the words the narrator hears her speak. "I not like woman. . . . I like man" are words that, in relation to Tie Co's masculine dress, queer her identity and make her illegible in terms of heteronormative understandings of sexuality and gender. But these observations are based on superficial and culturally manufactured notions of the masculine and the feminine. At the end of the story, after Tie Co jumps from a bridge to save Fabian from capture by American officers, the reader learns that "Tie Co's body was picked up the next day. Tie Co's body, and yet not Tie Co, for Tie Co was a youth, and the body found with Tie Co's face and dressed in Tie Co's clothes was the body of a girl—a woman."[31] Sui Sin Far surprises the reader at this moment in the narrative to reveal the misdirection associated with realist practices of observation and objectivity. There is, as Sui Sin Far implies here, nothing objective in these observations because the observations are always already indoctrinated in normative gender performance and in ethnic and racial stereotypes that prop up patriarchal and imperialist national programs.

Cross-dressing allows Sui Sin Far to raise concern for what realist novelists take to be true and for the methods they use to represent that truth. In his 1903 essay, "The Responsibilities of the Novelist," Norris begins with a long exposition about novels that "lie" to readers who "do not stop to separate true from false."[32] Norris's most pressing concern is that the novel—which he considers to be "essential" to relating modern life better than almost any other form of expression—has the most influence over people of all art forms and therefore has the most potential to sway public opinion.[33] Not only does Sui Sin Far dismiss the "essential" novel by conveying in her short sketch more truth than the realist and naturalist novel can do in all its hundreds of pages, but she also challenges what Norris identifies as "true" and "false." Donna Campbell has drawn connections between nineteenth-century realist and naturalist fiction and the era's scientific theories concerning the human body and its environment. Campbell suggests that "the true subject of the naturalistic text is the human body" and shows how women naturalists "add the tally of assaults [against the body] resulting from sexual violation and death in childbirth."[34] Campbell draws attention to the ways women naturalists reveal intimate knowledge about the female body that male naturalists overlook or exploit in misappropriated ways in their scientific observations of the body in its social environment. While Sui Sin Far certainly can be considered among the ranks of those women naturalists to whom Campbell refers, Sui Sin Far uses cross-dressing in her sketch to highlight not just what is missing in naturalist observations but also what is dangerously misleading about the scientific theories that inspire this kind of pseudo-scientific objectivity. In her sketches Sui Sin Far pushes against the notion that the body and the physically concrete—those observable aspects of human life—are enough to convey truth or to act as vehicles even to negotiate the truth philosophically. Rather, she places the physical body within the circulation of sociopolitical epistemologies that inscribe onto bodies certain identities based on a set of social codes.

Sui Sin Far's sketches expose the misleading ideologies behind dominant literary representation. By critiquing genre tropes such as objective observation and third-person narration, she draws attention to the nation's imperialist programs that underlie literary representation. As such, she is also insinuating that even the nation's most progressive programs are informed by an imperialist impulse. In "The Smuggling of Tie Co," for instance, Sui Sin Far condemns realist observation when, in the end, the meaning of the story is supposed to arrive through the observation of Tie Co's body and what it can tell us about her "real" identity and therefore her "real" self. However, the body found was both "Tie Co's body, and yet not Tie Co" because the physical body does not align with the culturally observed body described earlier in the story. Rather than revealing the truth about Tie Co, the conclusion disrupts the power of the outwardly observed body to convey Tie Co's real identity and instead layers the narrative with interlocking global histories and cultural knowledge that inform realists' treatment and containment of the physical body and that bring realist writers into an exploitative intimacy with their underrepresented subjects. Realist representation of Chinese bodies cooperates with the rhetoric of the restrictive immigration policies in North America, and in the West in particular, and undergirds an economic industry in which Anglo bodies economically benefit from the smuggling of Chinese bodies. Tie Co and Fabian are drawn into this exploitative economic intimacy because both are reliant on the other for economic survival. While Tie Co relies on Fabian to get her across the U.S.-Canada border, Fabian's financial livelihood also relies on Tie Co's need to move across international borders clandestinely. This intimacy remains rooted in the racialized but also the gendered hierarchies of bodies. Tie Co must disguise her gendered identity to gain access to this economic intimacy with Fabian, a move that only queers her romantically intimate feelings for him.

The histories that bring Tie Co and Fabian together are still imbued with an imbalanced distribution of power, emphasized by the sketch's deployment of a naturalistic determinism, which marks the physical body and catches each, Tie Co and Fabian, in what Lowe would call a "circuit" of intimate destinies. The concluding lines of the story reassure the reader that Fabian's smuggling business makes a strong recovery—something that the deceased Tie Co cannot do—but that "none of them [the commodified Chinese men he smuggles] are like Tie Co; and sometimes between whiles, Fabian finds himself pondering long and earnestly over the mystery of Tie Co's life—and death."[35] To broaden the purview through which naturalist texts are evaluated, Eric Carl Link argues for the ways naturalist authors such as Frank Norris and Jack London "necessarily turned toward symbol, allegory, [and] myth" in order to reach the "truth" about human experience rather than accuracy.[36] Link cites Norris's frustration with a literary realism that was "real" only on the surface and "regrettably confined to 'probabilities.'"[37] Link thus differentiates American literary naturalism from realism by arguing that naturalist writers recognize that "naturalist theory is elevated to the status of myth: it performs the function of providing a metaphysical backdrop upon which to build narratives of human experience and interaction."[38] In such a framework Fabian's "pondering" over the myth of Tie Co's transformation in death would serve to show the reader Fabian's interior self, emphasizing his humanness and expressing a "truth" about his earthly existence. However, Sui Sin Far underlines here that this centers and privileges one "truth" (Fabian's) over another (Tie Co's). As such, the sketch's ending emphasizes that there remain other Chinese immigrants to ensure Fabian's financial survival while for Tie Co there is no chance for survival. Tie Co is made visible in this narrative, but in deploying a nuanced version of a naturalist thematic rooted in scientific determinism, Sui Sin Far questions the productivity of that visibility and reminds readers that their privilege is made possible by the violence experienced by Chinese immigrants. "The Smuggling of Tie Co" ultimately suggests an undeniable and intimately violent relationship between privileged literary society and those it pushes to the fringes.

As Link and other recent critics have argued, the long-standing tendency to conflate American literary realism and naturalism or to situate naturalism as an offshoot of realism is problematic and limits our understanding of nineteenth-century American literary production. Authors such as Sui Sin Far, whose social commentary lies in the gray area between these literary modes, suggests that the more pressing problem is not in finding separation between realism and naturalism as literary modes, but in identifying the ways both are codified in a patriarchal and colonial American literary epistemology. Sui Sin Far's concerns lie in how literary realism and naturalism coopt the western American identity and how, in their attempt to know the West, realists and naturalists further instantiate negative and harmful stereotypes. Despite realist and naturalist claims that American literature should bring privileged readers into a "closeness" with life they themselves have not experienced, Sui Sin Far's works suggest that dominant literary texts reflect a xenophobic and racist orientation to the western American region, the nation, and the rest of the world, which creates distance in difference rather than "closeness."[39] As with her denunciation of realism's observation, Sui Sin Far illustrates the power imbalance in literary representation between the privileged reader and the minoritized subject.

In another of Sui Sin Far's sketches, "The Americanizing of Pau Tsu," Wan Lin Fo, a Chinese immigrant, establishes himself as a successful merchant in Seattle under the guidance of an American benefactress, Adah Raymond. Wan Lin Fo realizes one day while speaking to Adah that she has "inspired in [him] a love" for his wife in China.[40] He sends for his wife, Pau Tsu, who arrives in the United States to find that her husband values modern, American customs, a position that makes her uncomfortable. To Adah, Wan Lin Fo expresses his desire for Pau Tsu to "learn to speak like you [Adah]—and to be like you."[41] He buys his wife American dresses and encourages her to learn English, for as he tells her, "What is best for men is also best for women in this country."[42] The story reaches its climax in a moment of violation when Pau Tsu must see a doctor. Adah provides the name of her male physician, at which point Pau Tsu pleads for a female doctor instead. However, Wan Lin Fo declares: "We are in America. Pau Tsu shall be attended by [Adah's] physician."[43] The reader watches Pau Tsu's medical examination through Adah's perspective as she "closed her lips, feeling that if the wife would not dispute her husband's will it was not her place to do so; but her heart ached with compassion as she bared Pau Tsu's chest for the stethoscope."[44] Adah later writes to her sister: "It was like preparing a lamb for slaughter. . . . Pau Tsu was motionless, her eyes closed and her lips sealed, while the doctor remained; but after he had left and we two were alone she shuddered and moaned like one bereft of reason. I honestly believe that the examination was worse than death to that little Chinese woman. The modesty of generations of maternal ancestors was crucified as I rolled down the neck of her silk tunic."[45]

Here Sui Sin Far condemns an American Progressive Era rhetoric that may have "ached with compassion" for the plight of the immigrant woman but that nevertheless continued "preparing a lamb for slaughter" and took no responsibility for the crucifixion "of generations of maternal ancestors." While Wan Lin Fo dismisses his wife's requests and pressures her to Americanize, Adah, like the white western American charity women she represents, is responsible for setting the parameters of that Americanization. Out of his desire for economic security and opportunity, Wan Lin Fo internalizes the racist and gendered assumptions upon which American culture is built and suppresses his cultural knowledge for that acceptance. Sui Sin Far draws attention to the violence underlying a progressive literary agenda that aims to find "closeness" with the subjects of realist and naturalist writing through what Phillip Barrish calls the realists' "liberal guilt."[46]

For Adah does not want to "know" Wan Lin Fo and his wife. Rather, she derives a certain level of social capital and power as a charity woman working to Americanize Chinese immigrants in the West. Sui Sin Far makes this imbalanced set of relationships visible and reveals Americanization to be about the exchange and exposure of intimacies. Like Tie Co, Pau Tsu is forced to give up her body to scientific observation, which aims to determine the "truth" about her existence. Pau Tsu's experience is one "worse than death" because it is not just her body she is giving up but the "generations" of cultural knowledge and gendered orientations she has used to understand her role in the world. As a result of the sudden loss of this sense of cultural self, Pau Tsu breaks with her submissive orientation to her husband and requests that he "obtain a divorce, as is custom in America," and she disappears from their home.[47] Wan Lin Fo searches Chinatown with Adah, who blames him for forcing his wife to see the American doctor and for wanting "[his] wife to be an American woman while [he] remained a Chinaman." She asks him, "Do you think an American would dare treat his wife as you have treated yours?"⁴⁸ Wan Lin Fo is repelled by this version of Adah and wonders "how he could ever have wished his gentle Pau Tsu to be like this angry woman."⁴⁹ Wan Lin Fo finally finds his wife at the home of a female Chinese herbalist—a clear contrast to the male Western doctor—and asks Adah to leave them and "come to see my wife some other time—not today."⁵⁰ In this moment Adah and Wan Lin Fo see each other more truthfully than before. Adah recognizes that for her, Wan Lin Fo will never measure up to Anglo-American masculinity, and Wan Lin Fo realizes that no amount of cultural sacrifice will make him equal to Adah. For Americanization is about separating the Chinese immigrant from his intimacies with his home country, his wife, and his cultural epistemologies. But it is also about recapturing this separation as the immigrant's failure to maintain his intimate life and thereby his failure to be truly "American." Americanization is a mechanism through which the immigrant's intimacies are at once devalued and consumed by dominant forms of intimacy—as we see in Adah's charity work—to draw boundaries around democratic inclusion. Therefore Adah's and Wan Lin Fo's relationship must come to an end as Adah retreats from taking any responsibility for Pau Tsu's suffering at the hands of her charity work and Wan Lin Fo loses his deferent admiration for Adah and his aspirations for her American ways.

At each step in this sketch Sui Sin Far shows the misunderstandings and distance created between her Chinese immigrant characters and her Anglo-American characters. Benedict Anderson suggests that "the old-fashioned novel" and newsprint in the seventeenth and eighteenth centuries established a relation between an individual and her "240,000,000-odd fellow-Americans," whom she "[would] never meet, or even know the names of" and that made "it possible for rapidly growing numbers of people to think about themselves, and to relate themselves to others, in profoundly new ways."⁵¹ But as the relationship between Wan Lin Fo and Adah implies, at the turn of the twentieth century, the "profoundly new ways" in which Americans were coming to "know" one another were imbricated in the racialized and gendered histories that emerged in the post-Reconstruction and post-frontier eras. Adah wrongly perceives that Pau Tsu's pain stems from her assumption that she and Wan Lin Fo are having an affair or that, in the very least, Wan Lin Fo wants to have an affair with her. She soliloquizes to herself: "I ought to have known. What else could Pau Tsu have thought?—coming from a land where women have no men friends save their husbands. How she must have suffered under her smiles! Poor, brave little soul!"[52] Adah, as an East Coast white woman extending her charity in the West, is inculcated in the dominant notions that understand Anglo-American women to represent all that is desirable in American identity. Not only does she represent the privileged place of white society, but she also represents the reproductive and domestic promise of the West and, thereby, of the nation. As such, she misunderstands Pau Tsu's pain to be about her—"What else could Pau Tsu have thought?"—rather than about the individual loss Pau Tsu undergoes as she leaves her cultural identity behind. Therefore Sui Sin Far shows how the progressive strand in realist and naturalist writing cannot possibly "know" its subjects since the place whence it generates this "knowing" power is also the place that generates dominant ideologies that separate out privileged society from "othered" society. In revealing the deeply entrenched and overlapping oppressions that inform American cultural institutions, Sui Sin Far questions the ability for dominant literature to bring the increasingly diverse national population into "closeness" and for it to sustain a homogenous incorporation of the West in national identity.

Howells argues that the purpose of literature is in realizing the ways "men are more like than unlike one another."[53] However, Sui Sin Far's sketches identify that "men" is a limited category of people who, as she demonstrates in "The Inferior Woman," are allowed to know but not be known themselves. In his 1913 novel, *The Valley of the Moon*, for instance, Jack London narrates the economic and social decline of his two Anglo-American characters, Billy and Saxon Roberts, at the hands of labor strikes and increasing diversity in San Francisco. From the perspective of the novel, Billy and Saxon—characters with a long and, as Saxon's name indicates, proud Anglo-Saxon heritage—are the victims of Chinese immigrants who "smuggled" themselves into the nation and occupied jobs the novel otherwise reserves for Anglo-Americans.[54] Sui Sin Far deals directly in this negative stereotype in "The Smuggling of Tie Co," whose Chinese protagonist does not smuggle herself in but instead relies on a covert and economically lucrative system of Anglo-American smugglers to enter the country. London's novel follows what scholars have identified as a characteristically naturalist skepticism for humanity. However, while pessimism has served as an important critical theme in naturalist fiction, I agree with Link, who, in redefining literary naturalism as a thematic consideration of the era's scientific and philosophical trends "rather than [a] genre, methodology, convention, tone, or philosophy," frees the naturalist text from a strict adherence to pessimism and skepticism of humanity.[55] To take Link's argument further, Sui Sin Far's sketches indicate that rather than being a central tenet of the naturalist text, pessimism is in fact an expression of the Anglo-naturalist's racism and xenophobia. In the case of London's western city, the streets are filled with immigrant "scabs," "not men. They were beasts, fighting over bones, destroying one another for bones."[56] With each day, the city becomes more desperate, more violent, and more divided between the striker and the "scab." London's protagonists are pessimistic about their chances in San Francisco not because they feel crushed by an imbalanced global capitalist power but because the immigrant communities moving into the city threaten their privilege as white Americans and their attempts to dominate the western geography.

In clear contrast and written just one year before London's novel was published, Sui Sin Far's 1912 autobiographical article in the *Boston Globe* describes how she "fell in love with the City of the Golden Gate."[57] She identifies the city as "the place in which all the old ache in my bones fell away from them, never to return again," and tells of how she "looked out of [her] window, watched a continuously flowing stream of humanity, listened to the passing bands, inhaled the perfume of the curb stone flower sellers' wares and was very much interested."[58] For Sui Sin Far the city is a place of economic possibility for immigrants. In opposition to the Canadian and East Coast cities in which she had previously lived, San Francisco allows for immigrants to play their music, sell their merchandise, and cure the "old ache" with which they have lived. Where London sees filth, depravity, and the need for civilization, Sui Sin Far appreciates the diversity in the "flowing stream[s] of humanity," "passing bands," and "flower sellers wares" and sees true potential for the West to fulfill an American promise. While Billy and Saxon feel they must flee the city for their health and economic survival, the city cures "all the old ache" in Sui Sin Far's bones as she realizes a freedom previously denied to her and other ethnic Americans and immigrants.

London's *The Valley of the Moon* is an example of a naturalist novel that creates distance rather than "closeness" among American readers and that fails to see the romance in the diversity and bustling humanity of an international city like San Francisco. While London's novel might provide Anglo-American East Coast readers with a sense of the "immigrant problem" in the West, it is not intended to draw familiarity with those immigrants but to further dehumanize and demonize them as everything wrong with the western American experiment. Sui Sin Far's autobiographical article calls to the sentimental and romantic past not to dispel any notions of urban poverty, oppression, and difficulty—as we see in all the fictional sketches discussed thus far—but in order to recall what novels like London's miss: the individual histories that brought immigrants to a western city like San Francisco in the first place. In this autobiographical sketch, as in her *Mrs. Spring Fragrance* sketches, Sui Sin Far challenges the conclusions naturalist writers like London reach through their exploration of diverse American identities.

To do so, Sui Sin Far's sketches intervene in the dominant realist and naturalist novel's plot structures to uncover the subsumed individualities upon which Anglo-American centrism is built. Since her reintroduction into scholarly discussions, Sui Sin Far's use of the sketch has been a focal point for scholars. While early assessments considered Sui Sin Far's use of the sketch to be evidence that she was "trapped by experience,"[59] more recent scholars argue that "Sui Sin Far succeeded at what she attempted" and that "she did not share the mid-twentieth-century bias against short fiction, sketches, and vignettes as inferior 'sub-genres' of the novel."[60] I agree with this second argument and go further to suggest that Sui Sin Far not only "did not share the midtwentieth-century bias against short fiction," but she also recognized the dominant novel as an incommodious form in which to tell alternative narratives and to capture individuality. Anderson argues that the seventeenth- and eighteenth-century novel was able to draw the nation into an imagined community by deploying a "simultaneity in 'homogeneous, empty time'" that narrativized and accounted for the different daily occurrences individual Americans experienced at the same time.[61] But this also means that the novel had to be founded on a shared understanding of historical time for individuals to place their histories and daily experiences within a coherent and cooperative national framework. That is, the "old fashioned novel," as Anderson calls it, created a dominant imagined community that asserted one official national history and one official way to capture passing time, upon which individuals inscribed their individual, paralleling histories and knowledges.[62] In this sense the novel privileges the national collective over individuality and celebrates the individual's sacrifice to the nation. But Sui Sin Far ends her autobiographical essay by claiming "[to] have no nationality" and that she is "not anxious to claim any. Individuality is more than nationality. . . . I give my right hand to the Occidentals and my left to the Orientals, hoping that between them they will not utterly destroy the insignificant 'connecting link.' And that's all."[63] Sui Sin Far's biracial and immigrant experiences lead her to place more value on her personal history than on those competing and warring national histories from which her precise identity is derived.

Therefore Sui Sin Far's sketches respond to the obvious question: but what of the individuals who do not subscribe to the dominant historical narrative or whose individual historical narratives clash with what the nation believes to be true? Sui Sin Far's regional sketches transmit a different version of the American West and demand certain histories, cultures, and identities of the West be recognized rather than written away by the dominant realist and naturalist novel. The sketch, which is a more liberating literary form with which to work, gives Sui Sin Far license to explore the romantic and sentimental impulses Campbell and Link identify within the realist and naturalist novel and that allow a text to negotiate the "truth."[64] If Anderson suggests that the novelist "gives a hypnotic confirmation of the solidity of a single community,"[65] then Sui Sin Far's sketches lift the "hypnotic" trance American literature places on its readers to wrongly imagine the continuity of their experiences and the "solidity" of their "single community."

Sui Sin Far's own experience as a biracial and multinational woman in an increasingly nationalist society influences her treatment of biracial characters in her sketches and allows her to challenge the "hypnotic" trance and the imagined national community realists deploy in their narratives. In another of Sui Sin Far's regional sketches, "Its Wavering Image," a white reporter, Mark Carson, takes advantage of Pan, a half-Chinese and half-white woman, to gain access to the most culturally intimate spaces of San Francisco's Chinatown for an ethnographic news story. Once his romantic interest in Pan has secured him a story and he is about to leave Chinatown, Carson demands Pan give up her Chinese identity and leave Chinatown with him. He tells her: "You do not belong here. You are white—white."[66] When Pan challenges him by asserting that Chinatown is her home, Carson's argument becomes more violent. He demands that Pan "[has] no right to be here" and claims that her "real self is alien to [the Chinese]."[67] Carson reverses the rhetoric used to legally exclude Chinese immigrants from citizenship in the era's Chinese Exclusion Act by suggesting that the white half of Pan gives her "no right" to live in Chinatown and that it even makes her "alien" to her Chinese immigrant family and neighbors. Carson's literary mission is to write a feature on Chinatown for the amusement of an Anglo-American readership, but Carson is also representative of the era's anxieties around Anglo masculinity, and his literary forays in the West are Sui Sin Far's critique of a literary program that supports notions of the West as a playground upon which Anglo men can reassert their masculinity.[68] Carson's literary mission to expose what he considers to be the "mere superstition" of Chinese American communities is matched by his desire to rescue Pan's white half from the Chinese half that threatens to overwhelm her. While these cohabitating desires are certainly influenced by the era's anxieties over racial mixing, Sui Sin Far also captures in this story a realist literary strategy for acknowledging biracial identities and simultaneously articulating them as outside of the homogenous imagined community.

Carson's claim that Pan is white and that this whiteness gives her "no right" to be in Chinatown is at odds with his manipulation of Pan's Chinese identity to gain entry into Chinatown's culturally intimate spaces. When Pan refuses to accept the white identity Carson offers her at the expense of her Chinese self, his tone becomes increasingly angry because her refusal goes against the "hypnotic confirmation" that Carson and Pan are of a "single," shared community, a confirmation that would validate his romantic feelings for her and excuse him of any betrayal his ethnographic article might have been to her. In addition, Pan defies the "hypnotic confirmation" that miscegenation in the post-Reconstruction and early Jim Crow years is contained, and this throws Carson's intentions into crisis. While Carson exploits Pan's Chinese half to get the inside scoop on Chinatown, in private, as he declares his love to her, he denies her Chinese identity to rationalize his romantic feelings for her. Carson is willing to "know" Pan as a Chinese woman when it pays off in a story and she serves as his distanced "native informer," but he is unwilling to "know" Pan as a Chinese woman with whom he is intimately involved and with whom he holds reproductive potential. Therefore Sui Sin Far deconstructs how Carson's sense of Anglo masculinity relies upon Pan's acceptance of dominant Anglo-American society. In response to Carson's limiting demands that Pan choose to be either Chinese or white, Pan says: "I do not love you when you talk to me like that."[69] Pan refuses to participate in the myth that American identity is one thing rather than another and drains the power out of the dominant narratives that prop up and make necessary Carson's sense of white masculinity. Carson wants to believe that Pan is unhappy as a biracial woman. But in believing such, Carson is not concerned for Pan or her happiness. Rather, if Pan were to accept the opportunity to pass as white, she would reinforce Carson's sense of superiority and reaffirm his masculinity, which is just as much tied to his whiteness as it is to his sex. As such, "Its Wavering Image" documents Carson's identity crisis as a white man in a post-Reconstruction era rather than propagating racist notions that Pan, as a biracial woman, must suffer at the hands of her identity, as dominant realist narratives do. In privileging Pan's internal thoughts, Sui Sin Far counters dominant realist writers who capitalize off of engineered narratives of biracial identities—those writers who, like Carson, want to imagine Pan's biracial identity as a site of suffering—and who use biracial identities to emphasize difference rather than community between their readers and biracial subjects.

Ultimately "Its Wavering Image" offers insight into the ways Sui Sin Far negotiates biracial identity as that identity produces its own, alternative, intimate knowledges about family, domesticity, and citizenship. Pan's biracial negotiations can be best understood as the warring between her intimacy in reproductive relationships and her intimacy in interiority. Pan's romantic feelings for Carson are thus always considered against her desires for a romantic partner to fulfill her reproductive potential and her sexual identity and her desire for an intimate partner with whom she can share her private thoughts and interior self. Pan's biracial identity and her potential with Carson are antagonistic parts of her intimate identity, and Sui Sin Far recognizes how these forms of intimacy are in tension with one another in realist writing. For instance, in William Dean Howells's 1890 novel, *A Hazard of New Fortunes*, the "omniscient and focalized narration . . . goes in and out of various characters' consciousnesses," but "notably, the narration never attempts to give the reader a view from inside the consciousness of a striker. Nor do we ever see slum life from the perspective of somebody who lives there."[70] What Barrish identifies as Howells's struggle to actualize his interest in the plight of the urban poor in New York City is also evidence of his struggle with intimacy. Howells is willing to get "close to the canvas," as Norris would say, but he stops short of allowing himself to become "part of the picture."[71] That is, Howells is willing to walk his white protagonists down the impoverished streets of New York City, but he is unwilling to allow the individuals living on these streets to infiltrate the interior spaces of the Marches' minds. The Marches are not to become privy to these individuals' thoughts and desires, only to helplessly sympathize with them from a distance. In his foreword to the 1909 edition of the novel, Howells writes: "They who were then mindful of the poor have not forgotten them, and what is better the poor have not often forgotten themselves in violences such as offered me the material of tragedy and pathos in my story. In my quality of artist I could not regret these, and I gratefully realize that they offered me the opportunity of a more strenuous action, a more impressive catastrophe than I could have achieved without them. They tended to give the whole fable dignity and doubtless made for its success as a book."[72]

Like Helen Hunt Jackson, who used her position as Indian agent to find "the very perfection of coloring" to tell the sentimental story of Native Americans in the West, here Howells pays tribute to the urban poor subjects who, "not forgotten" these twenty years later, offered him "the material of tragedy and pathos" and who made his novel "more strenuous," "more impressive," and who gave it more "dignity" than he could have done without them. Howells credits the urban poor subjects of his narrative as the reason for his success but has failed here to consider how they felt in being that success for him. There is a physical "closeness" between the author who observes and the subject who is observed, but because these observations are inflected by the decades-long prejudices and cultural ideologies that situate the author as different than his subject, this intimacy is fractured—cut off at the subject's voice—and therefore inauthentic. As James says of the realist novel, "The province of art is all life, all feeling, all observation, all vision," and he calls this the author's "revelation—of freedom."[73] However, what James, Norris, and certainly Howells cannot realize from their privileged place is that in using their "freedom" to represent their previously underrepresented subjects, they are further stripping these individuals of their own representative power and freedom.

Pan and Carson in "Its Wavering Image" are Sui Sin Far's response to this kind of inauthentic intimacy. Sui Sin Far creates a romantic relationship between a biracial woman and a white ethnographic journalist to emphasize the ways dominant literary producers see only what they want to see or, in some instances, what they invent, in the underrepresented subjects they feature in their novels. In addition, Pan's and Carson's relationship shows that the problem is not that Pan has trouble reconciling her biracial identity but that Carson and the dominant Anglo-American literary society he represents have a problem committing to the inclusive programs their literatures espouse. Pan craves both romantic intimacy and interior intimacy with Carson, her "first white friend."[74] Her romantic feelings are inspired by the possibility that Carson, a white man, might truly take an interest in both parts of her identity, as she herself does. But like Howells's Marches, Carson is only capable of accepting Pan's physical intimacy and shies away from really seeing or hearing her interior self. When Carson tells Pan that "they [her Chinese community] do not understand you," Pan pushes back by telling him, "They have an interest in me."⁷⁵ It is ironic that Carson is in fact the one who does not understand, nor does he have a true interest in Pan. Nevertheless, he continues to tell Pan that she has "got to decide what [she] will be—Chinese or white," assuming that, when pressed to choose, Pan will choose to be white.⁷⁶ This is the same assumption Howells makes in *A Hazard of New Fortunes* and that Sui Sin Far critiques in the realist agenda more generally in "Its Wavering Image." Howells assumes that his urban poor subjects understand their own lives to be "tragic" and that they aspire for a life like the Marches or Howells himself. Similarly, Carson assumes Pan would be better off dismissing her Chinese half and fully committing herself to Anglo-American domestic life. While Sui Sin Far does not deny that Pan's life is difficult and that she suffers at the hands of a racist, capitalist society, she does suggest that realist writers contribute to the violence their subjects experience by assuming their lives to be pitiful and in need of rescue.

The realist and naturalist novel may delusion itself into thinking it "understands" its subjects, but what Sui Sin Far emphasizes in her sketches is that it does not take an authentic "interest." For the realist novel to take an interest it must center the individual histories and knowledges of its subjects and thereby feel secure in contradicting those nationally sanctioned histories and knowledges upon which the novel draws its form. In "Its Wavering Image" Pan's domestic space becomes an arena in which Sui Sin Far negotiates this fatal flaw of the realist novel. Each afternoon, after their travels through Chinatown, Pan and Carson reconvene in "that high room open to the stars, with its China bowls full of flowers and its big colored lanterns, shedding mellow light."⁷⁷ Below this "high room" are the bustling streets of San Francisco's Chinatown, complete with a Chinese band that "played three evenings a week in the gilded restaurant beneath them."⁷⁸ I read this "high room" as an extension of Pan's domestic space, and I recognize that Pan's domesticity is not contained within the walls of her dwelling. As this open "high room" suggests, Pan's domestic space is defined by the continuity between the street below, the skies above, and all the cultural places she took Carson to visit across Chinatown.

But, as with Tie Co's cross-dressing, Pan's domestic space is illegible to her white male counterpart, and as such, the "high room" does not represent the possibility of Pan's and Carson's equality, as others have suggested, but the different historical and cultural planes on which their epistemologies of intimacy operate.

If Pan's domesticity is defined by a continuity friendly to the possibility of Carson's inclusion, then Carson's domestic identity is indoctrinated in a strict nationalism that makes room for Pan only if she consents to relinquish her Chinese identity in favor of her white identity. Nineteenth-century Anglo-American domesticity was an exclusionary concept meant to further the imperial national project through its incorporation of Anglo-American women.[79] Carson's romantic pursuit of Pan is thus twofold: it is a project of romantic desire but also of rescue and, thereby, Anglo-American imperial takeover. As such, Carson is anxious by Pan's declaration of biracial identity, and his romantic feelings toward her motivate him to refuse Pan's interior self—the self that embraces both her white and Chinese identities—and demand that Pan choose to be either white or Chinese. Standing in the "high room," Carson "involuntarily" declares: "How beautiful above! How unbeautiful below."[80] Here Carson's impulse is to separate the stars above from the Chinese community below Pan's "high room." He finds beauty in one and disgust in the other, all the while failing to see that for Pan the "above" and "below" are inseparable from one another and that her "high room" is about bringing these continuous parts into a single vision, a single coherent, though complex, identity. Soon after this comment, Carson declares that Pan is white, a move that attempts to extricate Pan from Chinatown—the "foreigner within," as Kaplan would say[81]—and to restore her to the defined space of the domestic nation. While Pan's romantic feelings for Carson come from the possibility of Cason's inclusion, Carson's romantic intimacy with Pan is predicated on her removal from Chinatown.

This removal is reiterated in Carson's attempts to remove Pan from the ethnographic article he investigates with her help. Although Sui Sin Far doesn't tell us what Carson's news story is about—a move that refuses to give space or attention to literary inaccuracies and inventions about Chinese immigrants—Carson defends his betrayal of Pan by promising her "there was no word of you, dear. I was careful about that, not only for your sake, but for mine."[82] Once again we see the "hypnotic confirmation" on which Carson relies to bring himself and Pan into a "solid" imagined community. Carson assumes that what is best for him is also best for Pan. But while Carson's cultural histories and knowledges tell him that Pan's Chinatown community is "mere superstition" and that it has "got to be exposed and done away with,"[83] Pan questions whether he knew "that the sword which pierced her through others, would carry with it to her own heart the pain of all those others."[84] Of course the answer is that Carson did not know, nor did he care. Rather, Carson's ignorant betrayal is what Sui Sin Far recognizes in dominant realist and naturalist texts, and in "Its Wavering Image" Sui Sin Far condemns texts that represent this kind of treatment of individuals as normal, acceptable, and even progressive. The realist and naturalist novel and, as Sui Sin Far proves with Carson, ethnographic journalism intend to make their subjects "known" to a privileged reading audience. However, Sui Sin Far locates the imperial impulse in such a motivation and shows how in making their literary subjects known, Anglo-American society is better prepared to contain, control, dominate, and even remove them. Therefore I recognize that Sui Sin Far's sketches not only intervene in novelistic time—that "simultaneity of 'homogeneous, empty time'" that serves the "hypnotic confirmation" of the imagined community—to account for subsumed histories and cultural knowledges, but they also critique the ambivalence with which realist authors account for the sentimental and the romantic in their writing and thereby their ability to reach the "unplumbed depths" of the human individual.

As an ethnographic journalist indoctrinated in patriarchal literary conventions, Carson fails to consider Pan's emotional investment in her Chinese community and in the possibility she imagines of their romantic potential. In their final meeting Pan trades in her American dress for what Carson perceives to be a "Chinese costume."[85] Disturbed by this, Carson thinks to himself that Pan "did not even look herself" and asks Pan: "Why do you wear that dress?"[86] We can read this scene as another response to the superficial ways the observance of outer appearance—clothing, facial features, the physical body—serves realist writers in their claims to objective reality. With Tie Co, Sui Sin Far demonstrates the ways her gendered clothing along with her claims to "like men" queer her identity and mislead the reader to believe she is a man when in fact she is a woman. In "Its Wavering Image" Carson misreads Pan's cultural dress along with her biracial physical features and believes them to indicate that Pan's desire is to be white and that her romantic interest in him is an indication of her desire to escape Chinatown. By arriving one evening in her cultural Chinese dress, Pan tries to communicate to Carson in the only way he can be relied upon to understand—through the superficial observation of her physical appearance. Carson responds by accusing Pan of misleading him, insisting again to her, "You are a white woman—white. Did your kiss not promise me that?"[87] Even this physically intimate act is misread by Carson, who takes it to mean that in expressing her romantic desire for Carson, Pan dismisses her Chinese half and subscribes herself to the dominant Anglo-American cultural histories and customs that recognize Chinese culture to be "mere superstition." Link suggests that the naturalist novel borrows upon romantic impulses "to explore philosophical and scientific theories that offer an interpretation of nature and experience."[88] In so doing, these novels "had to rely on symbols and allegory, on the imaginative and the extreme."[89] But Sui Sin Far points out in this interaction between Carson and Pan all the ways "symbols" and "allegory" are misread or resisted by dominant society. Carson does not want to observe the truth conveyed in Pan's symbolic Chinese dress; he does not want to admit that her kiss was an expression of her romantic desire of him rather than the disavowal of the Chinese culture and community from which he believes himself to be rescuing her.

Throughout the sketch Carson is confused. He is confused about why Pan is hurt by his exploitative article, he is confused about why Pan will not submit to being "a white woman," and he is confused about why Pan finds beauty in her Chinatown community. Sui Sin Far recognizes that this confusion—this ignorance, really—is supported by the realist texts that certainly use romantic "symbols" and "allegory" but in ways that reaffirm stereotype and discredit alternative cultural knowledges as "mere superstition" rather than seeking out the truth in them. To emphasize what Carson has neglected to see, Sui Sin Far ends "Its Wavering Image" with an undeniably sentimental scene. Pan, "lying low" after "the element of Fire having raged so fiercely within her that it had almost shriveled up the childish frame," is greeted by "a little toddler who could scarcely speak. Climbing upon Pan's couch, she pressed her head upon the sick girl's bosom. The feel of that little head brought tears."[90] Looking upon them, the mother of the toddler says to Pan: "'Thou wilt bear a child thyself some day, and all the bitterness of this will pass away.' And Pan, being a Chinese woman, was comforted."[91] This toddler is an echo of Stowe's Little Eva and the moral healing powers exuded by innocent children in sentimental texts. But this interaction also leads the reader to see all that Carson has blocked from view—that Pan's hurt is one of divided intimacies. The very function of Carson's article is to separate Pan's reproductive intimacy (her sexual desire for the white Carson) from her interior intimacy (her pride and peace in her heritage) and to deny that these two parts of her can cohabitate in a single individual.

Many scholars have pondered whether or not "Its Wavering Image" has an autobiographical influence. Like Pan, Sui Sin Far is a biracial woman who spent her childhood and young adult years confronting her ambivalent society and even seems to have experienced the kind of intimate rejection Pan experiences with Carson. Scholars have speculated over an anecdote Sui Sin Far includes in her autobiographical essay, "Leaves from the Mental Portfolio of an Eurasian," in which she narrates the story of a Eurasian woman who becomes engaged to an Anglo-American man. According to Sui Sin Far, the Eurasian woman "discouraged [her white suitor] in every way possible, had warned him that she was half Chinese; that her people were poor."[92] And yet the "resolute and undaunted lover swore that it was a matter of indifference to him whether she was a Chinese or a Hottentot."[93] But then sometime later, when the Eurasian woman tells her white fiancé that she plans on giving "a Chinese party every month" and that the majority of the attendees would be "laundrymen and vegetable farmers," he responds by sinking "into a pensive mood" and wonders: "Wouldn't it be just a little pleasanter for us if, after we are married, we allowed it to be presumed that you were—er—Japanese?"[94] Because Sui Sin Far's own sister, Winnifred Eaton, adopted a Japanese persona in order to become a successful novelist herself and because Sui Sin Far harbored a grudge against her sister for doing so, scholars have questioned whether or not the Eurasian woman in this story is in fact Sui Sin Far. Ultimately the Eurasian woman ends the engagement and, like Pan in "Its Wavering Image," revels in being "free once more. Never again shall I be untrue to my own heart. Never again will I allow any one to 'hound' or 'sneer' me into matrimony."[95] Regardless of whether or not Sui Sin Far is narrating her own experience with marriage in this anecdote, this incident clearly influences Sui Sin Far's construction of "Its Wavering Image" and raises awareness for the ways even the most well-intentioned Anglo-American progressives and authors are imbricated in the long-standing prejudices that determine the intimate realms of American cultural society.

Sui Sin Far makes clear that what dooms Pan and Carson and the Eurasian woman and her white fiancé is the one-way exchange of cultural intimacies and knowledge. Carson refuses to recognize Pan as Chinese, and the white fiancé requests that the Eurasian woman trade in her Chinese identity for a more socially acceptable Japanese identity. In both examples the Anglo-American individual stops short of drawing his Chinese counterpart into his interiority. While intimacy as a romantic or reproductive relationship is easily obtained—we see this with Pan and Carson's kiss and the Eurasian and white fiancé's engagement—the white character grows anxious at inviting in the Chinese character's interior self. The point of violation for Anglo-American society, as Sui Sin Far depicts it, is not a sexual violation—as many have argued—but is rather, in Sui Sin Far's estimation, a violation of the interior self through a recognition and sharing of cultural knowledges, histories, and intimacies. Sui Sin Far marks this violation, which is not of reproduction but of self-realization, as the realist novel's ultimate ambivalence and struggle to self-actualization.

In chapter 2 I argued that Helen Hunt Jackson's sentimental novel, *Ramona*, is ambivalent to the project of Manifest Destiny rather than resistant to it. I suggested that Jackson at once celebrates national expansion and critiques the means to that expansion. Sui Sin Far's *Mrs. Spring Fragrance*, I argue, provides insight into the next era of national expansion as the United States moves into the twentieth century and to the new ways women writers in the American West—where discussions of national expansion and national identity continue to be rooted in the lived realities of global ports, international border disputes, and immigration—use genre to continue to resist the restrictive notion of national identity as it becomes more consolidated and yet more threatened amid the quickly globalizing world.

What is at stake for Sui Sin Far reaches beyond literary representation into the realm of lived loss. In an early piece of journalism, "The Land of the Free," published in the *Montreal Daily Witness* in 1890, and in its fictionalized version, "In the Land of the Free," published in *Mrs. Spring Fragrance* in 1912, Sui Sin Far engages with the forced sacrifices Chinese immigrants make as a condition of their entry into the nation. The article version is two paragraphs long and sends a winking message about immigration in North America. The article describes "Goon," a "Chinaman from New York" who is "desirous of taking up his residence in Montreal."[96] Once he "touched the free soil of Canada, he was pounced upon by a customs officer, A. Pare, who demanded in name of the Queen of this marvelously free country, $50 or his immediate departure."[97] The article seems to be building toward a climactic moment of tension between this Chinese immigrant and the customs officer. Instead Sui Sin Far abruptly ends the article by stating that the money was paid and "'Goon' is now 'washee-washee' as happy as a King."[98] Aside from mocking the racist language attributed to the Chinese, Sui Sin Far's journalistic voice also mocks the sensationalized reporting of the "real" in the era's newspaper industry. The lack of a climactic moment in this narrative suggests that such events were common and that Sui Sin Far found them to be ironic. Goon's experiences are declared common because he did not seem surprised by the customs officer's demands—was even prepared for them—and they are ironic because since this arrangement is so common, the article is not reporting on anything particularly "newsworthy." But when we read this article against the later sketch, "In the Land of the Free," this same narrative takes on more pressing criticisms.

"In the Land of the Free" is similar to its journalistic counterpart in that it is the story of a Chinese immigrant family who must pay to keep the family together in the United States. The story exudes an urgency not found in the journalistic version because the family member who is detained is Lae Choo's and Hom Hing's only child, their two-year-old son. The subtle title change from "*The* Land of the Free" to "*In* the Land of the Free" is also important because it indicates that immigrants face state-sanctioned violence not just at the time of crossing borders but also "in" their everyday lives "in" their new country. The story opens with Hom Hing, a Chinese merchant living in San Francisco, as he waits for his wife to return from China, where she gave birth to the couple's son. As they pull into the harbor, Lae Choo whispers to her child: "There is your home for years to come. It is very beautiful and thou wilt be very happy there."[99] Lae Choo's promises to her son rehearse the liberal American ideas of freedom and opportunity, but once Lae Choo and her son step onto the pier, her son is detained by the U.S. Coast Guard because there is "no proof" that he is their son or that he has permission to enter the country under the Chinese Exclusion Act's strict regulations.[100] As noted in Sui Sin Far's other sketches, American sociopolitical structures render Chinese intimacy suspicious. The Chinese couple is told their son will need to spend just one night away from them while the Coast Guard awaits authorization from Washington to return the child. Instead ten months go by, during which time the young boy is kept in a Catholic mission orphanage without any contact with his parents or his own culture. Only after Lae Choo pays a corrupt lawyer with her gold and jewels from China is she allowed to retrieve her son. When she spots him for the first time in ten months, Lae Choo "fell on her knees and stretched her hungry arms toward her son. But the Little One shrunk from her and tried to hide himself in the folds of the white woman's skirt."[101] It is with "'Go'way, go'way!' he bade his mother" that the story ends.[102]

In the fictional version of this narrative, Sui Sin Far is able to show readers what the anti-climactic journalistic version could not: that national histories subsume individual futures and use them as fodder to generate nationally sanctioned notions of intimacy and thereby personhood. In the journalistic version of this narrative, Sui Sin Far derides a realist narrative that fails to consider what Goon may be leaving behind or trying to emigrate toward. For readers his identity is flattened behind the stereotypes assigned to certain ethnic signifiers, and the possibility that he is a father, a spouse, or a son is foreclosed. He is stripped of these possibilities just as the Chinese couple and their son are stripped of them in the fictional retelling of this narrative. However, in the fictional version Sui Sin Far acutely portrays the loss sustained by this dehumanization. Whereas the money Goon pays to the immigration officer appears to be a small price to pay to gain entry into the country, the same payment is represented in "In the Land of the Free" as it is wrapped up in Lae Choo's intimate history. The jewelry she pays the corrupt lawyer includes a gold bracelet her parents gifted to her on her wedding day, suggesting that she is not exchanging just superficial monetary items to have her son back but the intimately symbolic objects of her identity, which are then traded to Anglo-American collectors as exotic knickknacks in the nineteenth-century Anglo-American home. As such, Lae Choo's gold bracelet and Goon's money circulate, to return to Lowe's terminology, in a "political economy of intimacy" that trivializes the Chinese immigrant family while it also funds dominant Anglo-American notions of interiority and personhood. The corrupt lawyer briefly hesitated before he "seized the jewels, thrust them into his coat pocket, and walked away rapidly."[103] Despite the lawyer's sense of his own wrongdoing, he cannot deny that the Chinese immigrant's sentimental objects hold a high price in an American sociocultural climate that wants to possess Chinese objects and individuals, as we saw with Adah and her charity work and with the mission orphanage that held Lae Choo's and Hom Hing's son as collateral for their family heirlooms. And like this lawyer, who felt shame but "seized" this Chinese immigrant family's intimate valuables nonetheless, Sui Sin Far places the realist writer in a similar orientation to the Chinese immigrant. The realist writer may proclaim to want to help the immigrant through literary representation—as the lawyer wants to help Lae Choo and Hom Hing get their son back—but that representation is always about exploiting Chinese intimacies in order to know and thereby possess them. And as long as Chinese immigrants and their intimacies are possessed by the realist text, they are refused a full-fledged personhood and, thus, inclusion in the nation as liberal persons with democratic potential. Ultimately Sui Sin Far's regional sketches are concerned with representational violence against immigrants, Americans of color, and women. Despite progressive programs, Sui Sin Far experiences dominant representational institutions such as American literature as oppressive forms that contribute to the systematic devaluation of certain American identities.

Contemporary readers of this book will recall twenty-first-century images of immigrant children being separated from their parents at the southwestern border and might be reminded of Sui Sin Far's Hom Hing and Lea Choo and the son with whom they are forced to part as they prove their belonging in the nation. Such similar circumstances over a century later only reinforce the importance of reading Sui Sin Far and the other authors brought together in this volume. Today's border strife and racist xenophobia are the residual legacies of an intolerant nationalism Sui Sin Far combatted in her literary ventures. Even more important, studying the women writers in this book reveals how the violence against immigrants from the nineteenth century through to our twenty-first-century moment has been supported by and is imbricated in a western American progressive ethos that remains oppressive and dangerously exclusive in its unreconciled ambivalence to national histories of racism and prejudice. In the next chapter I continue this examination by arguing that Eva Rutland also combats progressive political programs in the West that evade oppressive histories rather than confronting them. Together Sui Sin Far and Rutland reveal in their writing the insidious ways racism, xenophobia, and white supremacy are imbedded in progressive initiatives and curtail efforts to construct an equitable western American ecology.

4. An Autobiography of Western American Integration
Eva Rutland and Her Alternative Politics of Respectability

It is 1952 when Eva Rutland and her four young children board a train in Atlanta, Georgia, headed for Sacramento, California. The changing scenery as the train moves across the salt flats of Utah and over the Rocky Mountains seems impossible to Rutland in this moment. But this, she recognizes, is part of moving west. "I marveled at the beauty," she says, "the plains, the mountains rising behind, imagined the pioneers in circle with their covered wagons—perhaps Indians descending from the mountains. I was a pioneer too, I thought. How different was my journey!"[1] The journey for Rutland, a Black woman, is indeed different from those of the pioneers of the American West's mythological history. Regardless, the western American regional histories and myths influence how Rutland and her family come to know and navigate the mid-twentieth-century urban West.

Rutland begins her 1964 maternal memoir, *When We Were Colored*, with visions of "pioneers in circle with their covered wagons" and "Indians descending from the mountains," and thus she situates her experiences of the West in relation to the contentious nineteenth-century histories of American exceptionalism, Manifest Destiny, and the violent removal and genocide of Native American peoples. Rutland, who is herself moving away from the violence of the American South just as the civil rights movement is ramping up, imagines herself as a western pioneer as well. On a train instead of in a wagon, Rutland finds her own journey, different though it may be, to mimic the hardships faced by bands of mid-nineteenth-century pioneers headed west for new opportunities. She worries over the strained noises the train makes as it works to rise over the Rocky Mountains and thinks: "The pioneers had to be tough. How could one get a *wagon* over these mountains?"[2] And, perhaps echoing early pioneers arriving at their western American destination, Rutland writes: "Somehow, miraculously, we arrived safely."[3]

As I have demonstrated in other examples throughout this book, the West is not an easy destination to reach. But repeatedly literatures spanning the nineteenth and twentieth centuries indicate that the region's promise and potential make the dangerous journey worth it. In chapter 3 I argued that Sui Sin Far desired a literary representative apparatus that valued individuality over nationality. Her fictional sketches challenged the leading realist and naturalist novels of her era as they included ethnic and gendered subjects in their texts only to differentiate them from the imagined national community. But for her to pose this challenge to dominant literary society, Sui Sin Far had to believe in the national literary establishment's potential to support self-representation and individual representative autonomy. As much as she critiqued dominant images of the West and the ways dominant Anglo-American society coopted western American cultural identities, Sui Sin Far remained hopeful in the West's promise. We see this in her love of San Francisco as the city "in which all the old ache in my bones fell away from them, never to return again,"[4] and it is notable in her fictional sketches as they deal in the "poetry" and "fairy tales" subsumed under national narratives of progress.[5] Despite the violence, the women writers brought together in this book gravitate toward the West as a place of possibility and hope. If Sui Sin Far recognizes a path toward this possibility in prioritizing individual identity over a collective national identity, then Rutland, a woman far more indoctrinated in a middle-class, conformist culture, finds it in revising the collective national identity to embrace individual and regional cultural histories and knowledges.

Rutland's memoir is a regional narrative, but it is one that draws upon the movement of people and ideas and the corresponding shifts in definitions of "insider" and "outsider" that come to characterize the western region in relation to, as well as against, the nation. Originally published in 1964, *When We Were Colored* chronicles in ten witty chapters Rutland's experience with motherhood. The narrative begins with her own 1930s childhood in a Black neighborhood of Atlanta, Georgia; quickly moves to her marriage to Bill Rutland, a civilian engineer for the Tuskegee Airman; and leaves us in Sacramento, California, where Bill is eventually transferred after the integration and decentralization of the U.S. Air Force. Although Rutland's journey West begins with a rather conventional tale of pioneer struggle followed by the relief of touching western soil—a narrative to which Didion refers as the "redemptive West"—the rest of the memoir quickly recognizes the inconsistencies in this western American pioneer narrative. Most of the memoir goes on to debunk images of the American West as the progressive land of opportunity where the nation reaches its true democratic potential. Whether discussing matters as insignificant as the kinds of trees California has—"I had really expected palms like the ones on my husband's postcards, but elm was good enough"[6]—or as politically entangled as race politics, Rutland comes to realize that the West is more complicated than the utopic images distributed across the nation would make it seem. Her narrative also makes visible the tensions between the West's regional identity as a progressive "double for the US nation" and its denied relationship to the nation's violent histories of slavery, labor oppression, and class inequality.[7]

California is often considered separate from the rest of the western American region. Krista Comer calls California the "west of west" due to its associations with urban centers, such as Los Angeles and San Francisco, its "economic might and corresponding political clout, its population density and diversity, its unusual history of class formation and politics, [and] its home-base relationship to Hollywood."[8] According to Comer, California's exclusion from the "'real' West" is predicated on the fact that its history "echoes the dominant western story in that it is, fundamentally, one of paradise lost. The good days are always in the past."[9] Here Comer highlights an important aspect of the post-frontier western American psyche: as the nation moved into the twentieth century, the West struggled to keep its identity tied to the American "paradise" it had come to represent throughout the latter half of the nineteenth century. By the mid-twentieth century the West represented a "paradise lost," an opportunity lost, and a failure of the United States to reach its democratic ideal through Manifest Destiny. Therefore the twentieth-century American West—and California in particular—attempts to resurrect this sense of paradise in a hyper-progressive identity that is fundamentally an identity of loss and mourning for the pioneer history we see Rutland recount in her memoir and that sustains a sense of exceptionalism and hope for American democratic ideals. However, Rutland is not interested in mourning the loss of the western American paradise, as perhaps Didion is. Rutland recognizes that the western American paradise was always rhetorical, always something to struggle toward but something that is always just beyond the next frontier. Rather, she is motivated by the possibility of resurrecting the West's democratic potential. Rutland remains optimistic throughout the narrative and continues to dream the California Dream, even as she faces the West's insidious racisms and inequalities. Reading Rutland's memoir for how it traverses borders—regional, historical, and racial—draws attention to the ways regions are indeed discursive spaces but spaces that must negotiate the encrypted and oppositional situated knowledges nonetheless.[10]

As a region, the American West occupies a spot in the American imagination as a progressive space. As the other chapters of this book contend, the American West has been seen as a place of renewal for the American spirit, a place of opportunity to a disenfranchised and landless class of Anglo Americans, and a place of global economic growth. Since the pioneer era the terms of western American progress have changed to adapt to new sociopolitical and global situations. But the discursive West is always one that is preoccupied with what comes next, with that paradise just past the next frontier. As such, the West adopts both a historical and an ahistorical identity. It is historical in the sense that it always refers back to the possibilities of the frontier, but it is ahistorical in that the region pretends that there is no prior history to the frontier. The pioneers fled some unspeakable inequity, but that inequity is left behind, "redeemed," as Didion suggests, on the pioneer trail. And the "tabula rasa" rhetoric Didion confronts in her writing precludes any prior history of the region itself. Rutland's mid-twentieth-century maternal memoir demands a different orientation to the western American pioneer narrative. It is a narrative that begins in the South rather than in the West or on the pioneer trail. The first two chapters narrate Rutland's experiences with Jim Crow racism before she embarks on her journey west, a journey initiated by an uncomfortable encounter with a white ticket salesman at the train station. These experiences resituate the pioneer narrative by refusing to ignore the history that comes before. Western American progress in the memoir is filtered through the blatant racism Rutland experiences in the South and on her travels west. But instead of bolstering western American idealism, the racism in the South only shows the similar, though rearticulated, racisms Rutland must navigate in the West, thus demystifying much of the West's claims to racial equality.

Rutland's perspective as a member of the Black professional class in the American West offers a unique take on American racism. Although there are several studies on the late nineteenth- and early twentieth-century Black middle class, there are few inquiries into the ways the mid-twentieth-century Black middle class responded to civil rights activism and even fewer that look particularly to western American Black middle-class communities. Evelyn Brooks Higginbotham's work on Black club women's culture in the South has set the precedent for most studies on the Black middle class since the 1990s. Higginbotham argues that late nineteenth- and early twentieth-century Black club women responded to racial uplift with a "politics of respectability," which "equated public behavior with individual self-respect and with the advancement of African Americans as a group."[11] Black middle-class women, Higginbotham asserts, understood that "'respectable' behavior in public would earn their people a measure of esteem from white Americans, and hence they strove to win the Black lower class's psychological allegiance to temperance, industriousness, thrift, refined manners, and Victorian sexual morals."[12] As Higginbotham suggests, a political program rooted in "respectability" can also be understood as "assimilationist."[13] To value "respectability" is to value dominant notions of what "respectability" is, and therefore it required Black women to invest in certain normative standards and behaviors. But as Higginbotham also draws to our attention, a politics founded in "respectability" is simultaneously "progressive and conservative."[14] While the Black middle-class women in Higginbotham's study affirmed colonial and oppressive Anglo-American forms of respectability and social values, they also subverted the paternalistic racism of a society that defined "respectability" as white and that wanted to maintain Black dependency on white charity as a form of social control in the post-slavery decades.

Higginbotham's work has led to other studies that evaluate the Black middle class in similar ways. Mary Pattillo and Riché J. Daniel Barnes both consider twentieth-century Black middle-class communities through a "politics of respectability" framework and imply a continuity in Black middle-class political identity from the late nineteenth century through to the early twenty-first century. While Pattillo compares white and Black middle-class neighborhoods in Chicago, Barnes evaluates a professional class of Black women who leave their jobs to become stay-at-home mothers in the late twentieth century. Barnes argues that this professional class of Black women adapted the politics of respectability Higginbotham identified in the late nineteenth and early twentieth centuries into a "neo-politics of respectability." This politics remains indebted to conservative family values that privilege the heterosexual family unit even while it contends with new, late twentieth-century feminine pressures. Together, arguments such as Higginbotham's, Pattillo's, and Barnes's build a genealogy of Black middle-class identities that deploy dominant notions of "respectability" to prove themselves to white society and to dispel the stereotypes of Black family life that emerged in the slavery and Reconstruction eras.

Rutland disrupts this continuity. She is critical of dominant notions of respectability as they shape conservative family dynamics, and she holds both Black and white middle-class societies accountable for the violence inherent in a rhetoric of respectability. Rather than grouping Rutland in with the women of Barnes's study and calling her political expression a "neo-politics of respectability," I argue that Rutland strives for an *alternative politics of respectability*. As such, Rutland challenges what "respectability" means to both Black and white societies and attempts to reveal, and thereby do away with, the double standards placed on Black women.

As much as Rutland uses her memoir to intervene in the racist programs of her dominant white society, she also intervenes in the history of middle-class Black political advocacy and racial uplift ideologies. Her maternal memoir takes on a middle-class preoccupation with children, homemaking, and heterosexual marriage only to emphasize the oppressive programs such notions of respectability support. Her politics is thus still concerned with respectability, but it is more critical of how "respectability" is defined and hesitates to accept dominant renderings of family life. Rutland's politics is a radical politics compared with that of the Black women in Higginbotham's and Barnes's studies because she rejects dominant notions of respectability and instructs both Black and white middle-class women to reconfigure their "respectable" identities. Although Rutland and her editors attempted to distance her memoir from the more militant Black memoirs of the era (Malcolm X's and Stokely Carmichael's, to name a few)—Rutland likens Black Muslims to the Ku Klux Klan and believes that, like Ross Barnett of Mississippi, Malcolm X "preach[es] hate and racial supremacy"[15]— Rutland's anecdotes about raising Black children in the American West are underlined by the same urgency with which such leaders approached civil rights. Rutland's alternative politics of respectability translates the supposedly radical headlines, concerns, and approaches to racial justice into a maternal language that opens dialogues across racial divides without losing the urgency within these programs.

Therefore the politics in Rutland's memoir are just as radical as those of Malcolm X or Stokely Carmichael. Like them, she is asking for fundamental changes to American institutions that govern race, gender, and class. Even if the language Rutland uses seems to be rooted in a middle-class respectability, she uses this language to reflect back to dominant western American society and to the Black middle class in the West all that is encrypted in such an identity and seeks to restructure it. Black motherhood has been and continues to be political. Guided by their "neo-politics of respectability," Barnes suggests that the Black professional women in her study enact a "strategic motherhood," which accounts for "the myriad ways in which Black mothers continuously navigate and redefine their relationship with work to best fit the needs of their families and their communities."[16] Barnes uses the "strategic mothering" terminology "as a way to discuss African American women's roles as mothers and workers as multifold and multipurpose, often changing over the life course."[17] The "myriad," "multifold," and "multipurpose" roles Black mothers take on are "strategic" because they must always be aware of and prepared to confront the different systematic racisms that threaten their children, their communities, and themselves. Rutland is indeed a strategic mother, but again, unlike the women in Barnes's or Higginbotham's studies, Rutland must also contend with western American forms of early integration. Though the West's integration politics claim to have moved past issues of racial inequality and segregation, they lead to their own structures of institutional racism and discrimination. Therefore I recognize that Rutland's strategic motherhood must get even more strategic as it offers an alternative politics of respectability, one that questions what "respectability" means and how it is devised by dominant national institutions to covertly segregate an otherwise integrated society. Rutland's alternative politics of respectability and strategic motherhood demand that her color-blind western American society confront the exclusionary logic and imperialist impulses of traditional, middle-class domesticity as it undergirds the West's integration programs.

Thus Rutland's maternal memoir is not radical only because it asserts motherhood as a political role and demands a rethinking of conventional family structures but also because she does not conform to regional boundaries, gendered behaviors, or racial restrictions. Rutland is radical because she insists on foundational change to the systematic and institutional racisms that, though they manifest differently in different regions, plague the nation as a whole. Douglas Powell suggests that "region is always a relational term,"[18] and he offers "a model of region making as a practice of cultural politics."[19] Powell recognizes that the histories and stories on which a region relies for its identity are themselves "growing, changing conflicted cultural artifact[s], just like the region [they] help[] define," and he argues that "looking critically at the story itself provides a crucial starting place for understanding how the identity of the place is rooted in conflict and change as much as in permanence, stability, and continuity."[20] Powell's framework offers an opportunity to evaluate the American West's pioneer history and the myth of its progressive sociopolitical identity as a "cultural artifact" that is always "growing" and "changing." As such, I recognize that Rutland's western American story is critical of the story the West tells about itself and of the distance with which it treats the rest of the nation. While the American West imagines itself geographically and temporally separate from the rest of the nation—especially the American South and its history of race-based slavery—Rutland's memoir challenges this divide and reunites the American West with the rest of the nation's past and present practices in racism, imperialism, and racialized and gendered labor oppression. While her narrative remains loyal to a sense of western American idealism and hope for the future, I also argue that Rutland disrupts notions of western American exceptionalism and is skeptical of the West's self-proclaimed progressive regional identity.

Rutland's memoir draws upon a mostly southern, African American autobiographical tradition and a western American pioneer narrative tradition to bring the South and the West into regional commonality. Scholars of African American literature have long suggested that the autobiography played an important role in African American politics and literary contributions, noting that "African-American literary history begins with the self-consciously politicized autobiography."[21] Scholars have recognized the ways autobiography offered Black individuals an opportunity to create and recreate their identities in American history and culture from the slave era through emancipation to our contemporary moment. As Kenneth Mostern suggests, the very act of telling their life experiences is political in an American society that denies African Americans humanity, making the "tradition of African-American writing . . . one in which political commentary necessitates, invites, and assumes autobiography as its rhetorical form."[22] Telling of their lived experiences allowed for African Americans to build political identities and assimilate into American civic life.

Arguments such as Mostern's have led other scholars to consider the specific place Black women's autobiography occupies within this tradition, given that Black women, like white women, were not considered political beings until 1920, three years after Rutland was born. Johnnie Stover argues that nineteenth-century Black women "create a new form in autobiography—not so much a subgenre as a countergenre" to both white and Black men's autobiography that deploys a "mother tongue" (a Black women's coded language developed out of slave women's resistance strategies) and that "serves these Black women writers in challenging nineteenth-century sociopolitical and literary norms."[23] Stover recognizes that while Black, male autobiographers, including Booker T. Washington and W. E. B. Du Bois, were more assertively political and that their works "were more obviously individual-centered celebrations of heroism and freedom won," Black women had to make their texts "palatable" to a white, mostly female, audience.[24] Therefore their autobiographies not only had to create a cross-racial community with white women, but they also had to deal in the "bits and pieces" of domestic existence and the "'incidents' and 'sketches,' of one's life" that, as Stover quotes Harriet Jacobs, were also what provided the "loophole of resistance" in Black women's autobiographical writing.[25]

In addition, Angela Ards's analysis of contemporary Black women's autobiography suggests an "ethics of self-refashioning" and emphasizes the importance of reading Black women's autobiographical expressions for the cultural, geographic, and intellectual histories they feature.[26] Ards argues that the study of "black women's intellectual history requires that scholars consider not only geographies, that is, how place and history contextualize ideas, but also intellectual genealogies, the social discourses and various interlocutors subjects engage."[27] As such, Ards reads contemporary Black autobiographers for the ways they challenge dominant narratives of the 1960s civil rights movement as a fixed period, as a mission accomplished, and as a heroic history of progress.[28] Ards argues that "through engaging civil-rights cultural memory, these memoirs create a collective intimacy with readers, beyond solipsistic disclosure and market exchange, where mediated shared experience can forge new political discourses and allegiances."[29] In my reading of Rutland's maternal memoir, I align with Ards's call not only to find "new vocabularies for conceptualizing black identity" but also to find new national narratives and histories of citizenship.[30] Such a reading allows us to gauge the political import of Rutland's memoir by situating the domestic tales of raising children in relation to the nation's regionalization of certain histories, narratives, and identities. To pay attention to the geographies and "intellectual genealogies" in Rutland's narrative means to pay tribute to the ways Rutland takes the Black women's autobiographical tradition West; it means we read Rutland's narrative for the ways it brings together the histories of American slavery, American Manifest Destiny, and American civil rights.

While many of Rutland's narrative tactics stem from a tradition of Black women's autobiography and its "loophole[s] of resistance," her memoir also transcends the boundaries to which such autobiographical traditions adhere. For instance, Stover points to a "typical slave narrative form" in which Black women had to "establish themselves as 'American women,'" and this necessitates that the Black woman autobiographer start by "establishing who she is—where she was born, who her family was, and who her owners were."[31] Though Rutland is writing in the mid-twentieth-century American West, her narrative still begins by "establishing who she is" in Atlanta, Georgia, by introducing herself through her family lineage, including her grandfather, a former slave freed at emancipation. She stresses that "Grandpa was proud, and his shoe shop on Whitehall Street thrived. He brought sugar and flour in by the barrelfuls [*sic*], and he kept his children—all eleven of them—warmly clothed, and he didn't mean to see them in 'anybody's kitchen.'"[32] Because her grandfather is her first free and documented relative in the United States, Rutland starts her narrative by emphasizing his work ethic and success. This introduction is about situating her identity in relation to a hard-working, family-orientated Black male figure who provided for his family and raised his children to expect more out of life. It at once establishes Rutland as a product of the "American Dream," in which hard work pays off for future generations, and resists stereotypes of Black family structures in the post-slavery era.

But Rutland's narrative also deviates from the tradition Stover articulates for Black women's autobiography by taking it West. Out of necessity and in cooperation with her strategic motherhood, Rutland must adapt her "mother tongue" to speak a language of resistance that makes sense in the mid-twentieth century western American geographic and political region. If Stover recognizes that for Black women to find a publication outlet and a reading audience, they "had to deal with the duality that straddling two cultures necessarily created," then I find that Rutland's place in the integrated West encourages her to move past this "countergenre."[33] Rutland does not "deal" with the racist ways her society looks at her and her family. Rather, I credit the western American pioneer strain in Rutland's narrative as giving her a platform from which she can directly and far more openly confront a society that expects her to straddle two cultures. As mentioned, the West remains a beacon of hope even as the women writers collected here challenge the violence and oppression dominant national society wields against the region. But as Comer points out, the western American pioneer spirit also understands the West as "some lingering hope for a world less complicated by 'progress.'"[34] As indicated throughout this book, American pioneers were inspired to go west because industrial innovation and the nation's moves toward racial equality in the post–Civil War era were understood to be impediments and direct threats to their livelihoods. Anglo-American pioneers such as Ruiz de Burton's Darrell family and Jackson's Aunt Ri feared progress, and their choices to start anew in the West were as much about critiquing American progress as they were about finding new opportunities for themselves.

Rutland borrows upon this western American pioneer tradition to evoke hope but to also critique the "progress" the West claims to have made over the rest of the nation. For example, when Rutland declares that the "cloak was gone" in the American West, she is deploying a metaphor that has a clear relationship to Du Bois's theory of the veil, double consciousness, and a racism largely lived out at this time in the South. Du Bois deploys the veil metaphor to discuss the "second-sight" with which all African Americans must contend and that results in the African American individual always feeling "his twoness . . . two souls, two thoughts, two unreconciled strivings."[35] However, Rutland's cloak metaphor is inflected with her experiences traveling from the Jim Crow South to the seemingly less racist Ohio to the color-blind, supposedly integrated Sacramento, California. Just as we saw Jackson's experiences journeying West in *Bits of Travel at Home* show up in her political advocacy for Native Americans, so too do we see Rutland's understanding of herself and her Black community change as she traverses the Rocky Mountains. Rutland comes to recognize that it is not she or her children who are "twoness" but that it is her integrated, western American society that is struggling between "two unreconciled strivings." The cloak of segregation might be gone, but the racist spirit still lingers in the West. Sacramento's neighborhoods are at once "placid" and "unassuming" in their acceptance of Rutland's children, who mix and play with white children, and antagonistic in their judgments that "Negroes were dirty. Negroes were loud and uncouth. Negroes can't be trusted."[36] The cloak Rutland sheds then is her refusal to allow her community to dress her up in middle-class "respectability" and to call this integration; Rutland's narrative is a refusal to accept Sacramento's complacency in incomplete integration policies that she finds to be just as violent as the more overt Jim Crow segregation of the South.

In provocative ways Rutland's "strategic motherhood" is informed by her close ties to southern histories of slavery, emancipation, and a failed Reconstruction era. By recognizing the inequalities within integrated spaces in the West, Rutland deconstructs the rhetoric and politics of an American West that claims to be "beyond the racial problem" and shows how progressive programs such as integration are embedded in the social hierarchies built by the same racist histories that resulted in the Jim Crow South.[37] As such, I argue that Rutland's memoir resists regionalizing American racism and disrupts a national temporal narrative that suggests the nation is always forward moving and always progressing toward ideals of equality and justice in a geographic line that reads east to west and south to north. Rather, Rutland identifies how racist histories and institutions are recursive. She notes the patterns of cultural exchange that occur between the South and West and traces how these lead to the American West's institutionalization and entrenchment of new forms of racism adapted from the histories of southern American slavery and Jim Crow segregation.

In a chapter titled "Westward Ho!" Rutland confides to readers: "That's another thing about Mamas. We are neither broad minded nor progressive. We just want the children to be happy."[38] In this statement Rutland seems to want to depoliticize motherhood. However, because it is written at the point in her narrative when she moves from the South to the West, we can instead read this as her declaration of opposition to the kinds of "broad minded" and "progressive" politics championed in the West that lead to her "integration qualms."[39] Rutland's desire for happy children is the source of her political radicalism, and she goes on to document the strategic ways she deploys motherhood to achieve happy children. In "Happy Objects," Sara Ahmed questions what it means "to want 'just' happiness" for one's children. Ahmed points out that when people say they "just" want their child to be happy, they are typically speaking in a conciliatory manner that wants "to offer freedom of a certain indifference to the content of a future decision" for the child.[40] That is, Ahmed registers parents' anxiety in their desire for "'just' happiness." The anxiety is the fear that their child will not fit in or will be limited by a society that marks the child as different. The "happiness" desired has little to do with the child and everything to do with the normative standards of dominant society. But as a Black mother raising Black children in the integrated West, Rutland's desire for "just happy" children is not necessarily a fear her children will not fit in; at this moment her children's difference is already established by the color of their skin, and their exclusion from society is an expectation at birth. Rather, Rutland's desire for "just happy" children is a strategic and radical desire because it resists the "progress" her society claims to have made toward racial equality instead of resisting those parts of her children that mark them as different.

When Rutland says she "just want[s] the children to be happy," she is indeed expressing concern about how her children are to fit into normative society. But what makes Rutland's desire for happy children different from that of her white counterparts is that Rutland cannot even be sure what normative society is, given the covertly racist integration programs her children must navigate. Therefore Rutland's fear for her children's place in society is not one that sees something wrong with her children but one that sees something fundamentally wrong with her society. From her place in the American West Rutland looks upon seemingly progressive integration legislation, which eradicates segregation laws and presents a front of racial equality, and recognizes that it is not enough. Her children remain excluded even while sitting next to white children in the classroom or living next door to white families.

Therefore, to declare she wants "just happy" children is a strategic way of challenging the extent to which "progressive" western American society has achieved the racial equality it says it has. Stated another way, Rutland offers her opinion that "we could do with less *progress*" when that progress is serving new programs of de facto segregation rather than serving initiatives for true racial and gender equality.[41] She points out the problematic ways progress gets associated with "good" politics and social outcomes and how this rhetoric protects the West from sharing in the responsibility for the nation's histories of violence and oppression or for looking more critically at its own sociopolitical shortcomings. Rutland's motherhood must get strategic because it must fight against what is perceived to be the West's "good" politics and its moves toward progress.

As such, Rutland does not settle for the progress of the integrated classroom. Instead she compares her own childhood in Atlanta in the 1920s to that of her children's childhoods in Sacramento in the 1940s and 1950s. She points out that as a student in the all-Black school system of Atlanta, she "was educated in a segregated school where Negro history was a required part of the curriculum and where you learned about Crispus Attucks and Booker T. as well as George Washington."[42] The education Rutland received, which understands Black history and Black artists to be just as American as George Washington, is what gives Rutland the confidence to reassert her rights to citizenship in moments of racism by declaring, "I was emancipated," thereby making her just as entitled to safe housing, quality education, and participation in the democratic process.[43] While Rutland is indeed encouraged by the fact that the children in the western American, integrated classroom can shed the "warm cloak of segregation," she is also sensitive to the fact that "if you are a Negro child in an 'integrated' school, you don't exactly understand why the chip is there and you don't know what to do about it. You put your head on your desk when [white teachers] talk about slavery, and the other kids snicker and look at you."[44] Instead of feeling empowered by what they learn in school, Rutland fears that by shedding the "warm cloak of segregation," her children will also put their heads down on desks in shame of their family history. The shame, she realizes, is specific to her children's location in the mid-twentieth-century American West and "can lead you astray."⁴⁵ The integrated classroom is not to be celebrated for integration's sake but revisited as a new site of racial oppression. For Rutland the integrated classroom is less a sign of her society's progress and more a reminder of the deeply entrenched racisms that operate at the pervasive level of individuals.

State legislation may determine a Black student's right to enter the same classroom as white students, but Rutland quickly learns in the West that legislation does not necessarily mean white students, teachers, and school officials will receive her Black children with acceptance and welcome. As Rutland explains, the integrated classroom is integrated in formality only. There are a number of oppressive forces at work within it that segregate white students from students of color and that effectively rearticulate "separate but equal" for a western American geopolitical landscape. "Especially in California," Rutland narrates, "if you are not careful, you get categorized right out of school without even knowing it. They call it the XYZ program, wherein all pupils in high school are placed in three categories."⁴⁶ Rutland goes on to explain what these three categories are—"X (above average), Y (average), or Z (below average)"—and that based on the category in which students are placed, their chances for a college education and certain career paths are eliminated.⁴⁷ But as Rutland says, what bothers her are "the highly normal, slightly lazy Negro children like mine who just might slip into the wrong category."⁴⁸ For "it does seem a strange coincidence that . . . the majority of the children in the Z group . . . happened to be colored."⁴⁹ The XYZ program segregates school-aged children even while they sit next to one another in the physical classroom. And this segregation, Rutland suggests, is even more dangerous than the Jim Crow segregation in the South because it pretends to care about Black children without providing them anything more than the segregated schools in the South. In fact Rutland recognizes that Black students in the segregated school systems in the South are getting *more* out of their education because they are being exposed to Black history, artists, and leaders, an education that, in the very least, helps reaffirm their identities and sense of self-worth.

In the integrated West, however, Rutland demonstrates that there remains an impulse to segregate and that, problematically, this impulse is answered through an inauthentic rhetoric that pretends to care about Black children. Rutland worries that in the West, where students "get counseled out of careers, . . . we seem to be adopting England's class system."[50] She means that the XYZ curriculum and the daily interactions Black students have with white teachers and school counselors are influenced by racialized notions of labor that can be traced back to the legacies of American slavery and the failed Reconstruction era. Rutland complains that "way down deep the school just didn't care," even as it questioned: "'Can the son of this poor laborer really find happiness as a doctor?' 'Should I really advise this artistic Negro boy with definite skills in mechanical drawing to become an architect when the field for Negroes is so limited?' 'Should this boy with the limited vocabulary be encouraged in his ambitions to be a lawyer?'"[51] These are the wrong questions to ask, and it is clear to Rutland that these schoolteachers and counselors are not concerned about the Black child's "happiness." They are concerned about disrupting the social hierarchies that prop up their own superiority. But through a rhetoric of care, California feigns integration and a progressive approach to the era's civil strife while also maintaining a fundamentally segregated society. Therefore Rutland's declaration that she "just wants the children to be happy" makes a strategic demand that her children determine for themselves what makes them happy. The problem with this desire, Rutland implies, is that since the beginning of race-based slavery in the United States, the lives of Black individuals have been determined by what white society thinks makes them "happy" or what white society thinks they are best suited for in terms of labor and family life. In proclaiming she "just wants the children to be happy," Rutland insists that the progressive efforts and supposedly well-intentioned concerns of her integrated western American society are failing and that they are continuing to perpetuate a centuries-long oppressive approach in thinking they know what is best for Black individuals.

In the West, where dominant culture considers the histories of slavery and emancipation to be irrelevant to western American history and progressivism, Rutland fears her own children will feel irrelevant and will lack the self-knowledge and self-determination to participate in their societies and to assert themselves against the West's insidious racisms. Rutland reacts strategically when she chooses "to pass this [Black American] heritage on to my children" because it is a way for Rutland to move beyond condemning western American progressive integration and to start reconfiguring the pathways to a true democratic society.[52] When Elsie, Rutland's oldest daughter, must perform a poetry reading in front of her class, Rutland suggests a family favorite, Paul Laurence Dunbar's "Encouragement." "But," Rutland explains, "reading and laughing about ourselves in the confines of our own living room was quite different from displaying this bit of our past before an audience of white classmates."[53] Elsie fears having to read the dialect Dunbar uses in "Encouragement" to her class, so she chooses to go with "an especially good short [poem], 'Life.' Good—it was nondialect and would do."[54] When the teacher and the class praise Elsie's reading, Elsie, feeling "encouraged and proud, . . . timidly offered, 'I know some of his dialect poems,'" so the teacher asks her to share one with the class.[55] Reflecting on Elsie's success, Rutland claims that "by binding her to her heritage, I had set her free," and she marks this moment as Elsie's "emancipation."[56] Here Rutland deploys "emancipation" as a metaphor for the self-determination Elsie locates by embracing her Black history and ancestry. She is "set free" in the integrated western American classroom not by her proximity to white students and the "progress" of integration but by reasserting her Black heritage and her right to fully occupy an otherwise white space.

Elsie's poetry reading and the "emancipation" Rutland imagines she derives from it are about reciprocity and acknowledgment. Elsie already values Dunbar as a literary expression of her heritage, and therefore this moment does not represent Elsie's coming to know and appreciate her own identity. Rather, in reciting her favorite Dunbar poems to her white classmates, Elsie revels in the cultural and historical exchange she is afforded. This is liberating for Elsie because in this exchange is the possibility of a more collaborative and democratic future for the American West. In the Progressive Era Sui Sin Far took issue with the dominant literary establishment's ambivalent interest in underrepresented identities. With Pan and Carson in "Its Wavering Image," Sui Sin Far charges the literary establishment with an imbalanced exchange of cultural knowledges and histories and recognizes how the establishment thus fractures attempts to create a sense of national solidarity premised on equality but also on diversity. But unlike Sui Sin Far, who forecloses the possibility of national unity on the principle that national identity requires the sacrifice of individual autonomy, Rutland signals the potential for a national identity founded on individual diversity and acknowledgment. What is most "strategic" and radical about Rutland's motherhood, then, is the way it is informed by multiple regional knowledges and the way her maternal memoir seeks to make these knowledges known in cohesive, relational ways that change the "impressions" individuals have toward bodies that might differ from them in terms of race, gender, and class.

As Elsie's class poetry reading attests, Rutland's motherhood is a form of affective activism. Throughout the memoir Rutland encourages her children to participate in subtle forms of resistance—such as choosing a Black-authored poem for a class poetry assignment—as a means of reshaping the ways dominant western American individuals understand and interact with Black individuals. In affect theory bodies take the physical shape of social norms and guide individuals into an "ideal coupling" based on race and gender.[57] It is this affective segregation that Rutland combats in her memoir and that her strategic motherhood must navigate. For in the American West, where superficial forms of integration and a color-blind rhetoric generate the appearance of racial mixing and a doing away with "the fantasy of difference" (to use Ahmed's phrase), the idea of "ideal coupling" nevertheless continues to direct and "orient" white bodies and bodies of color away from one another. Rutland's memoir and the affective activism apparent therein are about reaching individuals and changing minds rather than changing legislation, which appears only to mask the problem. Rutland's memoir operates by purposefully making its readers uncomfortable, thus forcing their bodies to change shapes as they interact with those who appear different from them.

Rutland disorients what the white reader understands to be true—those "ideal couplings," the things that make "happy children," the terms of "respectability"—by shifting the perspective of dominant narratives of motherhood. Comfort, discomfort, happiness, and unhappiness are all measured against one another. That is, the "availability of comfort for some bodies may depend on the labour of others, and the burden of concealment."[58] As dominant notions stand, for some bodies to feel comfort, others must feel discomfort. When Rutland sees Black children's bodies curling in and dropping their heads upon their desks during a lesson on American slavery in the integrated western American classroom, she sees their "disorientation" and the "labour" these Black children put into their "burden of concealment" in order that they not make the snickering white children in the classroom any more uncomfortable with their presence. The shapes these Black bodies take are the consequence of the histories of enslavement that, even in the "progressive," integrated western American classroom "impress" upon them to curl in and conceal. At the same time, the snickering white bodies, which may raise a pointed finger or turn to other snickering white bodies for reassurance, are taking the shape of their concealed guilt or lack of understanding. Rutland's observation about the interactions between Black and white children in the integrated classroom reveal the racism of the American West to be about guilt and shame—the guilt and shame Black bodies have for not being able to hide the color of their skin in a society that does not want to see it and the guilt and shame white bodies have for the disjointed histories they are raised to ignore and push away as something of the past, something of the South. In either case the felt guilt and shame, which have a dramatic effect on the ways bodies are shaped and therefore "impress," derive from a lack of knowledge and shared responsibility for the histories of the nation.

With her memoir Rutland offers a new framework for evaluating western American progressivism as it intersects with other regional histories and knowledges. It is a framework that complicates our understanding of what "progressive" means to a western American regional identity that effaces racial tension by foreclosing any acknowledgement of race at all. As a tradition descended from the slave narrative, the Black autobiographical tradition focuses on images of the Black body as it undergoes egregious acts of violence. In the Black women's tradition more specifically, the Black body is depicted as it endures rape, childbirth, and the forced separation from children and other family members. In large part these images are tied to a southern American cultural history. However, Rutland's memoir about raising Black children in the integrated West draws upon this literary history and is also inflected by images of the Black body undergoing violence. But as we see in the above analysis of Black children curling into themselves as they endure whitewashed histories of slavery and racism in the integrated classroom, Rutland's images of the Black body in the West endure a rhetorical violence codified in historical notions of Manifest Destiny and American exceptionalism. Although Rutland begins her journey West imagining herself as a pioneer, she does not find the same open spaces and promise of upward social mobility in which white pioneers reveled as they arrived in California and that Didion celebrates. Rather, the Black bodies Rutland documents in her narrative are learning to curl in and to bear the burden of the coded rhetorical racisms of their integrated society. This is not to say that the kinds of physical violence typically depicted in southern Black autobiographies do not exist in the West. As Tomás Almageur and Ken Gonzales-Day show in their respective studies, the American West is not without its own history of lynching and physical violence against bodies of color. But Black women are also concerned with the family body and the ways dominant white society dismembers it, puts it on display, and displaces its history. It would be a mistake to think that this focus on family and on Black community in Black women's autobiography is any less political than that of Black men's focus on the heroic individual and the more apparent forms of racism, such as lynching.

Nevertheless, early reviews of Rutland's memoir enact a violence of perception against Rutland in their attempt to normalize the text's accounts of racism by depoliticizing the middle-class household. The reviews that followed the memoir's initial run clearly depict a literary establishment that wanted to position Rutland in opposition to the hyper-politicized Black voices dominating the nation's media channels in this era. For instance, the *Sacramento Union* wrote the following: "A delightfully entertaining book, timely and provocative, about the problems of contemporary American family life. With the wit of 'Cheaper by the Dozen' and the warmth of 'I Remember Mama,' the author compares her mother's slap-dash, child-rearing philosophy with today's highly pressurized-'organization family' approach."[59] It might be expected that this reviewer, writing in a Sacramento publication, would at least initiate a discussion about the questions the memoir raises about racism in the city. But evasively the reviewer instead focuses on the domestic entertainment the memoir provides and makes no mention of race at all. Although Rutland does consider the differences between her mother's mothering and her own, this is hardly what the book is about. The comparisons she offers are meant to raise critical awareness for the regional differences in raising Black children in the South versus in the West—and not in ways that congratulate western American progressive programs. And yet the reviewer packages the memoir as a domestic narrative in complete isolation from the political context from which it is written.

Most of the reviews follow this trend and sidestep the political themes that undergird Rutland's narrative in favor of advertising the memoir as a quaint tale of motherhood. *Publisher's Weekly*, for example, gives the book one line: "A Negro mother reflects on the universal as well as the special problems and satisfactions of rearing children."[60] This short review notes the "universal" themes Rutland covers, but it treats the memoir's considerations of race in a hushed language as "special problems and satisfactions." This is vague language that seems to avoid identifying not only Rutland's race but also the political commentary Rutland makes on those "universal" themes. In the *Atlanta World*, the book is reviewed at length, probably because Rutland was raised in Atlanta. But even this review is hesitant to address the politics in writing a maternal memoir about raising Black children in an integrated western American city. The reviewer begins by suggesting that Rutland "apparently didn't have enough to occupy her time, even with a husband, full time job and growing family, so, (you guessed it,) she wrote a book."[61] The reviewer situates Rutland as a bored housewife whose writing is an endearing hobby rather than a serious undertaking. But "get this," the review goes on to say. "Even in penning what seems to be a successful venture, she still couldn't get away from that family of hers. And the words and spirit of the novel reveal this: 'Mrs. Rutland has no problems of motherhood that she can't handle, and she's about as happy as a typical mother can be."[62] This part of the review recalls the stereotype to which Patricia Hill Collins refers as "the strong Black woman" or "matriarch," a stereotype, she argues, that is wielded against

Black women to condemn "[their] inability to model appropriate gender behavior" or, in other words, their inability to remain contained within domestic and family spaces.[63] The reviewer seems to imply that in writing a book, Rutland intended to "get away from that family of hers" and thereby to "get away" from her proper place in society. More than congratulating what "seems to be a successful venture," the reviewer is more concerned with censoring Rutland's authorship and policing the way her readers consume the text. Going further than the other two reviews, the Atlanta reviewer suggests that what makes Rutland successful is that she is "as happy as a typical mother can be." This misses the mark entirely as the narrative is all about the ways Rutland is dissatisfied with dominant society. But in advertising Rutland as a "happy" and "typical" mother, the reviewer depoliticizes Rutland and cautions that if she is not "happy," then she certainly should be.

In advertising Rutland's memoir as a witty tale of blissful domesticity, these reviewers separate Rutland's discussions of race from more militant discussions instigated by Malcolm X, James Baldwin, and (later) Angela Davis. The political nuance in Rutland's memoir is in the ways it demands a sharing of histories among her white and Black maternal readers, just as Elsie's poetry reading demands an exchange of cultural perspectives among her white and Black classmates. Understanding Rutland's narrative as one that intersects regions also allows us to understand that Rutland's intellectual genealogy (to use Ards's terminology) is one of varied maternal identities. Informed by her own childhood and the strategies her mother deployed to raise her to be a "happy child" in the South, Rutland also writes with the knowledge she garnered raising her own children in the integrated American West. Therefore Rutland's intellectual genealogy brings together Black and white mothers and their maternal knowledges to negotiate what western American history leaves behind in its efforts to start anew.

Although the reviews of Rutland's memoir attempt to frame Rutland's narrative as a superficially entertaining tale of motherhood, Rutland's female readers' responses to the narrative prove that she tapped into a maternal language that transcends race as much as it does region. In addition, Rutland's fan mail also suggests that the memoir resonates most with the reading public—Black and white—for her more politically inflected calls to unite under a shared humanity as mothers and women and to use this new community to combat racial and gendered oppressions. Rutland's memoir reaches readers who feel the instability of their mid-1960s moment and who are looking for answers to the unexplainable violence they see in the media. In 1968 a Detroit woman, Susan, writes to Rutland that because there was a long newspaper strike raging in Detroit, she went to the library and chose Rutland's book. Susan tells Rutland that, since she had four children herself, the book's "title appealed to [her]."[64] Susan continues: "Imagine my surprise to find you are a Negro mama."[65] This surprise registers for Susan as a reminder of their similarities and the importance in knowing one's "neighbors regardless of race, color or creed."[66] Susan tells Rutland that she could not stop reading the book and that when she "finally put the book down at 12:05 last evening," she decided she would write to Rutland in the morning.[67] "And then," Susan continues, "at 6:30 AM today I hear the shockingly horrible news that at this moment Senator Robert Kennedy lies in surgery. Dear God where will it all end? I'm not recovered from dear Martin Luther King yet."[68] More than anything, Susan's letter situates Rutland's narrative of Black motherhood within the turbulent 1960s decade and reveals its political pertinence to the decade's violence, as well as its progressive achievements.

Susan's experience of Senator Robert Kennedy's assassination is filtered through what she has just read in Rutland's maternal memoir. The memoir offers her, a woman with children of her own, a way to contemplate the 1960s political landscape. Susan concludes her letter with a promise to Rutland that she will "go on being a mama, like you, with 'imperfect children, all about to face an imperfect world.'"[69] In quoting this line from Rutland's memoir back to her, Susan reveals her key takeaway: that conventional middle-class family structures and norms are not enough to prepare children who are "about to face an imperfect world." Rather, it is up to mothers to raise "imperfect children," for they are the ones most equipped to deal with and change that "imperfect world." Susan recognizes the call Rutland makes for mothers to embrace new forms of respectability and to foster new familial relations that teach children to differentiate between true progress and "imperfect" progress.

Rutland's memoir is advertised as a "universal" and "typical" story of motherhood, but what Susan and the other "universal" and "typical" mothers who read it get out of it are new, alternative perspectives on what it means to raise children in an "imperfect world." Once white mothers begin to read the narrative, as Susan herself admits, Rutland accomplishes a "dialogue" that introduces these white women to maternal struggles to which they at once relate and cannot imagine. As one example, Rutland and her family quickly learn when they move to Sacramento that though "*there was no colored section*" of town in which they were forced to find housing, this did not necessarily mean they could live anywhere.[70] Rutland relates the "rollicking tale" of her husband's "experiences in a white hotel, served by *white* bellboys and *white* waiters, and his searching desperately through the hotel for a black face to direct him to the 'colored section' of town."[71] When he is finally told that "*there was no colored section*," Rutland explains that "the truth was that this left him rather naked. For he desperately needed a 'colored section.'"[72] That is, as Collins, Higginbotham, and Barnes all note, at least in the Jim Crow South there is a degree of protection to be found in the "colored section" of town. In the hushed racism of the West, however, the violence against Black bodies emerges through humiliation and a "desperately needed" sense of direction. Bill Rutland's white colleagues found "brand-new, better-than-average tract homes with an executive air, boasting of built-in modern appliances and situated near the air base where they worked. And for about $250 down, [there was] for Bill—nothing."[73] "After several rebuffs," Rutland explains, "he began to look for the 'unrestricted' notation and to rely on the real estate man to direct him to where 'they will sell to colored.'"[74] Rutland comes to learn that racism in the American West manifests in what is left unsaid or in what is implied by a coded language of exclusion. "Unrestricted," Rutland and her husband come to find out, is how the neighborhoods of the American West distinguish between "white" neighborhoods and "Black" neighborhoods. It isn't until Rutland matches the city's "subterfuge" with her own—employing a white friend to act as her proxy in the purchasing of a home while her husband is away on business—that she is able to rise above the power of this language and find a suitable home for her family.[75] The "universal" treatment western American programs of integration claim to deliver to all individuals, regardless of race, are exposed here as racially coded. By presenting her narrative as a "universal" tale of motherhood, Rutland is able to attract white readers and include them on observations of the violence perpetuated in the West's color-blind rhetoric and its initiatives to conditionally integrate Black and white communities.

Rutland's memoir gently, but no less politically, shows white women how their dominant notions of family life and maternal responsibilities obstruct racial progress. Though Rutland's move to purchase a home through a white friend speaks to the degree of freedom Black families have in the American West compared with in the American South, where this kind of "subterfuge" would have much more dire consequences, Rutland is nevertheless met with resistance by her white society. This resistance is expressed through the dominant rhetoric of respectable motherhood and therefore goes unrecognized by women such as Susan until Rutland's narrative brings it to their attention. Rutland relates how a "white acquaintance" questions her decision to move into an all-white neighborhood. The acquaintance asks Rutland if she will "be happy . . . knowing [the white neighbors] don't want [her]."[76] This question, which suggests not that dominant society is responsible for impacting Rutland's happiness by excluding her but that Rutland's desires for decent housing are contradictory to her own happiness, participates once again in an oppressive regime that positions white society as an authority on Black happiness and well-being. When Rutland responds that regardless of the neighbors, it is the right house for her family, the acquaintance rephrases the question in a way that falls back on a dominant rhetoric of motherhood: "But the children."[77] The acquaintance's "But the children" trails off to imply her belief that Rutland is not thinking about her children when she decides to move her family into the unofficially all-white neighborhood. The white acquaintance suggests that Rutland is deviating from her role as a mother by attempting a political insurrection rather than considering the safety and happiness of her children.

As dominant narratives of motherhood attest, politics has no place in family life, and the mother's role is to shield her family from the outside world of masculine business and politics. But Rutland's point in sharing this story with her audience is that when this "white acquaintance" says, "But the children," she is herself participating in the political programs that segregate Black families from white families and that reaffirm white supremacy. Rutland's message is that politics has always been the bedrock of dominant notions of middle-class motherhood, and as such, women have a great deal more power to change the political landscape than they might think. This message reaches Susan, as is evidenced by her vow to raise "imperfect children" to face an "imperfect world," and Rutland achieves this connection with her other readers by showing the receiving end of a white middle-class rhetoric of motherhood. Rather than registering the acquaintance's "But the children" comment as a genuine concern for her children, Rutland experiences it as a form of policing. Just as the Atlanta reviewer indicated that Rutland should be "happy" being a "typical" mother, this white acquaintance indicates to Rutland that she should be "happy" to have a home at all, even if it is in a less-desirable neighborhood. The woman's concerns are less for the safety of Rutland's children and more for her own unease at the prospect of Black families living on the same street as her family. In an integrated city racism cannot be spoken out loud, so it is hushed behind the rhetoric of a middle-class motherhood that hides behind dominant notions of respectably and that pretends to care for Black children while it also denies them access to certain neighborhoods and the corresponding residential schools and resources. Rutland's memoir deconstructs the rhetoric of motherhood to expose the "subterfuge" and how, like in the "unrestricted" notation on real estate listings, it uses a precise language of care to entrench new systems of racial oppression.

As readers like Susan demonstrate, Rutland's anecdotes about the subtle, often rhetorical racisms she encounters have profound impact on engaging her female readership in critical contemplation of racism in the American West and in the nation more broadly. Rutland repositions white readers to perceive the dominant rhetoric from new perspectives. She offers criticism on "respectability" and suggests that an alternative definition for respectability is needed to bridge the gaps erected between white and Black middle-class society. In response to the white acquaintance's "But the children," Rutland smiles and says, "'They'll survive.' And grow I thought to myself. I had not forgotten the vulnerability of their position. But this I had learned to accept and strangely enough to appreciate."[78] Rutland's willingness to make her children vulnerable does deviate from dominant notions of "respectable" motherhood, but vulnerability "involves a particular kind of bodily relation to the world, in which openness itself is read as a site of potential danger, and as demanding evasive actions."[79] Vulnerability functions to make us feel the "potential danger" of a situation and to demand our "evasive actions" to escape potentially harmful situations. The dominant rhetoric of motherhood responds to this sense of vulnerability by seeking ways to close off the "openness." When the white acquaintance says, "But the children," she reveals her own discomfort at the vulnerability she understands Rutland to create for her children. She prompts Rutland here to close her children off, to remove them from the site of vulnerability and potential danger. But as Toni Morrison helps us to see, the woman's "But the children" is a reflexive move that inquires not into Rutland's children but into her own. Rather than bringing her children together with Rutland's children, the acquaintance's unfinished question erects a division between the two and attempts to close both sides off from one another. The woman's concern is not with protecting Rutland's children but her own white children from the potential danger she imagines in racial mixing. Vulnerability is not actual, present danger; it is the "potential" for future danger, and it is reliant upon a social agreement about what is dangerous and what is not.

As Rutland's acquaintance expresses in "But the children," the dominant rhetoric of motherhood validates a sense of danger around integrated neighborhoods, at least in the middle- and upper-middle-class residential areas. Rutland's memoir is concerned with exposing this fabricated sense of vulnerability and danger by challenging dominant assumptions that her children are safe anywhere at all in the integrated western American city. Rather than seeking to close off her children as the dominant rhetoric of respectable motherhood does, Rutland's alternative politics of respectability acknowledges that dominant notions of motherhood prioritize the protection of white children over her own, and therefore she maintains her children's "openness" as a site for their potential growth as much as it is read as "a site of potential danger." By moving her family into a predominantly white neighborhood, Rutland strategically places her children at the crossroads of the dominant rhetoric of respectable motherhood and the West's claims to early integration and progressive race politics. She demonstrates that in any neighborhood in Sacramento her children face real vulnerability and real danger. In their previous home dilapidation and redlining threatened her children with physical harm and an attack on their environmental health. In the middle-class, white neighborhood into which she moves her children, the suppressed racism of her neighbors leads to her children's psychological and emotional insecurity. By pointing this out and contemplating which is the more productive vulnerability with which to burden her children, Rutland draws white readers' attention to the ways dominant middle-class notions of motherhood overlap with the West's ambivalence toward racial equality and integration policies.

Of course this remains a kind of politics of respectability in that Rutland continues to strive to provide her children with the same middle-class lifestyle that the white families in Sacramento have. However, Rutland's is an alternative politics of respectability because she does not allow her society to pretend that her children can have everything white children have if only they work hard enough or behave according to certain standards. Rutland's memoir acknowledges the histories of race and racism that place her children at a disadvantage, a disadvantage that only becomes harder to navigate in a western American city that refuses to acknowledge those histories. What Rutland's white acquaintance cannot see, and what Rutland is positioning her reading audience to reevaluate, is that Rutland's children are best served by her political actions, even if those political actions appear to deviate from a conventionally maternal role. To act politically is to expand her children's freedoms and to demand local, state, and national establishments to acknowledge and protect her children the same way they do white children. What makes Rutland's respectability an alternative to that of her mother's and grandmother's generation is that Rutland's hope for her children is not that they will just be able to possess the same houses, educations, and jobs as their white counterparts but that they will be able to attain these things without the "subterfuge" she herself had to deploy to get them. "Hope," according to Ahmed, "is when the 'not yet' impresses upon us in the present, such that we must act, politically, to make it our future."⁸⁰ As such, vulnerability opens the conditions for hope in that to have hope means to remain open to what is "not yet" and to imagine how the future is made in the impressions of it "upon us in the present." The close relationship between hope and vulnerability makes it clear that in Rutland's case, the "not yet" is racial equality in housing, and it entices her to act politically through subterfuge to "make it our future." While her actions may "impress" upon her white society in offensive ways—as seen with the white acquaintance—her actions are also forcing a vulnerability to dispel the notion that there is any "potential danger" in integrated neighborhoods. Her alternative politics of respectability opts for vulnerability not because it has the potential for danger but because it has the potential to redefine the social agreement about what constitutes danger, thus opening up the future to more genuine progress.

Rutland's alternative politics of respectability questions what it is the children really need protecting from. In so doing, Rutland is critical of the relationship between "respectable" middle-class values that preach clean houses, polite children, and obedient wives and the American West's programs for racial equality and integration. She writes about the year she became so over involved in PTA, Boy and Girl Scouts, and in supporting her children in other extracurricular activities to prove her maternal worth that, as she says, she "almost lost [her] husband."⁸¹ Rutland explains that the pressure to conform to respectable, middle-class standards and values was not exactly something she had been "trained" for but was something expected of her nonetheless.⁸² She describes her mother's house and form of mothering as "slapdash."⁸³ "In Mama's house," she says, "you never knew where anything belonged," and "[her] method of housekeeping was to fan a feather duster and pull down the shades. She always remembered flowers, though. Even now I can remember coming into a quiet, cool house, a fresh bowl of flowers on the bookcase in the hall and the sun filtering softly through the yellow shades of the dining room window. You had the illusion of peace and quiet order."⁸⁴ According to this account, it seems the politics of respectability, which positioned Black, middle-class women as "the caretaker[s] of the home, ergo the caretaker[s] of the race," and "charged" Black mothers "with the responsibility of maintaining disciplined and clean homes," is an "illusion" of "respectability."[85] While her mother never kept an organized home that was "a place-for-everything, everything-in-its place kind of operation," she was sure to always maintain fresh flowers, giving the "illusion" of cleanliness and "order" and thereby avoiding association with the racist images of dirty houses and unkempt children perpetuated by dominant society.[86] The flowers were meant to distract "the white gaze" that is constantly surveilling Black women and their roles as mothers and housekeepers. Rather than conforming to what dominant society suggests is respectable, Rutland defends herself against having to prop up this "illusion" and the superficial presentation of "peace and quiet."

Rutland's narrative points out the impact this "illusion" has on her and her family in their western American city. As mentioned above, Rutland indicates that being an involved mother almost cost her her marriage. The notion that mothers are first and foremost servants to their children is proven false as her overinvestment in her children nearly crumbled her marriage—the foundation of any heteronormative nuclear family structure. Rutland makes clear that the nuclear family structures and notions of respectable motherhood are impossible standards to meet, especially for Black women. They are impossible because they dictate that a mother's most important role is in protecting her children, but Rutland's society actively denies her the ability to find protection for her children. At a high school board meeting, for instance, Rutland relates that "it was election time and several burning issues were on the ballot that vitally affected the schools. When the legislative chairman asked what she should say about the ballot she was cautioned just to urge the people to vote and for goodness sake don't mention the issues that were too controversial and might spoil the board meeting."[87] The emphasis is on maintaining civility and not spoiling the meeting even while the "burning issues" are clearly disruptive enough to make their way onto the ballot in the first place. Like Rutland's mother's "slapdash" housekeeping, the school board privileges the "illusion" of progress rather than a more authentic version of it. Rutland "took issue with this position" and "rather vociferously" spoke up and demanded "*what was the school board for*" if not to democratically discuss and vote for these "burning issues."[88] But the rest of the board followed the advice of the legislative chairman and kept quiet on the "burning issues." Rutland later learned "that several felt as [she] did but were afraid to take a stand."[89] One board member told Rutland over the phone that she "was so glad [Rutland] spoke out at the board meeting. . . . I do feel we emphasize the wrong things. Keep it up, girl—lots of us are behind you."[90] In her reflection of this moment Rutland is "disheartened" by the fact that the board was "*behind* me—but not with me," and she suggests that "it takes more than one person to buck the tea-party trend and get down to the nitty gritty—the real and not always pleasant things that really affect the children."[91] Rutland recognizes that she cannot raise her children alone. She requires the support and participation of her society since raising children does not just occur within the four walls of her home but is "inevitably entwined in the small area of everyday living—the church, the school, the PTA, the boy next door, the girl in . . . class, the man across the street. . . . Here at home and in the streets and in the marketplaces the real battle for human dignity is being fought."[92]

In a narrative that has discussed the role of mothers and motherhood in general terms, Rutland takes this moment to get racially specific and to identify that this is the "trouble with being a *colored* mama."[93] Even in this western American city that prided itself on being progressive and integrated, the "nitty gritty" and the "things that really affect the children," especially Black children, are ignored to avoid conflict, defer blame, and maintain the appearance of social stability and progress. We can infer that the "controversial" and "burning issues" that are silenced at this board meeting are racial in nature. Other board members respond to Rutland's "vociferous" opposition at the meeting as evidence that she "cannot think beyond the racial problem," or they worry that "someone offended [her]."[94] Rutland tries to explain that "this was not a personal issue—that [she] was talking about something bigger than [herself]," but she "could see it was no use."[95] The danger in a society that fashions its progressive agendas on a color-blind rhetoric is that, as Rutland's frustration attests, it defers blame to the individual of color, who "cannot think beyond the racial problem."

The problem lies not with society but with the individual, even as the individual's problem is with the larger society. The challenge Rutland poses for herself and other mothers is to rise above an "illusion" of respectability and consequently an "illusion" of racial equality.

In another anecdote about her daughter Elsie, who comes home from school one day "screaming, 'This house is so dirty,'" Rutland comments on the internalized racism the politics of respectability has reinforced. While she admits that Elsie "had a point . . . as I collected the books and crayons and rescued the cracker box from one of the twins," Elsie goes on to say: "Dirty, dirty, that's what Janey's mother said. She said Negroes were all dirty and they kept dirty houses, and Janey can't play with me, even at school she can't."[96] Rutland tries to reassure her by saying: "'That's not true. Our house isn't really *dirty* and neither are. . . .' I mentioned a few of our friends who were immaculate housekeepers."[97] But later, when Rutland has time to reflect on this moment, she recognizes the inherent problem in her attempts to console Elsie in this way. "I wondered later why I was defending myself. Why should I try to prove to my own daughter that we were as good as anyone else and solely through the automatic, superficial process of keeping our faces and houses clean, of putting up a front?"[98] Respectability, as Rutland comes to understand it, is nothing more than "putting up a front." To talk about clean faces and clean houses is to avoid talking about the real issues. Just like the school board meeting, where civility is used as an excuse to avoid the "burning issues," domestic "respectability" becomes an excuse to avoid seeing racism at work. In this reflective moment Rutland vows to stop pretending about what makes someone "good" and to start holding her children and her society accountable for the front they put up when it comes to discussions of racism in the West.

Instead Rutland shifts to ask not whether her house is clean enough, her children composed enough, but to ask: "What about our hearts and minds?"[99] She realizes the unproductive nature of a politics of respectability as it achieves nothing more than reifying a social regime obsessed with appearances, including the color of one's skin. In her final reflection Rutland determines that "the next time the subject came up I would place it on a higher plane."[100] That "higher plane" leaves behind a nineteenth-century racial uplift ideology that allows

Black Americans access to dominant society through mimicking the same oppressive regimes dominant society has used to disenfranchise and exclude Black communities in the first place. In its place, Rutland instructs her readers, both white and Black, to embrace an alternative politics of respectability that reprioritizes the ways individuals are valued by society. This alternative politics of respectability may be messier, it may leave one more vulnerable, and it is certainly more assertive, but it remains grounded in mutual respect and exchange of cultural, regional, and individual knowledges. Most important, Rutland's alternative politics of respectability does not try to cover up the political in everyday domestic life. Rather, her politics becomes the cornerstone of her motherhood while her motherhood also becomes the cornerstone of her activism.

If Rutland acknowledges during the school board meeting that she cannot raise her children without the help of her community, then her motherhood and alternative politics of respectability also recognize that she must remain dedicated to a community of children that extends beyond her biological children so that she might reshape both regional and national communities. As Higginbotham, Barnes, and Pattillo all point out, the politics of respectability, as a racial uplift ideology, had to be about more than the nuclear family structure; it had to extend out into the larger Black community. As such, Black women became mothers not only to their own children but also to the community of Black children. Other scholars have described this phenomenon in Black maternal identity as "othermothering" (Patricia Hill Collins) and "m/othering" (Alexis Pauline Gumbs). Collins defines "othermothers" as "women who assist bloodmothers by sharing mothering responsibilities" and credits "othermothers" as "central to the institution of Black motherhood."[101] Likewise Gumbs argues that the "radical potential of the word 'mother' comes after the 'm.' It is the space that 'other' takes in our mouths when we say it."[102] Taken together, Collins's "othermothering" and Gumbs's "m/othering" reflect on the maternal role women play in raising more than just their own children. Gumbs expands upon this reflection to recognize the ways "Mamas who unlearn domination by refusing to dominant their children, extended family and friends" and the community are "breaking cycles of abuse by deciding what we want to replicate from the past and what we need urgently to transform."[103] Gumbs suggests for this reason that mothering "is a queer thing" because of its "creative power of transforming ourselves and the ways we relate to each other."[104] Rutland's memoir is certainly "breaking cycles of abuse" by "refusing to dominate" her and other children, and her affective activism certainly seeks to transform "the ways we relate to each other." Her motherhood is focused on creating space for children and young people to realize their own self-determination. She contemplates a politics "from the past," which places the Black middle-class mother in a position of moral superiority above Black men and children and appeals to mothers across the racial and regional divide to "urgently ... transform" such politics to allow for children to develop more organically and more communally. Essentially Rutland calls for new strategies for raising middle-class children. She proposes strategies that break down the intense individualism that has always been a foundation of the Anglo-American West and that embed children within community as much as they are embedded within family. This orientation makes children accountable to the communities in which they live just as much as to the family households in which they grow up, and it has the potential to circumvent the ignorance and individualism that serve much of the American West's twentieth-century forms of racism.

Rutland's call is a "radical" and "queer thing" because she questions the role of an outdated respectability not just in the nuclear household but also in local and state democratic institutions. As I pointed out above, Rutland notes a reluctance on the part of school board members to discuss the "burning issues." Rather than dealing in the controversial and making themselves vulnerable to unpleasantries, they mute themselves even while they acknowledge on the phone to Rutland that the "burning issues" were problems in need of address. In a similar story Rutland explains that she has attended "two state PTA conventions and [has] been so inspired to see *all those people* filling to the rafters the city auditorium—all sincere, dedicated women. But dedicated to what? Council luncheons, potlucks, and school carnivals—avoiding the vital controversial issues that might determine our children's future?"[105] She points out how the PTA and the school board depoliticize the youth and their education by focusing on "luncheons, potlucks, and school carnivals" rather than the important sociopolitical issues such as school busing programs aimed at integrating schools, public school curriculums that create racially imbalanced outcomes, or after-school programs that discriminate against children of color and children from low-income households. The legacy of respectability and normative gendered behavior follows Rutland's female readership into the political realms of PTAs and school boards. That these institutions are more interested in creating the façade of respectability and social coherence is illogical to Rutland, who inquires after the messier side of the democratic process, the side that may incite disagreement and debate but that also brings true progress and a more inclusive community and, thereby, national identity.

While Rutland's "motherwork" is political in and of itself, the memoir she writes about it and the stories she chooses to include expand her political reach and her subversive intentions to the national, not just the regional, stage. She becomes an "othermother" and a "m/other" to not just a Black community of children, nor just to a western American community of children, but to the nation's community of children. In a chapter titled "You Have to Be Rich," Rutland tells an endearing and timeless story of teaching her children about the true spirit of Christmas. Although she did not have a lot of money to give to her four children as allowance, Rutland "set up a system of jobs whereby the children could really earn their money for Christmas."[106] With her four children holding about two dollars each, Rutland takes all of them to the five-and-ten to purchase gifts for each of their family members. The experience was not without its challenges—one of Rutland's daughters ran out of money before finding something for her father, two of her children got their sibling the same gift, and Rutland received multiple condescending stares from other women over the chaos she and her children were causing in the store—but that Christmas Rutland watched her children "saying hello to the giving, the getting, the thoughtfulness, the pure loving kindness of Christmas."[107] For Rutland it was a win, and she said then, "God bless the five-and-ten."[108] But then this chapter about teaching children selflessness unexpectedly pivots to two short paragraphs that raise the political stakes of the story.

Rutland ends by imploring her readers to see that a nation that distributes rights and privileges based on race, gender, income, or region is not a true democratic nation at all. "It was a real wrench for me to pass up the five-and-ten when the pickets were there," Rutland explains. "You know the brave young people that decided segregation was wrong anywhere—schools, bus stations, lunch counters—and picketed all over the country. But pass it up I did. This was bigger than my pocketbook. These young people were bigger than me—and I could not let them down."[109] Despite being in the American West, where she is relatively accepted in the same stores and public places as white patrons, Rutland reminds her readers that regardless of regional privileges, racial privileges, or class privileges, the entire nation is at a loss when its citizens are not treated equally or provided with the same access to the democratic process. In concluding this chapter in this way, Rutland models for her readers an "othermothering" and "m/othering" relevant to the American West and connects western American communities to communities in the South. She shows how to stand in allegiance with those communities that do not have the same privileges and to see this allegiance as undeniably and necessarily American rather than anti-American, radical, or even controversial.

Rutland critiques the perversion of an American individualism and recenters the focus on the greater good. Her memoir is about networking with other mothers, but it is also about problematizing engineered narratives that instruct people on their differences rather than on their similarities. In her introduction to the 2008 republication of her memoir, Rutland explains that her "biggest trouble with being a mama, especially a black mama, was my unfamiliarity with the rapidly changing world into which my children were born."[110] "As I look back," she says of her childhood in Atlanta, "I realize that I lived in two worlds, one almost totally white and the other almost totally black—but not quite. For no matter where I was, policemen, streetcar conductors, and grocery clerks were white. . . . When my children were born, the two worlds had begun to mix and herein lies my story."[111] In reflecting on her memoir's first edition in this way, Rutland realizes that she is telling the story of a "rapidly changing world" and the increasing impossibility for the American West or for any individual mother to deny or remain "unfamiliar" with the nation's racial history. Rutland's story, which is one that lies in the "mix" of Black and white and South and West, elevates regional knowledges to national importance to disrupt the trajectory of the nation's progressive history. By bringing her experience in the Jim Crow South to bear upon western American notions of integration and racial equality, Rutland highlights the recursive nature of American historical identity and cautions her readers to see that which they have been encouraged to forget and ignore.

Rutland's narrative, which begins in the South with her own upbringing, travels to the West after she becomes a mother herself, and ends with a chapter titled "We the People," challenges the West's understanding of American progressive history. For instance, Rutland's critique of the school board is rooted in Sacramento society's perception of progress. When she confronts the board for trying to evade the "burning issues," Rutland's concerns are written off as her melancholic withdrawal into race. The other members of the board, including those "behind her," cannot fathom where the histories Rutland brings with her from the South fit into western American identity. Ahmed helps me to recognize that the Sacramento integration politics Rutland evidences in scenes such as this attempt to make "those histories [of race and slavery] disappear by reading them as a form of melancholia (as if you hold onto something that is already gone)."[112] Ahmed suggests that even in a society that portrays itself as integrated and progressive, "these histories have not gone: we would be letting go of that which persists in the present. To let go would be to keep those histories present."[113] By associating racism with "a form of melancholia," the American West's progressive rhetoric renders the problem of racism as "something that is already gone." And if it does affect individuals in the West, it is because those individuals choose to "hold onto [it]" rather than let it be in the past. When Rutland insists that the school board discuss the "burning issues" of racism, she is insisting the board open discussions that are potentially catastrophic to the ways the other board members—people who subscribe to similar histories as Didion—relate to their region and their local communities. Therefore Rutland's society is evasive, and it pushes the entirety of the burden onto Rutland and her inability to "think beyond the race problem." The histories and stories the West tells about itself are, Rutland recognizes, deceptive and prove to be the real obstacles to progressive social politics.

While Rutland acknowledges that state and national legislation cannot change individual minds, she also sees that state and national narratives still have a significant impact. In a letter Rutland received from a white reader, Rae Miller, in 1968, Miller tells Rutland that she used to live in Modesto, California, but recently moved to Fort Worth, Texas. Miller points out that "[she] went just the opposite route as [Rutland]," west to south, versus Rutland's move from south to west.[114] Miller explains that "[she has] always felt strongly about equality and human worth" but that since moving to Texas she has recognized an "irony" in her "humanitarianism."[115] She writes that she met a Black family in Texas whose children play with hers, and "with all the emphasis that has been put on the negro/white relationship" in Texas, she found herself "acutely aware of [differences in race]."[116] Miller confides to Rutland that when this Black family invited hers to go out dancing, "suddenly [she] was face to face with all [she] had mouthed [about equality]," and she worried: "What would I do when I was asked to dance? Especially in a Southern state?"[117] Though their date fell through, Miller says that "for the first time, [she] became *really* aware that [she] was white and they were black!"[118] For all Miller's indoctrination in western American progressivism and for all her strong support of western American integration, her identity performs a shift in Texas. Her "humanitarian" identity strains under the South's histories and knowledges and fractures the progressive continuity the American West represents for the nation.

Miller narrates in this letter all the dangers and contradictions Rutland warns of in her memoir about the American West's insistent declaration of its own progressive and racially tolerant identity. While in California, Miller never thought about race in the ways she was forced to confront "face to face" in the South. But when Miller does move to the South, though this does not stop her from making Black friends and allowing her children to play with Black children, it does make her "aware that [she] was white and they were black." Read next to the school board scene in which Rutland is blamed for not being able to "think beyond the race problem," Miller's comments to Rutland reveal that racism is not always about an individual's politics or "humanitarianism." Racism is also about the location and situated knowledges of those individuals and of those with whom they interact. Ideas about race and racism translate differently across different regional borders and press individuals to react differently in different regional situations. Once Miller traverses regional borders, the histories she might have pushed back onto Rutland as her individual melancholic concern are suddenly something she must become "aware" of. The color-blind rhetoric upon which Miller built her "humanitarian" identity in the West is no longer sustainable in Texas, where she now sees white and Black, even as she feels a conflicted resistance to such histories. In fact Miller's letter to Rutland expresses a crisis of national continuity—the "hypnotic confirmation," as Benedict Anderson would say—as she beings to realize that the histories she thought were past are still in progress in the South.[119] Miller's motivations are founded in her own sense of betrayal at the hands of national narratives that have taught her to believe so deeply that racism is over, that white Americans have been redeemed, and that the American West has led the way toward a more progressive and democratic national society. As Miller proves, Rutland teaches her readers about the danger in forgetting national histories in favor of regional ones. She knits back together the conflicting regional understandings of how race-based slavery, Jim Crow segregation, and modern forms of institutional racism impact national cohesion and serve aggrandized ideas about the nation's progressive moves into American modernity.

Rutland's narrative expresses concern for the ways regional knowledges take on different meanings as they navigate regional borders. She notes how these regional knowledges transform the bodies of individuals into different "shapes," as Ahmed would say, and affect the "impressions" they experience as they move across those regional borders. In a chapter in which Rutland narrates the pressures placed on the Black middle class "to join" certain clubs, organizations, and communities, she acutely points out the unspoken rules her children must follow in joining and how these rules are underscored by the nation's histories with slavery, a failed Reconstruction era, and Jim Crow segregation. Rutland admits that she is "all for integration, but it does have its problems. One of its biggest problems," she continues, "is sex."[120] Rutland describes how, as a kindergartner, her son Billy befriended a Jewish girl named Sally. Sally's mother praised Billy as "the most beautiful child [she] had ever seen, and . . . was so glad that Sally was so unconscious of race or color that it had not occurred to her to mention it."[121] Rutland is not deluded by this admiration, nor does she believe in Sally's "unconscious" orientation to race. She sees beyond Sally's mother's praise and recognizes, "That was at six. But suppose Sally should bring Billy home at sixteen"—what Rutland calls the "sex-conscious stage."[122] The point is that at six, Billy's Blackness is "beautiful" and unthreatening. However, "the same mother would shriek" if Sally brought Billy home at sixteen "because at six it is wonderful for Sally to be innocent and open-minded and democratic about race and such, but at sixteen the possibility exists that she might marry the boy, for heaven's sake."[123] While western American notions of integration allow Billy to go to school with Sally and play with Sally as a young child, the historical epistemologies invented in the postbellum South that understand Black men as sexual predators and a threat to the purity of white women still determine how Black and white bodies are to "impress" upon one another as they grow into adulthood. Though Rutland concedes that these histories translate differently in the American West and therefore must be navigated differently, they are present nonetheless. And sex, as Rutland states, is a problem of integration because western American integration does not change the nation's mind about her son's sexual identity. It does not change the way Sally's mother—or Sally at sixteen, for that matter—identifies herself in opposition to Rutland's son. The histories the West wants to write off as Rutland's melancholic responsibility still permeate western American progressivism and place limitations on its reach.

Histories are contorted but, as Rutland is clearly aware, western American progressivism is ambivalent when it comes to assimilating Black bodies into those compromised histories. As she suggests of the integrated classroom, Rutland's western American society does not want to see race at the same time that it cannot avoid seeing race. "Who has not asked, 'Who am I?' 'When did I come?'" Rutland questions.[124] "Many Americans can answer with pride, 'My forefathers came over on the Mayflower.' 'I can trace my ancestry to a castle in Scotland, to a nobleman of France, to an English peer.'"[125] Rutland admits that "it is true that some could be traced to a debtor's prison or an equal disgrace," but she also argues that "[this] shame has long been obliterated, buried, lost in the vast majority of white faces, leveled off in the leveling sea of American democracy."[126] Rutland considers how these histories of Anglo-European settlement in the Americas lend themselves to certain liberal scripts of American freedom, individuality, and equality. She recognizes that they undergird many an American's sense of self, including that of many of the white students in the integrated western American classroom. However, Rutland also deconstructs the ways these liberal scripts are imbricated in global histories of colonialism and slavery and how that imbrication has been silenced and even erased by dominant national narratives to promulgate notions of western American progressivism and American democratic identity. "But I," Rutland defiantly asserts, "have a trademark that shouts to the world that my ancestors came over in the belly of a slave ship. My roots go no further—from royal African tribe or scum, I know not. My ancestry beyond the slave ship is lost as surely as that of my white friends from the debtor's prison. But the mark of my slave ship is not. By the color of my skin ye shall know my shame."[127] Rutland draws attention to the ways her own body and the bodies of her children are not accounted for by national narratives of freedom, democracy, and opportunity. She points out how her history is fragmented at the historical juncture of the slave ship, all the history coming before that "lost" and insignificant to national archives. In stating "But I," Rutland asserts herself as proof of this past ignored history and makes it relevant to a western American identity that distances itself from histories of slavery, racism, and inequality at the same time it builds its liberal self atop them.

Rutland unsettles the stories the West tells about itself by telling a new story of western American pioneerism and struggle. In her mid-twentieth-century moment Rutland does not have the difficult task of crossing rugged geography and harsh climate the way the mid-nineteenth-century Anglo-American pioneers did. Instead she must forge the regional divides that are instantiated in geopolitical identities that refuse to acknowledge continuity across borders or relevance to ongoing national conflicts with racism. As Rutland's narrative carries

American histories of racism across regional borders, it becomes clear that dominant national narratives recognize the histories of slavery and racism as spatialized problems concerning the American South and as temporalized problems of the Civil War era. Not only does this separate the American South from the American West geopolitically, but it also relegates the American South to the nation's past, preserved, in a way, in that Civil War era as it continues to struggle with issues of race, while the American West is situated as the nation's progressive, forward-thinking future. Lisa Lowe argues that "the differentiations of 'race' or 'nation,' the geopolitical map of 'south,' 'north,' 'east,' and 'west,' or the modernization discourse of stages of development—these are the *traces* of liberal forgetting."[128] Though Lowe is discussing global regions, her argument helps me to conceptualize the ways the U.S. nation also spatializes and temporalizes certain histories and knowledges to enact a "liberal forgetting" that feeds into national scripts of freedom, equality, and opportunity. This framework for evaluating American regionalism fits with what Comer (among others) has pointed out as a trend in western American writing that understands the West "as a double for the US nation—the story of settling the West is the story of America," and it makes clear that a western American sense of progress, futurity, and idealism serves to consolidate the nation's past histories of slavery and racial segregation in the South.[129]

Rutland's narrative stands to challenge this consolidation—the pattern of forgetting, as I suggest in this book—in her physical and rhetorical movement across regional borders. When Rutland boycotts the five-and-ten in support of the Black youth in the American South and calls attention to the important Black histories her children miss out on in attending integrated western American schools, Rutland challenges national histories that, as Lowe helps us to see, "translate[] the world through an economy of affirmation and forgetting within a regime of desiring freedom."[130] The American West has created an identity out of Americans' desire for freedom and the failure of the nation to deliver on this promise to all Americans. If an American individual's situation in New England, the South, or even the Midwest fails to bring them the desired economic and sociopolitical capital, then that individual resorts to moving west for the opportunity to start over. Throughout this book I have shown this move. The Darrells, Ruiz de Burton's squatter family, move west in hopes of securing the financial freedom New England society has stifled for them; Helen Hunt Jackson's Aunt Ri leaves the labor-saturated South in a failed Reconstruction era; and Sui Sin Far's Chinese immigrants show us this same move on a more global scale as they travel from China to the U.S. West Coast. In each of these instances western American women writers and their diverse characters fail to be accounted for by national narratives and histories, so they accumulate debts, illnesses, and losses as they struggle against a system that promises them freedom and equality but that turns out to be the rhetoric of an empty progressivism. Rutland also travels west with the hope that the integrated cities in the West can offer her family something better than they could have in the South. However, just like Ruiz de Burton, Jackson, and Sui Sin Far, Rutland finds her move west creates new problems and obstacles as the region refuses to acknowledge the histories that led her to seek freedom and opportunity in the West in the first place. Rutland's memoir, with all its historical and cross-regional insight, draws attention to the "but I" that is left out of the American West's progressive histories and the nation's idealistic liberal scripts.

Regional and national amnesias are formidable in their ability to rewrite histories that become more readily consumable by the imagined national community. Although she asserts her "but I," Rutland also acknowledges the powerful allure of relinquishing her past to become an imagined but never fully realized member in what Didion referred to as a "we." In a reflective moment at the end of the memoir, Rutland critically engages with her own "amnesia" or her own pattern of forgetting. In the final chapter, "We the People," Rutland admits to pretending "that the problem [of racial violence] was far, far away."[131] As she watched the South's Black youth on television, "faced with the controversy over the integrated school, I thanked God that we were not involved," and she "shielded the children from the headlines" to protect them from even seeing the violence against Black children and adolescents from the relative safety of their living room.[132] But in this reflection Rutland recognizes the problems in thinking this way and understands the power of the manufactured histories and knowledges of the western American region that allow her to "pretend" her children were safe. She tells us that "in [her] selfishness, [she] thanked God that the children were in California, away from the controversy, the ugly strife and turmoil that surrounded boys and girls in some parts of our nation."[133] But then, "It was a lovely sunny day in California," when, across the country the Sixteenth Street Baptist Church is bombed in Birmingham, and Rutland, from her place in Sacramento, "came face to face with [her] beloved South."[134] And she was forced to ask herself, "Could I have forgotten so soon?"[135]

In this last chapter Rutland deconstructs national narratives that claim to be for "the people," just as she deconstructed the dominant rhetoric of middle-class motherhood. She points to the ways these narratives operate through "forgotten" histories, knowledges, and identities, in similar ways that the rhetoric of dominant middle-class motherhood operates through a language that predicates the protection of white children on the disregard for the protection of children of color. She sees the connections Sacramento has to Birmingham and how national narratives, which identify the U.S. nation as "this lighthouse across the sea, saying to the oppressed of Hungary and Syria, 'Give me your tired, your poor, your huddled masses yearning to breathe free,'" work through a discourse of forgetting that there are "tired," "poor," and "huddled masses yearning to breathe free" right there in the nation itself, right there in the American West, where the nation's ideals are said to reach their full potential.[136] Rutland thinks for a moment about how "Bill and [she] had both lived and worked in Birmingham, many times had attended the Sixteenth Street Baptist Church, would perhaps still be there if Bill had gotten the job he had applied for, right outside of Birmingham. . . . And next came the stabbing thought" that *"it could have been [her] girls."*[137] On that September Sunday, Rutland "admitted that [she] was not brave enough nor good enough. [She] could not love [her] enemies. If it were Pat or Billy or any of [her children], [she] would scream and fight and *kill!* [She] could not peacefully resist."[138]

Despite having claimed earlier in the narrative to be opposed to the more militant movements led by Malcolm X and Stokely Carmichael, Rutland admits in this moment of re-remembering that there is an emotional validity to their strategies. She says that if her own children were in the line of fire like those in the church bombing, she could not "peacefully resist." But it doesn't just stop there. Rutland's affective activism acquiesces to a politics of violence when she indicates that she would "scream and fight and *kill*" to protect her children from the violence of American racism. Not only does this leave Rutland's readers feeling the emotive power in her dueling regional identities, but it is also a conclusion that never would have shown up in the "politics of respectability" practiced by the generations of Black women before her. Rutland's alternative politics of respectability questions not only the racist practices of her national society but also the productivity in a respectable approach to equality if respectability is measured against a dominant Anglo-American sense of the word that has motivated and justified the oppression of so many.

Conclusion

*Joan Didion's Sacramento and
Arlie Russell Hochschild's "Deep Story"*

In an early autobiographical essay, "Notes from a Native Daughter" (1965), Joan Didion sets out to tell "what it is like to come from a place like Sacramento."¹ Published only one year after Eva Rutland's *When We Were Colored*, "Notes" traces Didion's ancestry back to the early pioneers of California and, in even more personal ways than in her first novel, *Run River*, captures the overwhelming sense of lost identity in the American West. Didion writes: "Because the land was rich, Sacramento became eventually a rich farm town, which meant houses in town, Cadillac dealers, a country club. In that gentle sleep Sacramento dreamed until perhaps 1950, when *something* happened. What happened was that Sacramento *woke* to the fact that the outside world was moving in, fast and hard. At the moment of its waking Sacramento lost, for better or for worse, its character, and that is part of what I want to tell you about."²

In this history of Sacramento Didion identifies that "something happened" in the 1950s, and it is this "something" that led to the loss of Sacramento's "character." When read in tandem with Rutland's memoir, the "something" that Didion does not or cannot name here shows itself as Rutland and the other diverse families that are moving into the city in these mid-twentieth-century decades and transforming Sacramento's social, economic, and urban infrastructures. Just like Lily and Martha in *Run River*, Didion was from the kind of wealthy farm family that had a "house[] in town," that bought from "Cadillac dealers," and that frequented the "country club." What Didion doesn't name, then, is the "something" that disrupts her own regional history and the epistemologies by which she recognizes her place in American narratives. But for Didion, Sacramento's loss, whether it be "for better or for worse," is "part of what [she] want[s] to tell you . . . for Sacramento *is* California."[3] Here Didion expresses the need to tell her own California story because it is incongruent with so much of her experience as a woman in the West.

In the introduction to this book I identify a consistent speechlessness throughout Didion's work and link this to her ambivalent relationship to the American West. I argue that Didion's speechlessness is evidence of an organic feminist response to a patriarchal literary industry that codifies dominant literary forms out of masculine language and tropes. Consequently women writers of the West, such as those collected in this book, write from within the interstices of dominant literary genres and narratives and, as I have shown in the previous four chapters, recall the cultural histories written over by national literary programs. Didion's "Notes" indicates her early frustration with a lack of appropriate language and the freedom of literary space to write her West. While the title of her essay, "Notes from a Native Daughter," captures a settler-colonial impulse to erase histories women like Ruiz de Burton and Sui Sin Far depict in their writing, Didion also recognizes that by 1950 Sacramento must "wake" from the "gentle sleep" induced by a national ideal that was only ever but a dream.

Didion wants to tell this story of a western American dream interrupted, or perhaps a western American dream dreamed for too long, because she wants us to understand how the West was seduced by a manufactured rhetoric that was never going to be sustainable. By the mid-twentieth century Didion recognizes the dream is but a "dreamtime," calcified under the weight of competing histories constantly in friction. Throughout this book I have shown those individual histories as they encounter one another and work out their tensions on the pages of American literature. The tensions manifest as Ruiz de Burton's contradictions, Jackson's ambivalence, Sui Sin Far's rejection of identity altogether, and Rutland's politicized, middle-class motherhood. As writers located in the American West, the women considered in this book are also located at that juncture between true histories and fabricated ones, and their literary productions are full of the insecurities that result because of this friction.

In the case of Didion's insecurities about Sacramento, we must read for what is left unwritten and absent from the page. This reading for the gaps is the kind of archival reading Lowe suggests we undertake to make our understanding of global histories more thorough.[4] It is also a reading practice for which Toni Morrison argues in *Playing in the Dark*. Morrison suggests that a key component of twentieth-century American literature is that it must contend in some way or another with the "other"—in Morrison's case, the "Africanist persona." Often, Morrison claims, the Africanist persona is evaded in a literary work, but this "evasion has fostered another, substitute language in which the issues are encoded" and in which "an Africanist persona is reflexive; an extraordinary meditation on the self; a powerful exploration of the fears and desires that reside in the writerly conscious."[5] Didion's language is indeed evasive. As much as she intends to, she avoids confronting the "something" that punctured Sacramento's dream, and the language is "reflexive" because that "something" is inherently antagonistic to the liberal idealism in which her pioneer family invests. But Didion's evasive maneuvers also go beyond "the fears and desires that reside in the writerly conscious."

Didion's speechlessness is, as I started off arguing in this book, anything but silent. Didion is a precise author, someone who seems to have the exact right words to describe the nation's most indecisive emotions—that is, until she doesn't. Her use of *"something"* in this passage cannot be ignored or read over. Rather, the word *"something"* is the rhetorical placeholder for what Didion perceives to be the traumatic disruption of Sacramento's character. In "Notes" Didion assumes that the "outside world," a wording that indicates a white western American tribalism, is encroaching on the West and fundamentally changing it. By referencing a "lost" Sacramento character, Didion implies the changes are a loss, a point of personal grievance, and she points to the de-regionalization of such western American cities as the "world" overrides what makes, in Didion's opinion, the West unique. This de-regionalization throws Sacramento's and the larger Western region's identities into flux as the region must contend with the histories and identities it has kept at bay through a frontier rhetoric and a western American idealism. In 1965 Didion is unable to name her loss, but she is curious enough to feel its relation to the world "moving in, fast and hard." And while the language Didion uses implies disruption at the hands of the "outside world," Morrison allows us to see this language as evasive. The "outside world" that Didion recognizes as "moving in, fast and hard" in the 1950s and that led to Sacramento's "waking" is that of diverse populations moving to Sacramento to fill jobs at the Aerojet factory, established in East Sacramento in 1951, or it references the Black population that is relocated to Sacramento's McClellan Air Force Base after the integration of the air force in 1948, a population of which Rutland and her family are part. These are global changes, altering the American West to position the nation as a global power. Already in 1965, before Didion has fully installed herself as an international journalist and the nation's "sharpest" critic—to recall President Barack Obama's accolades[6]—she feels a loss sustained by the western American region as the nation turns its attentions to the world. But where Didion mistakenly assumes that it is the world "moving in" to the West, her later works revise this to realize that it is in fact the American West moving out onto the world.

Didion's authorship provides an important insight into how the nation's nineteenth-century manufactured histories and narratives about the West are deployed on a global scale in the late twentieth century and sets up a framework for understanding how the consequences of these histories are playing out now in our contemporary era. As Didion's authorship continues past her 1963 first novel, *Run River*, she becomes more internationally aware. In her essay "Slouching towards Bethlehem," originally published in the *Saturday Evening Post* in 1967, Didion enmeshes herself in San Francisco's Haight-Ashbury neighborhood to expose the counterculture's flailing sense of disassociation with the nation. She declares that the youth are "less in rebellion against the society than ignorant of it, able only to feed back certain of its most publicized self-doubts, *Vietnam, Saran-Wrap, diet pills, the Bomb*."[7] Didion problematizes a counterculture that lacks depth or critical reflection on "certain of its most publicized self-doubts." True progress and truly progressive politics require reciprocal conversation, but as Didion says, the California counterculture is only able to "feed back" to the nation what it has fed them. Dynamic conversation is foreclosed when the terms of the debate are consolidated into an unempathetic, unreflective language served by the establishment, and Didion documents the damage this consolidation has on progressive movements and the young generations that sustain them.

Didion recognizes that the youths' disillusionment is a consequence of their dissatisfaction with national narratives but that their despondency is the result of having nothing else with which to fight back. Didion describes them as "sixteen, fifteen, fourteen years old, younger all the time, an army of children waiting to be given the words."[8] And while she has been associated with and often held up as a pinnacle example of an American postmodern literary movement, Didion's critique of the children lacking the "words" is a critique of that very postmodern and avant-garde program. But in identifying that the "army of children" lacks the right "words" to fight back, she pinpoints the problem the other women writers in this book also have.

Ruiz de Burton, Jackson, Sui Sin Far, and Rutland write outside the bounds of nationally prescribed histories and cultural knowledges. Therefore their narratives do not fit into dominant literary forms, nor do they follow conventional western American plot structures. From their specific positionalities to the nation and dominant literary society, this group of western American women writers understands that progress is discursive, so they adapt dominant literary forms to generate critical reflection. In chapter 1 I argued that Ruiz de Burton deployed autoethnographic sentimental heroines to bring awareness to the inconsistencies in the cult of domesticity and other women's programs as they impact the West. In chapter 2 I suggested that Jackson's use of the sentimental novel form uncovered the insecurities white women had even while they engaged in progressive work to emancipate slaves and advocate for Indigenous communities. I situated chapter 3 in the Progressive Era itself to show how Sui Sin Far represented supposedly progressive literary modes to draw attention to all the ways dominant realist and naturalist tropes further objectified ethnic American identities rather than incorporating them into national identity. In chapter 4 I introduced Rutland and the ways her maternal memoir combined features of the pioneer narrative and the African American autobiographical tradition to transcend regionalized histories of slavery and race and thereby generate a language to talk about a twentieth-century western American racism. In total, just as Didion critiques the counterculture's regurgitated progressive rhetoric, the women writers collected in this book also critique a western American literary industry that recycles imperialist and racist structures to imply progress.

Didion is aware that there is only so much manipulation one can do with dominant words and forms. Didion's 1960s literary works are fraught with the frustration that comes with not having the proper words and therefore with not having the right tools to communicate her dissatisfaction to the nation. For instance, "Slouching towards Bethlehem" was republished in a collection of essays Didion wrote throughout the 1960s that was also titled *Slouching towards Bethlehem*. In the preface to the collection Didion identifies "Slouching towards Bethlehem" as "the most imperative of all these pieces to write and the only one that made me despondent after it was printed."[9] She further explains that she decided to write about the Haight-Ashbury because she "had been paralyzed by the conviction that writing was an irrelevant act, that the world as [she] had understood it no longer existed." She states, "If I was to work again at all, it would be necessary for me to come to terms with disorder."[10] Didion remains "despondent" because, as she expresses it, she is "afflicted some of the time by the suspicion that nobody out there is listening," and those that are, miss the point entirely.[11] Here Didion relates her "work"—her writing—to the "disorder" she experiences in the years following *Run River* as she came face to face with the fact that "the world as I had understood it no longer existed." As critics have said in many ways, Didion writes to understand the world around her, and in large part that is what makes her work so intuitive. However, more than making Didion a vibrant writer, Didion's writing-to-understand also places her in relation to a genealogy of western American women writers who wrote to make others understand, and this is no easy task. Didion claims "Slouching towards Bethlehem" as the most "imperative" of her 1960s essays not only because at stake in the piece are America's youth but also because the essay taught her an important lesson about her audience and the high-brow literary culture into which she was stepping.

Although "Slouching towards Bethlehem" met immediate success and put Didion on the national literary map, Didion is unhappy with the way the essay was received. As quoted above, Didion is frustrated that "nobody out there is listening," even as the essay is widely read. This is consistent with all the women writers in this book. Ruiz de Burton was unhappy with the lack of attention her novels attracted; Jackson was displeased with critics' focus on *Ramona*'s sentimental plot instead of the political plot; Sui Sin Far constantly battled against the exoticization of her authorial identity; and (although outside the scope of this book) Rutland went on to challenge editors who felt her later works were "too defensive" for publication.[12] These women writers find that even their most successful works are misread, misinterpreted, and assigned alternative meanings to avoid the controversy they call up. Didion and her predecessors are writing from the interstices of a national ethos that only recognizes forward motion. Progress is the only narrative that makes sense to this national audience, and therefore, when Didion and the other women writers in this book propose a different trajectory, one that critiques American progress as a process of forgetting, the point is missed. Didion goes on to say that "it seemed to me then (perhaps because the piece was important to me) that I had never gotten a feedback so universally beside the point."[13] While critics congratulated Didion on having written "Slouching towards Bethlehem" "'just in time,' because 'the whole fad's dead now,'" Didion recognizes that this feedback is "beside the point."[14] Didion is not trying to capture either a social fad before it is "dead" or a timely counterhegemonic politic. Rather, Didion's intent is to expose the violence and disruption America's youth experience at the hands of this "fad," regardless of its being "dead now." Her focus is on the fatal consequences of a failed

American liberalism, and even while San Francisco counterculture seems to be "dead," Didion's "Slouching towards Bethlehem" fears its adaptation in the nation's global encounters.

Didion identifies San Francisco's youth as an unseen class of veterans. Though unsanctioned by the nation, their war is a war nonetheless. And like the Vietnam veterans of the same era, the counterculture's youth emerge from this "dead" war displaced and damaged, sometimes fatally so. Didion's "Slouching towards Bethlehem" shows her increasing awareness for the mid-twentieth century's globalization of a western American ethos. And although Didion is frustrated by the fact that her audience does not want to make these connections, she grows only more focused on this issue in her later works. Didion's late 1970s and 1980s novels and journalism are undeniably concentrated on the nation's international affairs. During this era Didion shifts from the American West to write the essays eventually collected in *The White Album* (1979), a collection far more globally minded than the American West–centric essays in her first collection, *Slouching towards Bethlehem*.[15] In addition, Didion caps off the 1970s with her third novel, *A Book of Common Prayer* (1977), which is her first literary venture to explicitly explore her international interests in novelistic form. Even so, the novel remains engaged with the American West's "dead" counterculture from a decade earlier.

A complexly plotted novel, *A Book of Common Prayer* begins with a wealthy San Francisco youth, Marin, who joins a militant anti-capitalist group that bombs San Francisco's Transamerica Building, the West Coast's symbol of global capitalism. Marin is a fugitive throughout the narrative and is relegated to the novel's fringes. She is, as Didion says of the youth in "Slouching towards Bethlehem," "missing" for much of the novel and is a representative member of the counterculture's "army of children." Although she is "missing," Marin haunts each page of the novel, and her radical behavior impacts the novel's intricate network of characters. The novel's focus is on Charlotte, Marin's mother, as she copes with the news that her daughter is both a domestic terrorist and "missing." Charlotte spends much of the novel in a Latin American country, Boca Grande, where she delivers American vaccines and birth control to the country's poor. But Charlotte also visits the airport every day, hoping to run into Marin. Charlotte is a rather mysterious character to whom the reader only gets as close as Grace Tabor, the novel's narrator, allows us to.

Grace, an American expatriate, is Boca Grande's recently widowed matriarch. Her perspective offers the novel a filter through which western American progressive radicalism negotiates with American global intervention. For instance, Grace meets with Marin, estranged from her mother, in a Buffalo, New York, hotel room while Marin is on the run. During this meeting Grace and Marin talk about Charlotte. When Marin asks Grace what her mother does in Boca Grande, Grace answers that she "did some work in a clinic."[16] Marin scoffs at this reply, answering back, "Charity," while Grace feels the "indictment [that] lay between" them.[17] Grace tries to emphasize the importance of Charlotte's work by explaining to Marin that she has helped control the country's cholera outbreak. But "Marin Bogart shrugged."[18] She shrugged, Grace realizes, because "Cholera was something Marin Bogart had been protected against, along with diphtheria, pertussis, tetanus, tuberculosis, poliomyelitis, and undue dental decay."[19] So Grace concludes, "Cholera was one more word Marin Bogart did not understand."[20] Marin's privilege as a white middle-class American informs her orientation to the world, and in failing to acknowledge that privilege as central to her progressive epistemology, Marin also fails to register her relation to imperial projects. This scene documents Marin's inability to account for different and complex systems of power working simultaneously. While Marin deems her mother's distribution of birth control as "*the* most flagrant example of how the ruling class practices genocide," she also sits on a hotel bed next to an M-3, leaving Grace to counter back, "Maybe not *the* most flagrant."[21] Through Grace, Didion compares and links together the white savior complex in Charlotte's international reproductive activism and Marin's militaristic approach to end cultural imperialism. The birth control Charlotte distributes and the M-3 Marin holds across her lap are but different iterations of the same progressive problem. Each one sets out to do something "right," but each one becomes mired in a progressive overstep in which the "right" thing turns violent. Progress and the pathway to a more progressive state, Didion contemplates here, are defined by power as much as the "flagrant" imperialism and capitalist takeover associated with more conservative movements.

To Grace, therefore, Marin is but a "lost daughter . . . who never had much use for words but had finally learned to string them together so that they sounded almost like sentences."[22] While Marin deplores her mother for being "on the wrong side of a 'people's revolution,'" Grace, who has lived through the violent rhythms of revolutions and military coups in Boca Grande as a consequence of American capitalism's destabilizing effects in other parts of the world, tries to explain to Marin that "there was no 'right side.' . . . *There were only personalities.*"[23] Here Grace tries to capture the waste in a culture war fought via extremism. Each side finds its justification in the same claims to American freedom and liberty, and each side justifies violence, whether it be physical or rhetorical, as a necessary means to a win, to achieve progress. But Marin still does not get it. Instead she answers back: "*A typically bourgeois view of the revolutionary process.*"[24] The "revolutionary process" in which Marin invests is less a process, according to Didion, and more an unproductive chaos. As Didion ponders in "Slouching toward Bethlehem," "It is possible for people to be the unconscious instruments of values they would strenuously reject on a conscious level."[25] For Didion the problem with Marin is that she is an "unconscious instrument" of the revolution rather than an agent of it. Marin recycles the words of the counterculture, words she has assumed but of which she has no real understanding.

This is not to say that Marin lacks intelligence or self-awareness. In fact many of Marin's intentions and observations of dominant society hold merit. However, Marin serves Didion in problematizing a mid-twentieth-century progressive radicalism because it is linked to a century-old western American rhetoric rooted in exceptionalism and intense individualism. Grace suggests Marin can form "almost" sentences, but the words in these sentences are just as misplaced as Marin's violent protests because Marin lacks the critical understanding of the histories of imperial violence from which her words descend and, therefore, of the meanings they inherit along that history. Grace observes that Marin was a "lost child in a dirty room in Buffalo. A child who claimed no interest in the past. Or the future. Or the present."[26] To be "lost" or (as Didion says in "Slouching towards Bethlehem") to be "missing" is to be detached from the histories that bring us to our present and to be uninterested in the way our present actions impact the future. In many ways the conversation between Grace and Marin depicts the obvious fact that the past, present, and future are related, but Didion's nuance is in how she diagnoses the counterculture's ineffectiveness as a kind of historical amnesia and certainly a future disinvestment. Grace ends her meeting with Marin thinking that "maybe there is no motive role in this narrative. Maybe it is just something that happened."[27] Marin's actions, her bombing of the Transamerica Building, are catastrophic, but as Grace questions here, for what? Nobody benefits from Marin's bombing of the Transamerica Building, and even more discouragingly for Didion, Marin represents a "lost" generation whose words and behaviors only serve to incite a wasteful culture war and, in so doing, feed into global patterns of violence and imperial takeover.

A Book of Common Prayer is mobilized by a rhetorical fatalism that Didion associates with the West but that she also sees making global moves. But even in this 1977 novel Didion resists or evades placing the criticism on any one camp or any one character. While she does clearly articulate that Marin is "lost" in a rhetorical program she does not fully comprehend, Didion also mourns for Marin as a western American woman who bears the brunt of a failed dream. Marin turns to the counterculture to cope with her lack of appropriate words and her dissatisfaction with national scripts. The counterculture supplies these words and an outlet for her pain, but as Grace notes in her conversation with Marin, Marin is just as taken advantage of by the counterculture as she was by dominant culture. Didion puts it another way in a 1965 essay, "On Morality," in which she says: "I want to be quite obstinate about insisting that we have no way of knowing—beyond that fundamental loyalty to the social code—what is 'right' and what is 'wrong,' what is 'good' and what is 'evil.'"[28] The fictionalized telling of 1960s San Francisco counterculture through the "missing" Marin, who believes herself to be on the "right side" of a "people's revolution," allows Didion to draw out the larger, global consequences of the liberal movements germinating in the West. These movements rely on notions of a western American progressivism and idealism that, as we saw in numerous different ways throughout this book, are largely fabricated by dominant national narratives to sustain a continuous national identity without taking responsibility for the nation's past. There is no "right" or "wrong," no "truth" or "lie," in these rhetorical wars. Marin throws out phrases like "ruling class," "people's revolution," and "bourgeois," but these words are empty signifiers that support equally empty political identities. They are, as Arlie Russell Hochschild would say, indicators of a western American "deep story" that cannot move past the way it feels to consider the way things are.[29]

Hochschild's 2016 *New York Times* best-selling book, *Strangers in Their Own Land*, is the next iteration in a genealogy of western American women's critiques of the region's progressive identity. As a well-revered Berkeley, California, academic and social critic, Hochschild confronts the ways the nation's conservative nationalism, largely associated with the American South, and the West's liberal progressivism are intertwined even as they position themselves in opposition to one another. That is, Hochschild offers insight into how a western American progressive identity and the South's conservatism are born out of the same political philosophy, American liberalism. Of course, as Hochschild documents, the terms of American liberalism are interpreted differently in the different regions, and thus different political and regional identities develop. Hochschild's concern, as she sets out for the American South's Gulf Coast at a time when the nation's "polarization, and the increasing reality that we simply don't know each other, makes it too easy to settle for dislike and contempt," is for *why* different regional communities interpret notions of "freedom," "equality," and "consent of the governed" differently.[30] Hochschild's ethnographic approach—an approach driven by "a keen interest in how life *feels* to people on the right"[31]—involves her with several Louisiana communities, including rural communities, working-class communities, religious communities, and local political communities. Hochschild shares conversations she has with these communities about their urgent climate change disasters, accelerated by unregulated industrial pollution; the nation's social inequalities; and the upcoming 2016 presidential election between Donald Trump and Hilary Clinton. Hochschild's aim is to understand what she calls "the great paradox," the southern states' resistance to federal aid programs even though these are also the states that could benefit the most from those programs.³²

What it comes down to, Hochschild concludes, is the "deep stories" that inform regional cultural knowledge and that create the dissociative gaps between the nation's regional and political factions. Hochschild defines the "deep story" as "a story that *feels as if* it were true."³³ It is, Hochschild continues, "the story feelings tell, in the language of symbols. It removes judgement. It removes fact. It tells us how things feel."³⁴ And everyone, Hochschild stresses, has a deep story. It is how we relate our experiences—the way we "*feel*"—to the way things appear to be in a world of politics and social organization. It is a powerful story in that it is something we can inherit, a "feeling" we can adopt from our ancestors—as Didion stands to show—and it is a story that guides our very social and political identities within the nation.

Hochschild recognizes that though told from different perspectives, the South's "deep story" and the West's "deep story" are imbricated in the same national promise, the promise of the "American Dream," which is also a "dream of progress—the idea that you're better off than your forebears just as they superseded their parents before you—and extends beyond money and stuff."³⁵ But the term "progress," as I have shown, does little to clarify the vague concept of the American Dream or its purpose to a nation that imagines itself equitable enough. While Hochschild identifies that the southern "deep story" relates to American progress through "long hours, layoffs, and exposure to dangerous chemicals at work [to show a] moral character through trial by fire," the western "deep story" relates through the "redemptive power of the crossing," which many do not survive.³⁶ In each instance "progress" does not actually *feel* like progress. In each instance "progress" is defined through individual loss—loss of economic power, loss of environmental health, loss of life. Didion's Marin is an example of this loss as well, as her "revolutionary process" leads her to destroy the Transamerica Building and forfeit her freedom to make a point for the counterculture. And yet, as Hochschild uncovers through interactions in the South, this individual loss is forgotten in American narratives of progress, or in the case of Marin, it is dismissed as a necessary evil.

Deep stories are stories of mourning. They mourn for the loss sustained on the road to progress, but they also mourn for the thing progress works toward but remains forever out of grasp. Central to anyone's "deep story" is a "larger institutional forgetting" or, as Hochschild rephrases it, "a structural amnesia" that facilitates the erasure of personal loss at the behest of American "progress."[37] Even as the families Hochschild meets contend with the individual losses and consequences of the nation's gross negligence of the environment and corporate greed, they continue to politically support conservative agendas and offer their labor to the very same companies that destroy their homes with toxic waste. Although these families sometimes do not have any other choice but to find employment in the chemical companies polluting their waterways, Hochschild marvels over their fierce defense of the companies' legal rights to shirk responsibility and, in some cases, economically benefit from the environmental disasters they create. This contradiction breeds in a rhetoric of American liberalism (and now neoliberalism). As Hochschild notes at a meeting she sits in on for the Republican Women of Southwest Louisiana, the women spoke "a great deal about freedom in the sense of freedom *to*," but "there was almost no talk about *freedom from*."[38] While the women spoke about their freedom *to* openly carry guns, there was no consideration of the people's freedom *from* gun violence. Louisianans discuss corporations' freedom *to* increase their profit margins, but they do not mention the local residents' and employees' freedom *from* harmful chemical agents in their water supply or in their work environments, even as those freedoms *from* directly impact them. Put succinctly, American liberalism, an always already contradictory ideology, fuels "structural amnesia" with a one-sided rhetoric of freedom.

The western American women writers considered in *California Dreams and American Contradictions* work from within the cracks of this rhetoric and the forgotten histories it writes over by not only addressing the ethnic, gendered, and immigrant individuals excluded from American liberal identity but also by reframing dominant genres to account for the freedom *from* perspective in American liberal conversations. Ruiz de Burton's autoethnographic heroines reshape sentimental tropes that emphasize a woman's freedom *to* domesticate into a freedom *from* the restrictive gender roles that only imagine American women's liberal autonomy. Jackson enters a similar conversation but from the sentimentalized perspective of a disenfranchised class of Anglo Americans to posit their freedom *from* industrial labor strife and capitalist "progress." In the Progressive Era Sui Sin Far dismantles the realist novel's self-proclaimed freedom *to* represent American outliers and erects a new language for ethnic immigrants' freedom *from* dominant realists and their literary machines. Likewise Rutland questions western American integration policies to advocate for a freedom *from* respectability and a western American sense of social progressivism. And finally, as this conclusion has emphasized, Didion reconceptualizes dominant historical and literary myths concerning the American West to negotiate between her proclivities for a freedom *to* be western American and her fear that this identity requires a freedom *from* a progressivism coopted by the West's 1960s counterculture. Together these western American women writers trace a century-long struggle to justly disseminate liberty. Their literatures realize the contradictions in American liberal foundations and the slippages between American individualism and American progress.

Hochschild delivers this criticism to a twenty-first-century audience at a time when all progressive pretense in American neoliberalism is quickly being overtaken by an extreme vein of American populism. In his recent book *What Was Liberalism?*, journalist James Traub names the "rise of illiberalism" as the "greatest shock of my political life."[39] It is precisely because American illiberalism is a "shock" to so many in the twenty-first century that the western American women writers collected here are so important. For I do not think any of them, from Ruiz de Burton all the way through to Hochschild, would find the rise of American illiberalism particularly shocking. Traub situates his "shock" in a dual-party system that posits to "liberals and conservatives . . . that the greatest threat to the American future was one another."[40] He suggests that this bipartisan fantasy led his generation astray. "They were wrong," Traub admits, and adds that the "greatest threat is that we will normalize violence and hatred; that we will abandon science, facts, and reason itself; that we will marginalize and persecute minorities."[41] What Traub realizes is of course true; American liberalism is at odds with itself. However, his "shock" is part of the problem and is the unfortunate consequence of a progressive ethos that has allowed the nation to overlook that violence and hatred have always been normalized in the United States; that science, facts, and reason have always been challenged by self-serving political institutions; and that minorities have always been marginalized and persecuted by the nation. The rhetoric of "progress," which I have traced throughout this book, operates to make Americans *feel* the nation has rectified its histories of oppression, but in actuality, it is a passive rhetoric that evades historical reconciliation. Authors such as those collected in this volume have stood against the feeling of progress to show that the least progressive thing about American society is its progress.

Together María Amparo Ruiz de Burton, Helen Hunt Jackson, Sui Sin Far, and Eva Rutland provide the twenty-first-century United States an undeniable and urgently needed history of cautionary tales about the illiberal veins of American liberalism. In the foreword to Didion's *South and West*, Nathaniel Rich makes a case for the relevance of Didion's 1970s notes about American regions in our twenty-first-century moment. He argues that today Didion's "observations read like a warning unheeded. They suggest that California's dreamers of the golden dream were just that—dreamers—while the 'dense obsessiveness' of the South, and all the vindictiveness that comes with it, was the true American condition, the condition to which we will always inevitably return."[42] I agree but also suggest that Didion is a part of a genealogy of "warning[s] unheeded" and that the "dense obsessiveness" from which Didion retracts in the South is also what has stoked the California dream and allowed the warnings to go unheeded. For obsessiveness is an intense curiosity for that which we do not understand. If, as Didion identifies, the South is densely obsessed with "race, class, heritage, style, and the absence of style," it is so because these conversations are drawing the South toward an unresolved past. This brand of American obsessiveness—I say "American" rather than "southern" for it has been my work here to de-regionalize such histories—has led to successful political campaigns that run on "making America great again." The obvious critique here is that many Americans have not experienced a time when America was great, just as many Americans do not recognize progress in progressive campaigns. In addition, "make America great again" is a regressive notion, positioning "progress" in the past. This is fundamentally at odds with a western American progressive identity. As I have traced throughout this book, the American West is rendered as always looking forward, but as Didion eloquently articulates, it is also rendered through "the frontier ethic which teaches western children to deny [the past] and to leave [it] deliberately unmentioned."[43] The western American identity is equally obsessed with a future it imagines to be better and locates progress—"a great America," we could say—in the perpetual, unreachable future. The "warning unheeded" is thus a caution about how regional and political fractioning is the consequence of "deep stories," underwritten by similar national narratives, that redirect one region to obsess about the past and the other region to obsess about never looking to the past. In this regional and political stasis American liberalism is being tugged in opposing directions, and American "progress" is recognized as a regional affect.

As I drafted early versions of this conclusion, the nation was living out a particularly violent iteration of this tug, and certain regional communities were doubling down on their affective investment in their brand of American progress. On January 6, 2021, a mob of alt-right conservatives invaded the nation's Capitol Building in protest of President-elect Joe Biden's confirmation. The protestors believed President Biden had won the 2020 election unfairly, and this led them to push down barricades, break windows, threaten democratic congressional leaders, and damage historic property belonging to American citizens. I paused in my writing, when I was thinking through Hochschild's observations about "freedom *to*" versus "freedom *from*," to watch the unprecedented desecration of *the* symbol of American liberal democracy on live television. I was struck by the realization that the scene I was watching unfold was the consequence of "warnings unheeded" and of "nobody out there listening." For the January insurrection depicted different ideas of progress clashing—quite literally. The insurrection was an event in which those who locate progress in the past took a stand against those who locate progress in the future, irrespective of the past. So we saw on January 6, 2021, what is at stake in the western American narratives collected in this book. These narratives document a national initiation of progress through Manifest Destiny (Ruiz de Burton), complicate progress as non-inclusive (Jackson), reject progress in its attempt to coopt representative power (Sui Sin Far), and change the terms of a complacent progress (Rutland).

In *California Dreams and American Contradictions* I have sought to install an intersectional literary analysis in historical and present conversations of American progress as a means of understanding the centuries-long struggles for American democratic liberalism. I have centered complexity and contradictions to understand the intimately emotional investment individuals and cultural communities—regional, ethnic, gendered—place in narratives of progress, and I have excavated language and literary forms for their multiplicity of meanings and histories. Out of this work American progress is no longer recognized as a complete project. In fact it is not even recognized as a single, coherent project but many projects underwritten by competing histories, cultural knowledges, and varying national support. As such, I join Hochschild in asking for "a full understanding of emotion in politics,"[44] but I also posit a new language with which we discuss American progress. This new language is intersectional and unbound by national narratives, and it draws together seemingly disparate identities into the nation's vision for the future.

NOTES

INTRODUCTION

1. Didion, *Where I Was From*, 16.
2. Didion, *Where I Was From*, 16–17.
3. Didion, *Where I Was From*, 17.
4. Didion, *Where I Was From*, 17.
5. Didion, *Where I Was From*, 17.
6. Didion, *South and West*, 117.
7. Homans, "California Screamin'."
8. Didion, *South and West*, 14.
9. Didion, *South and West*, 117.
10. Didion, *South and West*, 117.
11. Didion, *South and West*, 21.
12. Didion, *South and West*, 117
13. Didion, *South and West*, 14.
14. Duncan, *Tell This Silence*, 9.
15. Duncan, *Tell This Silence*, 14–15.
16. Randisi, "The Journey Nowhere," 41.
17. Cited in Henderson, "Run River," 91.
18. Review of Joan Didion's *Run River*, *New Yorker*, 1963, 13.
19. Kaplan, "Manifest Domesticity."
20. Didion, *Run River*, 264.

21. Didion, *Run River*, 264.
22. Didion, "Notes from a Native Daughter," 172.
23. Didion, "Notes from a Native Daughter," 172.
24. Morrison, *Playing in the Dark*, 6.
25. Morrison, *Playing in the Dark*, 17.
26. Morrison, *Playing in the Dark*, 17.
27. Morrison, *Playing in the Dark*, 9.
28. Anderson, *Imagined Communities*, 195; emphasis in original.
29. Anderson, *Imagined Communities*, 205.
30. Mexal, *Reading for Liberalism*, 6; emphasis in original.
31. Mexal, *Reading for Liberalism*, 215; emphasis in original.
32. Mead, *How the Vote Was Won*, 2.
33. Mead, *How the Vote Was Won*, 2.
34. Didion, *Run River*, 214–15.
35. Henderson, "Run River," 99.
36. Didion, *Run River*, 63.
37. Didion, *Run River*, 63.
38. Lamont, "Big Books Wanted," 312.
39. Halverson, *Maverick Autobiographies*, 147.
40. Halverson, *Maverick Autobiographies*, 147.
41. Anderson, *Imagined Communities*, 24.
42. Anderson, *Imagined Communities*, 36.
43. Foote, *Regional Fictions*, 6.
44. Campbell, *Bitter Tastes*, 4–5.
45. Sui Sin Far, "Leaves from the Mental Portfolio of an Eurasian," in Sui Sin Far, *Mrs. Spring Fragrance*, 230.
46. Mexal, *Reading for Liberalism*, 12.
47. Mexal, *Reading for Liberalism*, 33.
48. Lowe, *The Intimacies of Four Continents*, 17–18.
49. Lowe, *The Intimacies of Four Continents*, 16.
50. Amy Kaplan, "Manifest Domesticity," in Kaplan, *The Anarchy of Empire*.
51. Jacobs, "Mixed-Bloods, Mestizas, and Pintos," 226.
52. San Diego History Center, "Ephraim W. Morse (1823–1906)."
53. As I have suggested in McDade, "Neither Here Nor There," in the wake of her husband's death, Ruiz de Burton began writing to Ephraim W. Morse to continue her and her husband's project of securing rights to their San Diego land. However, Morse frequently ignored Ruiz de Burton's letters, and growing frustrated, Ruiz de Burton became more and more candid in her correspondence with him. In a letter from 1869, for

instance, Ruiz de Burton writes: "Tell me too please how much I must pay in advanced [sic], you say, and what the costs of the court, etc. Explain it all well to me, remember that women can't vote yet and we are very ignorant individuals" (Ruiz de Burton, *Conflicts of Interest*, 296). This response clearly indicates Ruiz de Burton's frustration with Morse, who continues to ignore her letters even as his correspondence with Jackson appears prompt and helpful. Together, these letters indicate a difference in Morse's attitude toward Californio and Anglo-American women that contributed to both Ruiz de Burton's struggles as an author and as a San Diego landowner.

54. Rutland, *When We Were Colored*, 4.
55. Rutland, *When We Were Colored*, 15.
56. Eva Rutland Papers.
57. Lamont, "Big Books Wanted," 312.
58. Rich, "Introduction," xix.
59. Rich, "Introduction," xix.
60. Rich, "Introduction," xix.
61. Hochschild, *Strangers in Their Own Land*, xi.

1. "AUTOETHNOGRAPHIC" HEROINES

1. Cited in Ruiz de Burton, *Conflicts of Interest*, 604.
2. Cited in Ruiz de Burton, *Conflicts of Interest*, 604.
3. Cited in Ruiz de Burton, *Conflicts of Interest*, 605.
4. Kaplan, *The Anarchy of Empire*, 582.
5. McCullough, *Regions of Identity*, 133. José Aranda also argues that the marriages in Ruiz de Burton's novels represent a "union between two colonial enterprises" ("Contradictory Impulses," 569).
6. Goldman, "Who Ever Heard of a Blue-Eyed Mexican?," 74; Aranda, "Contradictory Impulses," 22.
7. Molina, *How Race Was Made in America*, 45.
8. Beecher, *Treatise on Domestic Economy*, 26.
9. Beecher, *Treatise on Domestic Economy*, 27.
10. Beecher, *Treatise on Domestic Economy*, 27–28.
11. Beecher, *Treatise on Domestic Economy*, 26.
12. Perkins Gilman, *Women and Economics*.
13. Beecher, *Treatise on Domestic Economy*, 27.
14. Ruiz de Burton, *Who Would Have Though It?*, 8.
15. In their introduction to *The Squatter and the Don*, Sánchez and Pita suggest that *Squatter* "demands a double reading, both as a romance and

as a historical novel. The tension between the two discourses enables us to read one against the other. As we shall see, romance invites a closure and resolution that the historical narrative rejects" (in Ruiz de Burton, *The Squatter and the Don*, 15). While I agree that there are two plots, I do not separate them out from one another as Sánchez and Pita do. Rather, I see them as intrinsically and complicatedly intertwined. In my reading of these plots I do not see the romance as "closure." Rather, Ruiz de Burton purposefully resists closure, as I argue later in this chapter.

16. Pratt defines "contact zones" as "social spaces where disparate cultures meet, clash, and grapple with each other, often in highly asymmetrical relations of domination and subordination," and she encourages us to find these "asymmetrical relations" of power in literary manifestations (*Imperial Eyes*, 7).
17. Pratt, *Imperial Eyes*, 9.
18. Pratt, *Imperial Eyes*, 9.
19. Douglas, *The Feminization of American Culture*, 4.
20. Douglas, *The Feminization of American Culture*, 4.
21. Dillon, *The Gender of Freedom*, 205; emphasis in original.
22. In *Federalist* 10, James Madison warns against factions, which he defines as "a number of citizens, whether amounting to a majority or a minority of the whole, who are united and actuated by some common impulse of passion, or of interest, adverse to the rights of other citizens, or to the permanent and aggregate interests of the community."
23. Cited in Ruiz de Burton, *Conflicts of Interest*, 570.
24. Ruiz de Burton, *Conflicts of Interest*, 572.
25. In their introduction to *The Squatter and the Don*, Sánchez and Pita argue that the correspondent "did not accede to her request and in fact published a review of her novel giving the author's name and speaking of the 'descriptive and narrative power' of the work as well as of the author's 'critical though perhaps too cynical habit of observation'" (in Ruiz de Burton, *The Squatter and the Don*, vii).
26. Tompkins, *Sensational Designs*, 162.
27. As Ruiz de Burton's letters to both her Californio friends and her Anglo-American financial and business advisers suggest, she felt her oppression as a woman in both Californio and American society. As Sánchez and Pita conclude in their analysis of Ruiz de Burton's letters, Ruiz de Burton's "sense of gender constraints is particularly painful . . . , as she feels dismissed by Morse and her lawyers for being merely a woman, one

already sufficiently constrained by her own culture" (in Ruiz de Burton, *Conflicts of Interest*, 229).
28. Ruiz de Burton, *Who Would Have Thought It?*, 5.
29. Ruiz de Burton, *Who Would Have Thought It?*, 7.
30. Kaplan, *The Anarchy of Empire*, 43.
31. Kaplan, *The Anarchy of Empire*, 44.
32. Kaplan, *The Anarchy of Empire*, 44.
33. Ruiz de Burton, *Who Would Have Thought It?*, 75, 40.
34. Ruiz de Burton, *Who Would Have Thought It?*, 49–50.
35. Ruiz de Burton, *Who Would Have Thought It?*, 9.
36. Ruiz de Burton, *Who Would Have Thought It?*, 8.
37. Ruiz de Burton, *Who Would Have Thought It?*, 8.
38. Ruiz de Burton, *Who Would Have Thought It?*, 8.
39. Ruiz de Burton, *Who Would Have Thought It?*, 10.
40. Ruiz de Burton, *Who Would Have Thought It?*, 50.
41. Ruiz de Burton, *Who Would Have Thought It?*, 23–24.
42. Ruiz de Burton, *Who Would Have Thought It?*, 24.
43. Ruiz de Burton, *Who Would Have Thought It?*, 30.
44. Ruiz de Burton, *Who Would Have Thought It?*, 24.
45. Goldman, "Who Ever Heard of a Blue-Eyed Mexican?," 64.
46. Kaplan, *The Anarchy of Empire*, 583.
47. Ruiz de Burton, *Who Would Have Thought It?*, 20.
48. Ruiz de Burton, *Who Would Have Thought It?*, 20.
49. Ruiz de Burton, *Who Would Have Thought It?*, 21.
50. Ruiz de Burton, *Who Would Have Thought It?*, 220; emphasis in original.
51. Ruiz de Burton, *Who Would Have Thought It?*, 227.
52. Ruiz de Burton, *Who Would Have Thought It?*, 261.
53. Ruiz de Burton, *Who Would Have Thought It?*, 132.
54. Ruiz de Burton, *Who Would Have Thought It?*, 219.
55. Ruiz de Burton, *Who Would Have Thought It?*, 225.
56. Ruiz de Burton, *Who Would Have Thought It?*, 131.
57. Ruiz de Burton, *Who Would Have Thought It?*, 131.
58. Ruiz de Burton, *Who Would Have Thought It?*, 132; emphasis in original.
59. Ruiz de Burton, *Who Would Have Thought It?*, 18.
60. Ruiz de Burton, *Who Would Have Thought It?*, 81.
61. Ruiz de Burton, *Who Would Have Thought It?*, 81.
62. Ruiz de Burton, *Who Would Have Thought It?*, 81–82.
63. Ruiz de Burton, *Who Would Have Thought It?*, 82.
64. Ruiz de Burton, *Who Would Have Thought It?*, 81.

65. Ruiz de Burton, *Who Would Have Thought It?*, 97.
66. Ruiz de Burton, *Who Would Have Thought It?*, 100–101.
67. Ruiz de Burton, *Who Would Have Thought It?*, 102.
68. Ruiz de Burton, *Who Would Have Thought It?*, 102.
69. Ruiz de Burton, *Who Would Have Thought It?*, 100.
70. Ruiz de Burton, *Who Would Have Thought It?*, 102.
71. Berlant, *The Female Complaint*.
72. Ruiz de Burton, *Who Would Have Thought It?*, 132.
73. Ruiz de Burton, *The Squatter and the Don*, 169.
74. Ruiz de Burton, *The Squatter and the Don*, 169.
75. Ruiz de Burton, *Conflicts of Interest*, 438.
76. Ruiz de Burton, *The Squatter and the Don*, 180.
77. Ruiz de Burton, *The Squatter and the Don*, 178.
78. Theodore Roosevelt's 1899 essay, "The Strenuous Life," builds upon Beecher's notions of femininity to exert a masculine identity rooted in ostentatious displays of strength that counter the perceived feminization of a professional class of men. The rhetoric Selden uses to "dream" of Mercedes echoes Roosevelt's masculine directives.
79. Ruiz de Burton, *The Squatter and the Don*, 156.
80. Ruiz de Burton, *The Squatter and the Don*, 156.
81. Ruiz de Burton, *The Squatter and the Don*, 156.
82. Ruiz de Burton, *The Squatter and the Don*, 157.
83. Ruiz de Burton, *The Squatter and the Don*, 175.
84. Ruiz de Burton, *The Squatter and the Don*, 181.
85. McCullough, *Regions of Identity*, 463.
86. Ruiz de Burton, *Who Would Have Thought It?*, 242.
87. Ruiz de Burton, *The Squatter and the Don*, 299.
88. Ruiz de Burton is thought to have written two articles in the *San Diego Union* in which she documented her own successful ventures in castor bean cultivation and her investment in Southern California irrigation (Ruiz de Burton, *Conflicts of Interest*, 573–76).
89. Ruiz de Burton, *The Squatter and the Don*, 299.
90. Ruiz de Burton, *The Squatter and the Don*, 336.
91. Ruiz de Burton, *The Squatter and the Don*, 341, 340.
92. Ruiz de Burton, *Who Would Have Thought It?*, 290–91.
93. Ruiz de Burton, *Who Would Have Thought It?*, 271.
94. Ruiz de Burton, *Who Would Have Thought It?*, 271.
95. Ruiz de Burton, *Who Would Have Thought It?*, 293.
96. Ruiz de Burton, *Who Would Have Thought It?*, 196.

97. Ruiz de Burton, *Who Would Have Thought It?*, 196, 197.
98. Ruiz de Burton, *Who Would Have Thought It?*, 197; emphasis in original.
99. Ruiz de Burton, *Who Would Have Thought It?*, 200.
100. Ruiz de Burton, *Who Would Have Thought It?*, 200; emphasis in original.
101. Pratt, *Imperial Eyes*, 9.
102. Ruiz de Burton, *The Squatter and the Don*, 61.
103. Ruiz de Burton, *The Squatter and the Don*, 61.
104. Ruiz de Burton, *The Squatter and the Don*, 84.
105. Ruiz de Burton, *The Squatter and the Don*, 235–36.
106. Ruiz de Burton, *The Squatter and the Don*, 236.

2. THE LIBERAL FANTASY

1. Jackson, *Ramona*, 304.
2. Jackson, *Ramona*, 304.
3. Jackson, *Ramona*, 304.
4. Jackson, *Ramona*, 305.
5. Pratt, *Imperial Eyes*, 9.
6. Pratt, *Imperial Eyes*, 9.
7. Jackson, *Ramona*, 95.
8. Jackson, *Ramona*, 388.
9. Gonzalez, "The Warp of Whiteness," 437.
10. Senier, *Voices of American Indian Assimilation and Resistance*, 59.
11. Jackson, *Ramona*, 307.
12. Jackson, *The Indian Reform Letters*, 84.
13. Jackson, *The Indian Reform Letters*, 65–66; emphasis in original.
14. Jackson, *The Indian Reform Letters*, 49.
15. Jackson, *A Century of Dishonor*, 9.
16. Jackson, *The Indian Reform Letters*, 150.
17. Jackson, *The Indian Reform Letters*, 307.
18. Berlant, *The Female Complaint*, 40.
19. Berlant, *The Female Complaint*, 19; emphasis in original.
20. Berlant, *The Female Complaint*, 19.
21. Berlant, *The Female Complaint*, 2.
22. Fichtelberg, *Critical Fictions*, 1.
23. Lisa Lowe traces the ways the abolition of slavery in the Caribbean replaced "African enslaved labor with Chinese 'free' labor there and elsewhere" (*The Intimacies of Four Continents*, 18). I use this framework to also think about the ways the abolition of slavery in the United States resulted in new forms of "free" labor.

24. Lowe suggests that "a colonial division of intimacy . . . charts the historically differentiated access to the domains of liberal personhood" (*The Intimacies of Four Continents*, 18). In this framework Lowe suggests that having access to domestic intimacy serves as a prerequisite to liberal personhood. But as Lowe traces throughout her book, domestic intimacy is restricted through certain forms of labor that replace the fully enslaved laboring body with a "free" (as in free to move) laboring body whose constant movement in search of labor is rendered a new form restricted access to domestic intimacy.
25. Phillips, *Helen Hunt Jackson*, 82.
26. Cited in Phillips, *Helen Hunt Jackson*, 84; emphasis in original.
27. Cited in Phillips, *Helen Hunt Jackson*, 84; emphasis in original.
28. Jackson, *Bits of Travel at Home*, 81.
29. O'Sullivan, "Annexation," 34.
30. Jackson, *A Century of Dishonor*, 340.
31. Jackson, *Glimpses of Three Coasts*, 35.
32. Jackson, *Glimpses of Three Coasts*, 35.
33. Jackson, *Ramona*, 2.
34. Jackson, *Ramona*, 23.
35. Jackson, *Ramona*, 2.
36. Jackson, *Ramona*, 3.
37. Jackson, *Ramona*, 73.
38. Jackson, *Ramona*, 57.
39. Jackson, *Ramona*, 72.
40. Jackson, *Ramona*, 72.
41. Jackson, *Ramona*, 72.
42. Jackson, *Ramona*, 72–73.
43. Jackson, *Ramona*, 5.
44. Jackson, *Ramona*, 26.
45. Jackson, *Ramona*, 2.
46. Jackson, *Ramona*, 1.
47. Jackson, *Ramona*, 11.
48. Jackson, *Ramona*, 11–12.
49. Jackson, *Ramona*, 305.
50. Jackson, *Ramona*, 308.
51. Jackson, *Ramona*, 308.
52. Jackson, *Ramona*, 305.
53. Jackson, *Ramona*, 308.
54. Jackson, *Ramona*, 308.

55. Jackson, *Ramona*, 308.
56. O'Sullivan, "Annexation," 32.
57. O'Sullivan, "Annexation," 33.
58. As a pioneer writing for an East Coast audience, Jackson was at the center of U.S. settler-colonial activity. It is Kate Phillips's understanding that despite Jackson's involvement in settler colonialism in Colorado and the exploitative travel writing industry, she "became a champion of tolerance and grew to possess an unusual appreciation for racial, ethnic, and religious diversity" (*Helen Hunt Jackson*, 27). Similarly scholars such as James Weaver have argued that Jackson's travel writings reveal that she "comes to embrace an intimacy with nature and with other people [in the West] that reveals her shifting sensibility towards the US imperial imperative," a shift that leads her to problematize "the idea of 'conquering' people and places" ("Being In and Not Among," 215, 216). While scholars have wanted to situate Jackson as an anti-imperialist voice in nineteenth-century literary culture, her location at the center of American imperialism and settler colonialism complicates this impulse, making it difficult to parse the relationships between her supposed anti-imperialist agendas and her representations of and advocacy for Native Americans. Her advocacy does not, for instance, attempt to dissuade Americans from settling the West, a stance that by definition resulted in the taking of lands that belonged to Native Americans. In fact, her western American writings often encourage settlers and travelers to the region.
59. Jackson, *Ramona*, 309.
60. Padget, "Travel Writing," 849–50.
61. Jackson, *Ramona*, 304.
62. Jackson, *Ramona*, 304.
63. Jackson, *Ramona*, 318.
64. Jackson, *Ramona*, 318.
65. Jackson, *Ramona*, 318.
66. Jackson, *Ramona*, 318–19.
67. Jackson, *Ramona*, 320.
68. Jackson, *Ramona*, 320.
69. Jackson, *A Century of Dishonor*, 340.
70. Jackson, *Ramona*, 318.
71. Jackson, *Ramona*, 318.
72. Jackson, *Ramona*, 318.
73. Jackson, *Ramona*, 319.

74. Jackson, *Ramona*, 322.
75. Jackson, *Ramona*, 323.
76. Kaplan, *The Anarchy of Empire*, 26–30.
77. Jackson, *The Indian Reform Letters*, 65–66.
78. Jackson, *The Indian Reform Letters*, 341.
79. Jackson, *The Indian Reform Letters*, 341.
80. Jackson, *The Indian Reform Letters*, 341.
81. Jackson, *The Indian Reform Letters*, 341.
82. Jackson, *The Indian Reform Letters*, 352.
83. Jackson, *The Indian Reform Letters*, 342.
84. Jackson, *The Indian Reform Letters*, 342.
85. Jackson, *The Indian Reform Letters*, 342; emphasis in original.
86. Jackson, *Ramona*, 307.
87. Tuttle, "The Symptoms of Conquest," 59, 58.
88. Tuttle, "The Symptoms of Conquest," 59.
89. Jackson, *Ramona*, 307.
90. Jackson, *Ramona*, 313.
91. Jackson, *Ramona*, 313, 314.
92. Jackson, *Ramona*, 314.
93. Jackson, *Ramona*, 314.
94. Jackson, *Ramona*, 314.
95. Jackson, *Ramona*, 314.
96. Jackson, *Ramona*, 314.
97. Jackson, *Ramona*, 314.
98. Jackson, *Ramona*, 318.
99. Jackson, *Ramona*, 318.
100. Jackson, *Ramona*, 380.
101. Jackson, *Ramona*, 312.
102. David Roediger helps us see this context of the novel more clearly when he argues in *The Wages of Whiteness* that "the working class formation and the systematic development of a sense of whiteness went hand in hand for the US white working class" (8). During and just after the Civil War, Roediger points out, "workers nurtured a sense of grievance based on the notion that they were being exploited as whites and that favor was being, or was about to be, lavished on Blacks" (171). The confusion over how definitions of "free" were to be interpreted—now that "no longer could a counterpoint with slaves define whites as 'free labor'"—was accompanied by the poor working whites' need to separate themselves from the formerly enslaved (175). With the distinction between free and

unfree labor collapsed, wage labor itself, a form of labor that places the laborer in a position of dependency, became a way to distinguish between citizens and the disenfranchised, encouraging the white working class to turn to race as a way of distancing itself from the newly freed Black population. Whiteness, Roediger argues, emerges as an identity only after Emancipation and serves to alleviate anxieties about citizenship and national belonging among a class of poor working-class whites. Though Roediger's study focuses on the consequences of Emancipation on the urban North, reading *Ramona* as a post-Reconstruction novel rather than confining it to a traditional "western American" analytical framework helps us identify the ways Jackson's Native American advocacy is also concerned with the parameters of citizenship and national belonging now that labor no longer serves as a proper distinction. It helps us read scenes where Aunt Ri's attention to Ramona seems charitable with an eye for the power struggle happening between them as the new national conditions make a meeting such as the one between Aunt Ri and Ramona in the mountains of the American West precarious and unstable. Roediger's study mostly focuses on the tensions between Black and white labor in the urban North, but his findings encourage us to consider the tension that also arose between the freed slave populations in the South and poor white farmers; although many of these farmers owned their land, they labored on it themselves, unlike the owners of large plantations who employed workers to work the land for them. In a similar way that the white workers of the industrialized North felt their wages and labor power threatened by freed slaves, so too can we understand Aunt Ri and her family as threatened by the changing tides of rural labor in the South.

103. Lowe, *The Intimacies of Four Continents*, 24.
104. Jackson, *Ramona*, 95.
105. Jackson, *Ramona*, 95–96.
106. Jackson, *Ramona*, 96.
107. Jackson, *Ramona*, 107.
108. Jackson, *Ramona*, 232.
109. Jackson, *Ramona*, 232.
110. Jackson, *Ramona*, 233.
111. Jackson, *Ramona*, 233.
112. Jackson, *Ramona*, 233.
113. Jackson, *Ramona*, 233.
114. Jackson, *Ramona*, 95.
115. Jackson, *Ramona*, 53.

116. Jackson, *Ramona*, 56.
117. Jackson, *Ramona*, 59.
118. Jackson, *The Indian Reform Letters*, 313.
119. Jackson, *The Indian Reform Letters*, 313.
120. Jackson, *The Indian Reform Letters*, 314.

3. SUI SIN FAR'S GENRE OF INTERVENTION

1. Sui Sin Far, *Mrs. Spring Fragrance*, 28.
2. Sui Sin Far, *Mrs. Spring Fragrance*, 34, 28.
3. Lowe, *The Intimacy of Four Continents*, 21.
4. Lowe, *The Intimacy of Four Continents*, 21.
5. Sui Sin Far, *Mrs. Spring Fragrance*, 36.
6. Sui Sin Far, *Mrs. Spring Fragrance*, 41.
7. Lowe, *The Intimacy of Four Continents*, 18.
8. Lowe, *The Intimacy of Four Continents*, 18.
9. Sui Sin Far, *Mrs. Spring Fragrance*, 39.
10. Sui Sin Far, *Mrs. Spring Fragrance*, 36.
11. Sui Sin Far, *Mrs. Spring Fragrance*, 23.
12. Lowe, *The Intimacy of Four Continents*, 17–18.
13. Lowe, *The Intimacy of Four Continents*, 18.
14. Ling, *Between Worlds*, 109.
15. Wang, "Reading Sui Sin Far," 244.
16. Diana, "Biracial/Bicultural Identity in the Writings of Sui Sin Far," 160.
17. Sui Sin Far, *Mrs. Spring Fragrance*, 222; emphasis in original.
18. In *The Responsibilities of the Novelist*, Frank Norris does plead for a romantic take on realism. However, Norris places strict qualifications on romanticism. He disagrees that "romance must be an affair of cloaks and daggers, or moonlight and golden hair" and instead asserts that the "true Romance is a more serious business than this" (229). Norris's "more serious business" does not align with the "fairy tales" and "heroic pieces" Sui Sin Far seems to aspire to (*Mrs. Spring Fragrance*, 222). It is "serious" because it is about categorizing and controlling identities rather than allowing identities to speak for themselves, as Sui Sin Far suggests.
19. Link, *The Vast and Terrible Drama*, 67.
20. Link, *The Vast and Terrible Drama*, 67.
21. Link, *The Vast and Terrible Drama*, 67.
22. Hamilton, *America's Sketchbook*, 15.

23. Benedict Anderson's argument in *Imagined Communities* is that the eighteenth-century novel facilitated national identity by creating an "imagined community" through a novelistic time rooted in simultaneity or the idea that multiple lives can be lived all at the same time. This simultaneity brings otherwise disparate narratives into a single, cohesive timeline that is always moving forward to produce national histories as well as national futures.
24. In "Psychoanalyzing the Narrative Logics of Naturalism: *The Call of the Wild*," Pease situates literary naturalism within a biopolitical framework within which he argues literary naturalists had "complicitous relations between their fictions and the more pervasive systems of social control" (14).
25. Kaplan, *The Social Construction of American Realism*, 1.
26. Kaplan, *The Social Construction of American Realism*, 7.
27. Cited in Barrish, *The Cambridge Introduction to American Literary Realism*, 47.
28. James, "The Art of Fiction," 390; Norris, *The Responsibilities of the Novelist*, 20.
29. James, "The Art of Fiction," 399.
30. Sui Sin Far, *Mrs. Spring Fragrance*, 107.
31. Sui Sin Far, *Mrs. Spring Fragrance*, 108.
32. Norris, *The Responsibilities of the Novelist*, 8.
33. Norris, *The Responsibilities of the Novelist*, 8.
34. Campbell, *Bitter Tastes*, 9.
35. Sui Sin Far, *Mrs. Spring Fragrance*, 109.
36. Link, *The Vast and Terrible Drama*, 67.
37. Link, *The Vast and Terrible Drama*, 66.
38. Link, *The Vast and Terrible Drama*, 67.
39. In "The Art of Fiction" Henry James indicates that the "motive" of writing "is simply experience. As people feel life, so they will feel the art that is most closely related to it. This closeness of relation is what we should never forget in talking of the effort of the novel" (397). James argues that the realist novel is about giving the readers an "experience" that they otherwise would not experience. In so doing, the writer draws the readers into "closeness" with the novel's subjects.
40. Sui Sin Far, *Mrs. Spring Fragrance*, 84.
41. Sui Sin Far, *Mrs. Spring Fragrance*, 85.
42. Sui Sin Far, *Mrs. Spring Fragrance*, 86.
43. Sui Sin Far, *Mrs. Spring Fragrance*, 88–89.

44. Sui Sin Far, *Mrs. Spring Fragrance*, 89.
45. Sui Sin Far, *Mrs. Spring Fragrance*, 89.
46. Barrish, *The Cambridge Introduction to American Literary Realism*, 103.
47. Sui Sin Far, *Mrs. Spring Fragrance*, 90.
48. Sui Sin Far, *Mrs. Spring Fragrance*, 91.
49. Sui Sin Far, *Mrs. Spring Fragrance*, 91.
50. Sui Sin Far, *Mrs. Spring Fragrance*, 92.
51. Anderson, *Imagined Communities*, 26, 36.
52. Sui Sin Far, *Mrs. Spring Fragrance*, 92.
53. Cited in Barrish, *The Cambridge Introduction to American Literary Realism*, 6.
54. London, *The Valley of the Moon*, 45.
55. Link, *The Vast and Terrible Drama*, 18, 4.
56. London, *The Valley of the Moon*, 124.
57. Sui Sin Far, *Mrs. Spring Fragrance*, 294.
58. Sui Sin Far, *Mrs. Spring Fragrance*, 293.
59. Solberg, "Sui Sin Far/Edith Eaton," 32.
60. Ammons, *Conflicting Stories*, 117.
61. Anderson, *Imagined Communities*, 25.
62. Anderson, *Imagined Communities*, 24.
63. Sui Sin Far, *Mrs. Spring Fragrance*, 230.
64. In her book-length study of the sketch form, Kristie Hamilton suggests that "it is plain that the sketch's association with privacy and with that phase of the artistic process preceding formal fixity" gave authors "license" to be freer in their expression than if they were to write novels (*America's Sketchbook*, 15). Hamilton describes the sketch as a kind of "pre-writing" that does not take itself seriously and does not expect to be taken seriously by a reading audience. Hamilton's assessment of the sketch form allows us to see that Sui Sin Far, as a sketch writer, has the ability to be honest in her artistic representation even if that does not necessarily mean "real."
65. Anderson, *Imagined Communities*, 26–27.
66. Sui Sin Far, *Mrs. Spring Fragrance*, 63.
67. Sui Sin Far, *Mrs. Spring Fragrance*, 63.
68. Kimberly Macellaro argues that Carson represents the "epistemological crisis of white masculinity as it played out in the white American anxieties about Chinese-white miscegenation" ("Sui Sin Far's Jekyll and Hyde," 49). He is, as Vanessa Holford Diana also argues, portrayed as "a predator and unscrupulous ethnographer, posing a double threat of sexual and

cultural violation," but this predatory characterization is complicated by Carson's indoctrination in "his cultural blindness," which recognizes Pan as white and therefore "abandoned among foreigners" ("Biracial/Bicultural Identity in the Writings of Sui Sin Far," 173–74).
69. Sui Sin Far, *Mrs. Spring Fragrance*, 63.
70. Barrish, *The Cambridge Introduction to American Literary Realism*, 103–4.
71. Norris, *The Responsibilities of the Author*, 20.
72. Howells, *A Hazard of New Fortune*, 6–7.
73. James, "The Art of Fiction," 75.
74. Sui Sin Far, *Mrs. Spring Fragrance*, 62.
75. Sui Sin Far, *Mrs. Spring Fragrance*, 63.
76. Sui Sin Far, *Mrs. Spring Fragrance*, 63.
77. Sui Sin Far, *Mrs. Spring Fragrance*, 62.
78. Sui Sin Far, *Mrs. Spring Fragrance*, 62.
79. Kaplan argues that domesticity as cultural knowledge showed up in the nation's sentimental literatures to erect "the home as a bounded and rigidly ordered interior space" as the nation was "boundless and undifferentiated" in its rapid expansion ("Manifest Domesticity," 583). The "bounded and rigidly ordered" home helped compensate for the anxiety accompanying the open national borders.
80. Sui Sin Far, *Mrs. Spring Fragrance*, 63.
81. Kaplan, *The Anarchy of Empire*, 582.
82. Sui Sin Far, *Mrs. Spring Fragrance*, 65.
83. Sui Sin Far, *Mrs. Spring Fragrance*, 65.
84. Sui Sin Far, *Mrs. Spring Fragrance*, 64.
85. Sui Sin Far, *Mrs. Spring Fragrance*, 66.
86. Sui Sin Far, *Mrs. Spring Fragrance*, 66.
87. Sui Sin Far, *Mrs. Spring Fragrance*, 66.
88. Link, *The Vast and Terrible Drama*, 93.
89. Link, *The Vast and Terrible Drama*, 94.
90. Sui Sin Far, *Mrs. Spring Fragrance*, 66.
91. Sui Sin Far, *Mrs. Spring Fragrance*, 66.
92. Sui Sin Far, *Mrs. Spring Fragrance*, 228.
93. Sui Sin Far, *Mrs. Spring Fragrance*, 228.
94. Sui Sin Far, *Mrs. Spring Fragrance*, 229.
95. Sui Sin Far, *Mrs. Spring Fragrance*, 230.
96. Sui Sin Far, *Mrs. Spring Fragrance*, 179.
97. Sui Sin Far, *Mrs. Spring Fragrance*, 179.
98. Sui Sin Far, *Mrs. Spring Fragrance*, 179.

99. Sui Sin Far, *Mrs. Spring Fragrance*, 93.
100. Sui Sin Far, *Mrs. Spring Fragrance*, 94.
101. Sui Sin Far, *Mrs. Spring Fragrance*, 101.
102. Sui Sin Far, *Mrs. Spring Fragrance*, 101.
103. Sui Sin Far, *Mrs. Spring Fragrance*, 100.

4. AN AUTOBIOGRAPHY OF INTEGRATION

1. Rutland, *When We Were Colored*, 38.
2. Rutland, *When We Were Colored*, 39; emphasis in original.
3. Rutland, *When We Were Colored*, 39.
4. Sui Sin Far, *Mrs. Spring Fragrance*, 293.
5. Sui Sin Far, *Mrs. Spring Fragrance*, 222.
6. Rutland, *When We Were Colored*, 40.
7. Comer, "Accountabilities," 419.
8. Comer, "Accountabilities," 68.
9. Comer, "Accountabilities," 68.
10. Critical regionalism forges a new framework for analyzing regionalism by recognizing the interconnectedness rather than the isolation of regions and the always-in-flux identities of individuals within a region. Douglas Powell, like Fetterely and Pryse in *Writing Out of Place*, argues in *Critical Regionalism* that regionalism is not a genre of place per se; instead he defines it as a "strategy" deployed to "provide a rhetorical basis for making claims about how spaces and places are connected to spatially and conceptually broader patterns of meaning" (4). "When we talk about a region," Powell continues, "we are talking not about a stable, boundaried, autonomous place but about a cultural history, the cumulative, generative effect of the interplay among the various, competing definitions of that region" (5).
11. Higginbotham, *Righteous Discontent*, 14.
12. Higginbotham, *Righteous Discontent*, 14.
13. Higginbotham, *Righteous Discontent*, 200.
14. Higginbotham, *Righteous Discontent*, 26.
15. Rutland, *When We Were Colored*, 128.
16. Barnes, *Raising the Race*, 2.
17. Barnes, *Raising the Race*, 2–3.
18. Powell, *Critical Regionalism*, 4.
19. Powell, *Critical Regionalism*, 8.
20. Powell, *Critical Regionalism*, 14.
21. Mostern, *Autobiography and Black Identity Politics*, 11.

22. Mostern, *Autobiography and Black Identity Politics*, 11.
23. Stover, *Rhetoric and Resistance in Black Women's Autobiography*, 15, 16.
24. Stover, *Rhetoric and Resistance in Black Women's Autobiography*, 28, 35.
25. Stover, *Rhetoric and Resistance in Black Women's Autobiography*, 51, 17.
26. Ards, *Words of Witness*, 4.
27. Ards, *Words of Witness*, 5.
28. Ards, *Words of Witness*, 7.
29. Ards, *Words of Witness*, 18.
30. Ards, *Words of Witness*, 10.
31. Stover, *Rhetoric and Resistance in Black Women's Autobiography*, 93.
32. Rutland, *When We Were Colored*, 4.
33. Stover, *Rhetoric and Resistance in Black Women's Autobiography*, 28.
34. Comer, *Landscapes*, 24.
35. Du Bois, *The Souls of Black Folk*, 13.
36. Rutland, *When We Were Colored*, 41, 46.
37. Rutland, *When We Were Colored*, 72.
38. Rutland, *When We Were Colored*, 40.
39. Rutland, *When We Were Colored*, 40.
40. Ahmed, "Happy Objects," 42.
41. Rutland, *When We Were Colored*, 97; emphasis in original.
42. Rutland, *When We Were Colored*, 104.
43. Rutland, *When We Were Colored*, 45.
44. Rutland, *When We Were Colored*, 102–3.
45. Rutland, *When We Were Colored*, 103.
46. Rutland, *When We Were Colored*, 98.
47. Rutland, *When We Were Colored*, 98.
48. Rutland, *When We Were Colored*, 98.
49. Rutland, *When We Were Colored*, 99.
50. Rutland, *When We Were Colored*, 100.
51. Rutland, *When We Were Colored*, 100–101.
52. Rutland, *When We Were Colored*, 105.
53. Rutland, *When We Were Colored*, 105.
54. Rutland, *When We Were Colored*, 105.
55. Rutland, *When We Were Colored*, 106.
56. Rutland, *When We Were Colored*, 106.
57. In her analysis of the bodily effects of emotional responses, Ahmed argues that "bodies take the shape of norms that are repeated over time and with force" (*The Cultural Politics of Emotion*, 145). Social norms determine not only how a person thinks but how the body interacts in physical society as

well. Ahmed argues that norms that shape are derived from "the narrative of heterosexuality as an ideal coupling," and she thereby suggests that heteronormative narratives of love, sexuality, and family dictate which bodies are "ideal" for each other (145). This same idea can be applied to the ways bodies of different races are also instructed toward "an ideal coupling." The concept of "an ideal coupling" serves to "orient" certain bodies "towards some objects and not others, objects that are secured as ideal through the fantasy of difference" (145). Heteronormative notions of love and, as I argue here, race define bodies in relation to one another and create affective forms of segregation as the "fantasy of difference" determines who is "ideal" for whom.

58. Ahmed, *The Cultural Politics of Emotion*, 149.
59. Cited in Eva Rutland Papers.
60. Cited in Eva Rutland Papers.
61. Cited in Eva Rutland Papers.
62. Cited in Eva Rutland Papers.
63. Collins, *Black Feminist Thought*, 84.
64. Cited in Eva Rutland Papers.
65. Cited in Eva Rutland Papers.
66. Cited in Eva Rutland Papers.
67. Cited in Eva Rutland Papers.
68. Cited in Eva Rutland Papers.
69. Cited in Eva Rutland Papers.
70. Rutland, *When We Were Colored*, 36; emphasis in original.
71. Rutland, *When We Were Colored*, 36; emphasis in original.
72. Rutland, *When We Were Colored*, 36; emphasis in original.
73. Rutland, *When We Were Colored*, 36–37.
74. Rutland, *When We Were Colored*, 37.
75. Rutland, *When We Were Colored*, 43.
76. Rutland, *When We Were Colored*, 45.
77. Rutland, *When We Were Colored*, 45.
78. Rutland, *When We Were Colored*, 45.
79. Ahmed, *The Cultural Politics of Emotion*, 69.
80. Ahmed, *The Cultural Politics of Emotion*, 184.
81. Rutland, *When We Were Colored*, 70.
82. Rutland, *When We Were Colored*, 13.
83. Rutland, *When We Were Colored*, 67.
84. Rutland, *When We Were Colored*, 67–68.
85. Higginbotham, *Righteous Discontent*, 202.

86. Rutland, *When We Were Colored*, 67.
87. Rutland, *When We Were Colored*, 71.
88. Rutland, *When We Were Colored*, 71; emphasis in original.
89. Rutland, *When We Were Colored*, 71.
90. Rutland, *When We Were Colored*, 71.
91. Rutland, *When We Were Colored*, 71–72; emphasis in original.
92. Rutland, *When We Were Colored*, 130.
93. Rutland, *When We Were Colored*, 72; emphasis in original.
94. Rutland, *When We Were Colored*, 72.
95. Rutland, *When We Were Colored*, 72.
96. Rutland, *When We Were Colored*, 46.
97. Rutland, *When We Were Colored*, 46; emphasis in original.
98. Rutland, *When We Were Colored*, 46.
99. Rutland, *When We Were Colored*, 46.
100. Rutland, *When We Were Colored*, 46.
101. Collins, "Shifting the Center," 192.
102. Gumbs, "Introduction," 21.
103. Gumbs, "Introduction," 21–22.
104. Gumbs, "Introduction," 23.
105. Rutland, *When We Were Colored*, 72; emphasis in original.
106. Rutland, *When We Were Colored*, 86.
107. Rutland, *When We Were Colored*, 91.
108. Rutland, *When We Were Colored*, 91.
109. Rutland, *When We Were Colored*, 91–92.
110. Rutland, *When We Were Colored*, vii.
111. Rutland, *When We Were Colored*, ix.
112. Ahmed, "Happy Objects," 50.
113. Ahmed, "Happy Objects," 50.
114. Cited in Eva Rutland Papers.
115. Cited in Eva Rutland Papers.
116. Cited in Eva Rutland Papers.
117. Cited in Eva Rutland Papers.
118. Cited in Eva Rutland Papers; emphasis in original.
119. Anderson, *Imagined Communities*, 26–27.
120. Rutland, *When We Were Colored*, 109.
121. Rutland, *When We Were Colored*, 113.
122. Rutland, *When We Were Colored*, 113, 112.
123. Rutland, *When We Were Colored*, 113.
124. Rutland, *When We Were Colored*, 102.

125. Rutland, *When We Were Colored*, 102.
126. Rutland, *When We Were Colored*, 102.
127. Rutland, *When We Were Colored*, 102.
128. Lowe, *The Intimacies of Four Continents*, 39.
129. Comer, "Accountabilities," 419–20.
130. Lowe, *The Intimacies of Four Continents*, 39.
131. Rutland, *When We Were Colored*, 137.
132. Rutland, *When We Were Colored*, 137.
133. Rutland, *When We Were Colored*, 138.
134. Rutland, *When We Were Colored*, 146.
135. Rutland, *When We Were Colored*, 144.
136. Rutland, *When We Were Colored*, 141; emphasis in original.
137. Rutland, *When We Were Colored*, 145.
138. Rutland, *When We Were Colored*, 147.

CONCLUSION

1. Didion, "Notes from a Native Daughter," 172.
2. Didion, "Notes from a Native Daughter," 173; emphasis in original.
3. Didion, "Notes from a Native Daughter," 172; emphasis in original.
4. Borrowing from Raymond Williams, Lisa Lowe argues that late eighteenth- and early nineteenth-century forms "of national liberal republics made less available the residual intimacies of colonialism and slavery that nonetheless continued as the practical conditions for liberal forms of personhood, society, and government; in other words, settler practices and the afterlife of slavery are residues that continue beyond declarations of independence and emancipation" (*The Intimacies of Four Continents*, 19). Lowe suggests a method for bringing together fragmented and dispersed pieces of the archive that makes visible the contingency of liberal notions of sovereignty, citizenship, and human rights—as they are iterated through individual interiority and privileges of the private home—on what Lowe calls the "emergent," or "new," articulations of otherwise residual or lingering histories of enslavement and exploitation (19).
5. Morrison, *Playing in the Dark*, 9.
6. Obama, "2012 National Medal of Arts and Humanities Award Ceremony."
7. Didion, *Slouching towards Bethlehem*, 122; emphasis in original.
8. Didion, *Slouching towards Bethlehem*, 123.
9. Didion, *Slouching towards Bethlehem*, xi.
10. Didion, *Slouching towards Bethlehem*, xi–xii.
11. Didion, *Slouching towards Bethlehem*, xii.

12. Though Rutland's manuscript for "In Defense of Uncle Tom" met with initial excitement from both her agent and her representative at Abingdon Press, Robert Hill, early concerns ranged from the manuscript's "defensive attitude" about the role of "Uncle Toms" (Rutland to Hill, 1969, in Eva Rutland Papers) to the manuscript's moderate political tone in an age where the Black Panthers and Black militant groups were drawing headlines (Margolis to Rutland, 1969, in Eva Rutland Papers). The contract for "In Defense of Uncle Tom" was finally withdrawn in November 1970, when it became clear that Rutland and Abingdon Press had different opinions on the direction the manuscript should take. In response to the first draft of the manuscript, delivered in August 1970, Hill regretfully sends a "discouraging report" in which he accuses Rutland of deviating from her "original thesis that any real achievement in society is the result of compromise plus determination and individual effort" (Hill to Rutland, 1970, in Eva Rutland Papers). After asking her in November 1969 to change the title from "In Defense of Uncle Tom" to "Don't Call Me an Uncle Tom," Hill, in a final assessment of the manuscript, still charges Rutland with taking a "defensive posture" (Hill to Rutland, 1970, in Eva Rutland Papers). He writes: "Again and again you are on the defensive in your case for the middle-class black parents and others classed as Uncle Toms" (Hill to Rutland, 1970, in Eva Rutland Papers). He finds her to "vacillate" between being "proud of the term" and being offended by it (Hill to Rutland, 1970, in Eva Rutland Papers). To prove his point and supposedly add credibility to his opinion of Rutland's manuscript, Hill shares with Rutland "the comments of a black staff member" who, in addition to finding Rutland's premise offensive, is quoted as saying, "I find that I am wholeheartedly in agreement with much of what Mrs. Rutland is trying to say. However, it seems to me that the attempt is much too defensive and personal" (Hill to Rutland, 1970, in Eva Rutland Papers).
13. Didion, *Slouching towards Bethlehem*, xii.
14. Didion, *Slouching towards Bethlehem*, xii.
15. Didion's *Slouching towards Bethlehem* collection features articles on California housewives who murder their husbands ("Some Dreamers of the Golden Dream"), John Wayne and his western movies ("John Wayne: A Love Song"), and autobiographic essays of Didion's own experiences in the West ("On Going Home" and "Notes from a Native Daughter").
16. Didion, *A Book of Common Prayer*, 213.
17. Didion, *A Book of Common Prayer*, 213.

18. Didion, *A Book of Common Prayer*, 213.
19. Didion, *A Book of Common Prayer*, 213.
20. Didion, *A Book of Common Prayer*, 213.
21. Didion, *A Book of Common Prayer*, 213, 214; emphasis in original.
22. Didion, *A Book of Common Prayer*, 214.
23. Didion, *A Book of Common Prayer*, 214; emphasis in original.
24. Didion, *A Book of Common Prayer*, 214; emphasis in original.
25. Didion, *Slouching towards Bethlehem*, 113.
26. Didion, *A Book of Common Prayer*, 213.
27. Didion, *A Book of Common Prayer*, 214.
28. Joan Didion, "On Morality," in Didion, *Slouching towards Bethlehem*, 162.
29. Hochschild, *Strangers in Their Own Land*, 16.
30. Hochschild, *Strangers in Their Own Land*, xiv.
31. Hochschild, *Strangers in Their Own Land*, xi.
32. Hochschild, *Strangers in Their Own Land*, 8.
33. Hochschild, *Strangers in Their Own Land*, 16; emphasis in original.
34. Hochschild, *Strangers in Their Own Land*, 135.
35. Hochschild, *Strangers in Their Own Land*, 136.
36. Hochschild, *Strangers in Their Own Land*, 136; Didion, *Where I Was From*, 37.
37. Hochschild, *Strangers in Their Own Land*, 49, 52.
38. Hochschild, *Strangers in Their Own Land*, 71; emphasis in original.
39. Traub, *What Was Liberalism?*, 3.
40. Traub, *What Was Liberalism?*, 3.
41. Traub, *What Was Liberalism?*, 3.
42. Rich, "Introduction," xix–xx.
43. Didion, *South and West*, 21.
44. Hochschild, *Strangers in Their Own Land*, 15.

BIBLIOGRAPHY

Ahmed, Sara. *The Cultural Politics of Emotion*. Oxfordshire: Routledge, 2004.
———. "Happy Objects." In *The Affect Theory Reader*, edited by Melissa Gregg and Gregory J. Seigworth, 29–51. Durham NC: Duke University Press, 2010.
Almaguer, Tomás. *Racial Fault Lines*. Berkeley and Los Angeles: University of California Press, 2009.
Ammons, Elizabeth. *Conflicting Stories: American Women Writers and the Turn of the Twentieth Century*. New York: Oxford University Press, 1992.
Anderson, Benedict. *Imagined Communities*. London: Verso, 2006.
Aranda, Jose F., Jr. "Contradictory Impulses: María Amparo Ruiz de Burton, Resistance Theory, and the Politics of Chicano/a Studies." *American Literature* 70, no. 3 (1998): 551–79.
Ards, Angela. *Words of Witness: Black Women's Autobiography in the Post-Brown Era*. Madison: University of Wisconsin Press, 2015.
Barnes, Riché J. Daniel. *Raising the Race: Black Career Women Redefine Marriage, Motherhood, and Community*. New Brunswick NJ: Rutgers University Press, 2016.
Barrish, Phillip J. *The Cambridge Introduction to American Literary Realism*. Cambridge: Cambridge University Press, 2011.
Beecher, Catherine. *Treatise on Domestic Economy*. New York: Harper and Brothers, 1845.

Berlant, Lauren. *The Female Complaint: The Unfinished Business of Sentimentality in American Culture.* Durham NC: Duke University Press, 2008.

Campbell, Donna. *Bitter Tastes: Literary Naturalism and Early Cinema in American Women's Writing.* Athens: University of Georgia Press, 2016.

Carmichael, Stokely. "What We Want." *New York Review*, September 1966.

Collins, Patricia Hill. *Black Feminist Thought.* Oxfordshire: Routledge, 2000.

———. "Shifting the Center: Race, Class, and Feminist Theorizing about Motherhood." In *American Families: A Multicultural Reader*, 2nd ed., edited by Stephanie Coontz, Maya Parson, and Gabrielle Raley, 173–87. Oxfordshire: Routledge, 2008.

Comer, Krista. "Accountabilities: Authority, Feminism, West." *Studies in the Novel* 49, no. 3 (2017): 419–25.

———. *Landscapes of the New West.* Chapel Hill: University of North Carolina Press, 1999.

Diana, Vanessa Holford. "Biracial/Bicultural Identity in the Writings of Sui Sin Far." MELUS 26, no. 2 (2001): 159–86.

Didion, Joan. *A Book of Common Prayer.* New York: Vintage International, 1977.

———. "Notes from a Native Daughter." In Didion, *Slouching towards Bethlehem*, 171–86.

———. "A Preface." In Didion, *Slouching towards Bethlehem*, xi–xiv.

———. *Run River.* New York: Vintage International, 1994.

———. *Slouching towards Bethlehem.* New York: Farrar, Straus and Giroux, 1968.

———. "Slouching towards Bethlehem." In Didion, *Slouching towards Bethlehem*, 84–128.

———. *South and West.* New York: Alfred A. Knopf, 2017.

———. *Where I Was From.* New York: Vintage International, 2003.

Dillon, Elizabeth Maddock. *The Gender of Freedom: Fictions of Liberalism and the Literary Public Sphere.* Stanford CA: Stanford University Press, 2004.

Douglas, Ann. *The Feminization of American Culture.* New York: Alfred A. Knopf, 1977.

Du Bois, W. E. B. *The Souls of Black Folk.* New York: Start Publishing, 2012.

Duncan, Patti. *Tell This Silence: Asian American Women Writers and the Politics of Speech.* Ames: University of Iowa Press, 2004.

Eva Rutland Papers. Edited by Eva Rutland and Kathryn Crosby. Coll. 063, 1949–1979. Special Collections and University Archives, University of Oregon Libraries, Eugene.

Fetterley, Judith, and Marjorie Pryse. *Writing Out of Place: Regionalism,*

Women, and American Literary Culture. Champaign: University of Illinois Press, 2003.

Fichtelberg, Joseph. *Critical Fictions: Sentiment and the American Market, 1780–1870*. Athens: University of Georgia Press, 2003.

Foote, Stephanie. *Regional Fictions: Culture and Identity in Nineteenth-Century American Literature*. Madison: University of Wisconsin Press, 2001.

Goldman, Anne. "'Who Ever Heard of a Blue-Eyed Mexican?': Satire and Sentimentality in María Amparo Ruiz de Burton's *Who Would Have Thought It?*" In *Recovering the U.S. Hispanic Literary Heritage*, vol. 2, edited by Erlinda Gonzales-Berry and Chuck Tatum, 59–78. Houston: Arte Público Press, 1996.

Gonzalez, John M. "The Warp of Whiteness: Domesticity and Empire in Helen Hunt Jackson's 'Ramona.'" *American Literary History* 16, no. 3 (2004): 437–65.

Gonzalez-Day, Ken. *Lynching in the West, 1850–1935*. Durham NC: Duke University Press, 2006.

Gumbs, Alexis Pauline. "Introduction." In *Revolutionary Mothering: Love on the Front Lines*, edited by Alexis Pauline Gumbs, China Martens, and Mai'a Williams, 115–16. Oakland CA: PM Press, 2019.

Halverson, Cathryn. *Maverick Autobiographies: Women Writers and the American West, 1900–1936*. Madison: University of Wisconsin Press, 2004.

Hamilton, Kristie. *America's Sketchbook: The Cultural Life of a Nineteenth Century Literary Genre*. Athens: Ohio University Press, 1998.

Henderson, Katherine U. "*Run River*: Edenic Vision and Wasteland Nightmare." In *Joan Didion: Essays and Conversations*, edited by Joan Didion and Ellen G. Friedman, 91–104. New York: Ontario Review Press, 1984.

Higginbotham, Evelyn Brooks. *Righteous Discontent: The Women's Movement in the Black Baptist Church, 1880–1920*. Cambridge MA: Harvard University Press, 1993.

Hochschild, Arlie Russell. *Strangers in Their Own Land*. New York: New Press, 2016.

Homans, John. "California Screamin'." *New York Magazine*, October 6, 2003.

Howells, William Dean. *A Hazard of New Fortune*. E-Artnow, 2015.

Jackson, Helen Hunt. *Bits of Travel at Home*. New York: Little, Brown, 1904.

———. *A Century of Dishonor*. Mineola NY: Dover Publications, 2003.

———. *Glimpses of Three Coasts*. Boston: Roberts Brothers, 1886.

———. *The Indian Reform Letters of Helen Hunt Jackson, 1879–1885*. Edited by Valerie Sherer Mathes. Norman: University of Oklahoma Press, 1997.

———. *Ramona*. New York: Signet Classics, 2002.

Jacobs, Margaret D. "Mixed-Bloods, Mestizas, and Pintos: Race, Gender, and Claims to Whiteness in Helen Hunt Jackson's 'Ramona' and María Amparo Ruiz de Burton's 'Who Would Have Thought It?'" *Western American Literature* 36, no. 3 (2003): 212–31.

James, Henry. "The Art of Fiction." In *Partial Portraits*, 375–408. New York: Macmillan, 1894.

Kaplan, Amy. *The Anarchy of Empire in the Making of U.S. Culture*. Cambridge MA: Harvard University Press, 2002.

———. "Manifest Domesticity." *American Literature* 70, no. 3 (1998): 581–606.

———. *The Social Construction of American Realism*. Chicago: University of Chicago Press, 1988.

Lamont, Victoria. "Big Books Wanted: Women and Western American Literature in the Twenty-First Century." *Legacy* 31, no. 2 (2014): 311–26.

———. *Westerns: A Woman's History*, Lincoln: University of Nebraska Press, 2016.

Ling, Amy. *Between Worlds: Women Writers of Chinese Ancestry*. Oxford: Pergamon Press, 1990.

Link, Eric Carl. *The Vast and Terrible Drama: American Literary Naturalism in the Late Nineteenth Century*. Tuscaloosa: University of Alabama Press, 2004.

London, Jack. *The Valley of the Moon*. 1913.

Lowe, Lisa. *The Intimacies of Four Continents*. Durham NC: Duke University Press, 2015.

Macellaro, Kimberly. "Sui Sin Far's Jekyll and Hyde: Divided Subjects and Utopian Alternatives." *Modern Fiction Studies* 61, no. 1 (Spring 2015): 47–65.

Madison, James. *Federalist*, no. 10. In *The Federalist Papers*. Washington DC: Library of Congress. https://guides.loc.gov/federalist-papers/full-text.

Mathes, Valerie Sherer. "Helen Hunt Jackson, Amelia Stone Quinton, and the Mission Indians of California." *Southern California Quarterly* 96, no. 2 (2014): 172–205.

McCullough, Kate. *Regions of Identity*. Stanford CA: Stanford University Press, 1999.

McDade, Monique. "Neither Here Nor There: Ruiz De Burton's Genres of Resistance." *Nineteenth-Century Prose* 46, no. 2 (2019): 1–26.

Mead, Rebecca. *How the Vote Was Won: Woman Suffrage in the Western United States, 1868–1914*. New York: New York University Press, 2004.

Mexal, Stephen J. *Reading for Liberalism: The Overland Monthly and the Writing of the Modern American West*. Lincoln: University of Nebraska Press, 2013.

Molina, Natalia. *How Race Was Made in America: Immigration, Citizenship, and the Historical Power of Racial Scripts*. Berkeley: University of California Press, 2014.

Morrison, Toni. *Playing in the Dark*. New York: First Vintage Books, 1993.

Mostern, Kenneth. *Autobiography and Black Identity Politics: Racialization in Twentieth-Century America*. Cambridge: Cambridge University Press, 1999.

Norris, Frank. "A Plea for Romantic Fiction." In Norris, *The Responsibilities of the Novelist*.

———. *The Responsibilities of the Novelist: And Other Literary Essays*. New York: Doubleday, Page, 1903.

———. "The Responsibilities of the Novelist." In Norris, *The Responsibilities of the Novelist*, 1–12.

Obama, Barack. "2012 National Medal of Arts and Humanities Award Ceremony." Washington DC, July 2013. https://www.youtube.com/watch?v=EciDRwKHONk&t=314s.

O'Sullivan, John. "Annexation." 1845. https://www.billofrightsinstitute.org/activities/john-osullivan-annexation-1845.

Padget, Martin. "Travel Writing, Sentimental Romance, and Indian Rights Advocacy: The Politics of Helen Hunt Jackson's Ramona." *Journal of the Southwest* 42, no. 4 (2000): 833–76.

Pattillo, Mary. *Black Picket Fences: Privilege and Peril among the Black Middle Class*. 2nd ed. Chicago: University of Chicago Press, 2013.

Pease, Donald E. "Psychoanalyzing the Narrative Logics of Naturalism: *The Call of the Wild*." *Journal of Modern Literature* 25, nos. 3–4 (2002).

Perkins Gilman, Charlotte. *Women and Economics: A Study of the Economic Relationship between Men and Women as a Factor in Social Evolution*. Boston: Small, Maynard, 1898.

Phillips, Kate. *Helen Hunt Jackson: A Literary Life*. Berkeley: University of California Press, 2003.

Powell, Douglas Reichert. *Critical Regionalism: Connecting Politics and Culture in the American Landscape*. Chapel Hill: University of North Carolina Press, 2007.

Pratt, Mary Louise. *Imperial Eyes: Travel Writing and Transculturation*. 2nd ed. Oxfordshire: Routledge, 2008.

Randisi, Jennifer L. "The Journey Nowhere: Didion's *Run River*." *Markham Review* 11 (1982): 41–43.

Review of Joan Didion's *Run River*. *New Yorker*, 1963.

Rich, Nathaniel. "Introduction." In Didion, *South and West*.

Roediger, David R. *The Wages of Whiteness: Race and the Making of the American Working Class*. London: Verso, 1991.

Roosevelt, Theodore. *The Strenuous Life*. New York: P. F. Collier and Son, 1899.

Ruiz de Burton, María Amparo. *Conflicts of Interest: The Letters of María Amparo Ruiz de Burton*. Edited by Rosaura Sánchez and Beatrice Pita. Houston: Arte Público Press, 2001.

———. *The Squatter and the Don*. Edited by Rosaura Sánchez and Beatrice Pita. Houston: Arte Público Press, 1997.

———. *Who Would Have Thought It?* New York: Penguin Books, 2009.

Rutland, Eva. *When We Were Colored: A Mother's Story*. Arlington VA: IWP, 2007.

Sánchez, Rosaura, and Beatrice Pita. "Introduction." In *Who Would Have Thought It?*, by María Amparo Ruiz de Burton, vii–lxv. Houston: Arte Público Press, 1995.

San Diego History Center. "Ephraim W. Morse (1823–1906)."

Senier, Siobhan. *Voices of American Indian Assimilation and Resistance: Helen Hunt Jackson, Sarah Winnemucca, and Victoria Howard*. Norman: University of Oklahoma Press, 2001.

Solberg, S. E. "Sui Sin Far/Edith Eaton: First Chinese-American Fictionist." *MELUS* 8, no. 1 (1981): 27–39.

Stover, Johnnie M. *Rhetoric and Resistance in Black Women's Autobiography*. Gainesville: University Press of Florida, 2003.

Sui Sin Far. *Mrs. Spring Fragrance and Other Writings*. Edited by Amy Ling and Annette White-Parks. Champaign: University of Illinois Press, 1995.

Tompkins, Jane. *Sensational Designs: The Cultural Work of American Fiction, 1790–1860*. Oxford: Oxford University Press, 1985.

Traub, James. *What Was Liberalism? The Past, Present, and Promise of a Noble Idea*. New York: Basic Books, 2019.

Tuttle, Jennifer. "The Symptoms of Conquest: Race, Class, and the Nervous Body in the *Squatter and the Don*." In *María Amparo Ruiz de Burton: Critical and Pedagogical Perspectives*, edited by Amelia María de la Luz Montes and Anne Elizabeth Goldman. Lincoln: University of Nebraska Press, 2004.

Wang, Bo. "Rereading Sui Sin Far." In *Representations: Doing Asian American Rhetoric*, edited by LuMing Mao and Morris Young, 244–65. Boulder: University Press of Colorado, 2008.

Weaver, James. "Being In and Not Among: The Anti-Imperial Impulses of Helen Hunt Jackson's *Bits of Travel at Home*." *Legacy* 32, no. 2 (2015): 214–35.

INDEX

Abingdon Press, 30
abolition, 46, 85, 87
abolitionists, 41, 53
Aerojet factory, 202
affective activism, 171, 187, 198
affect theory, 171
African American autobiography, 160–63
Ahmed, Sara, 166, 171, 181–82, 190, 192, 233n57
Aldrich, Thomas Baily, 105
Almageur, Tómas, 173
alternative politics of respectability, 158–59, 179, 181, 187, 198
American dream, 163, 211
American exceptionalism, 3, 5, 12, 24, 32, 36, 76, 97, 153, 173, 208
American individualism, 46, 73, 76, 208
Americanization, 132–33

"The Americanizing of Pau Tsu" (Sui Sin Far), 131–34
American paradox, 9
amnesia, historical, 209
Anderson, Benedict, 12, 20–21, 22, 133, 136–37, 192, 229n23
"Annexation" (O'Sullivan), 97
antebellum America, 37
anti-conquerors. *See* anti-conquest
anti-conquest, 80, 82, 83
archives, 23–24, 30–31, 88
Ards, Angela, 162, 176
"The Art of Fiction" (James), 229n39
assault plot, 66
Atlanta GA, 153, 163, 189
Atlanta World, 174
Atlantic Monthly, 21
autoethnographic heroine, 26, 43, 50, 58, 212

245

autoethnography, 43, 74

Baldwin, James, 31, 176
Barnes, Riché J. Daniel, 158, 177, 186
Barnett, Ross, 159
Barrish, Phillip, 132, 140
Baym, Nina, 18
Beecher, Catherine, 40, 61, 63
Berlant, Lauren, 28, 66, 84, 85
Biden, Joe, 215
biracial identity, 138–143, 145, 146
Bits of Travel at Home (Jackson), 89, 164
Black middle class, 157–59, 173
Black motherhood, 31, 159, 166, 174–75, 176, 183, 186–87
Black Muslims, 159
Black women's autobiography, 161–63
A Book of Common Prayer (Didion), 32, 206
borders, 148–49, 151, 156
Boston Globe, 135
Burton, Henry S., 35, 60

California, 8, 15, 27, 89, 92, 156, 200
California dream, 2–3, 4, 8, 10–11, 156, 214
Californios, 25, 27–28, 38, 39, 72, 108
Campbell, Donna, 21, 22, 123, 128
capitalism, 33, 69–70
Capitol Building, 215
captivity narrative, 57
Carmichael, Stokely, 31, 159, 197
Century Magazine, 21, 91, 93, 111
A Century of Dishonor (Jackson), 18, 26, 83–84, 91, 105

Chief Standing Bear, 83
Chinese Americans, 122–23
Chinese Exclusion Act, 122, 138, 149
Choices (Rutland), 30
citizenship, 26, 32, 38–39, 90–91, 108
civic identity, 85, 87, 104, 116
civil rights activism, 157, 162
Civil War, 46, 86
Cleveland, Grover, 105
Clinton, Hilary, 210
Cody, Buffalo Bill, 98
Collins, Patricia Hill, 31, 174–75, 177, 186
Comer, Krista, 17, 18, 155, 164, 195
Congress, 83, 108
consent: of the governed, 14–15, 100; sexual, 16–17
counterculture, 32, 203, 208, 211
critical regionalism, 31, 232n10
Critical Regionalism (Powell), 232n10
cult of domesticity, 40, 45, 46, 56, 64, 75
The Cultural Politics of Emotion (Ahmed), 233n57
culture war, 207
Cummins, Maria Susanna, 42

Daily Alta California, 47
Davenport, Guy, 6
Davis, Angela, 176
Davis, Jefferson, 46
Dawes, Henry, 84
deep story, 211–12, 215
Diana, Vanessa Holford, 123, 230n68
Didion, Joan, 190; *A Book of Common Prayer*, 32, 206; "Notes from a Native Daughter," 199; "On Morality," 209; *Run River*,

5–9, 15–17, 126, 200; "Slouching Towards Bethlehem," 32, 202–3, 204–6; *South and West*, 33, 214; and "we" concept, 196; *Where I Was From*, 1; *The White Album*, 206
Dillon, Elizabeth Maddock, 44
domesticity, 26, 162, 188; in comparison to labor, 28, 86, 111–12; and domestic spaces, 142–43; and imperialism, 14; and slavery, 45
Dreiser, Theodore, 122
Du Boise, W. E. B., 162, 164
Dunbar, Paul Lawrence, 170
Duncan, Patti, 5

Eaton, Winifred, 147
emancipation, 163, 168, 170
"Encouragement" (Dunbar), 170
Eva (character), 43–44, 46, 146
extremism, 207

family, 40, 46, 176–78
Federalist 10 (Madison), 220n22
femininity, 134
feminism, 17, 18
Fetterley, Judith, 17, 232n10
Fitchelberg, Joseph, 85
five-and-ten stores, 188–89, 195
Foote, Mary Hallock, 7
Foote, Stephanie, 21
Fort Worth TX, 191
Fourteenth Amendment, 39, 104
Franciscans, 89, 91, 93
frontier, American, 1, 13, 32, 33, 107; closing of, 36, 37; language of, 5, 201; post-frontier, 29, 156; writers, 14

gender, 40
genre, 19–20, 24, 124, 148, 200; conventions, 26, 43, 44, 50, 54–55; realism, 21, 29, 126, 130, 213; sentimental, 26, 38, 41, 44, 62, 85, 115–16; women's, 83, 104
Girlfriends (Rutland), 30
Goldman, Anne, 57
Gonzales-Day, Ken, 173
government, 14, 100–101, 107–8, 113
Gumbs, Alexis Pauline, 186

Haight Ashbury CA, 202–3, 204
Halverson, Cathryn, 19
Hamilton, Kristie, 124, 230n64
"Happy Objects" (Ahmed), 166
Harlequin Books, 30
Harper Paperbacks, 30
Harper's, 21
A Hazard of New Fortunes (Howells), 140
health tourism, 106
Henderson, Katherine, 16
Higginbotham, Evelyn Brooks, 31, 157, 177, 186
Hobbes, Thomas, 13
Hochschild, Arlie Russell, 33, 210–12, 215, 216
Homestead Acts, 75, 87
Howells, William Dean, 105–6, 122, 125–26, 134, 140
How the Vote Was Won (Mead), 14–15

illiberalism, 213
immigrant children, 148, 151
imperialism, 36, 43, 52, 80, 98–99, 112, 207

"In Defense of Uncle Tom" (Rutland), 30, 236n12
Indian agents, 100, 109
"The Inferior Woman" (Sui Sin Far), 117–21, 125
integration: and the integrated classroom, 168, 170–71; and integrated neighborhoods, 180–81; and a rhetoric of care, 169, 179; western American, 160, 165, 193
intersectionalism, 19, 25
"In the Land of the Free" (Sui Sin Far), 148–49
The Intimacies of Four Continents (Lowe), 23, 28, 45, 86, 201, 223n23, 224n24, 236n4
intimacy, 41, 53; complexity of, 118; domestic, 86, 112, 121; economic, 129; epistemologies of, 143; exchange of, 132–33, 134, 147; fractured, 141, 146; "as heuristic," 23, 118, 121; network of, 119; sexual, 64, 140
"It's Wavering Image" (Sui Sin Far), 138–46, 170–71

Jackson, Helen Hunt, 26–27, 141, 164; in comparison to María Amparo Ruiz de Burton, 25; and imperialism, 225n58; and Native American advocacy, 226n102; and progressive politics, 87–89, 113–14
Jackson, William Sharpless, 83
Jacobs, Harriet, 162
James, Henry, 105–6, 127, 229n39
January 6 insurrection, 215
Jim Crow segregation, 30–31, 157, 164; in comparison to western American integration, 168, 177, 190, 192

Kaplan, Amy, 8, 21, 26, 36, 143; "Manifest Domesticity," 55, 58, 231n79; and realism, 125; and Republican motherhood, 103; and sentimental tropes, 51
Kennedy, Robert, 176
King, Martin Luther, Jr., 176
knowledge: cultural, 12, 19, 118, 129, 132, 144, 203; exchange of, 52, 132, 147, 165, 170, 188; gendered, 121; as imperial violence, 80, 118, 131, 134, 144; intimate, 119, 128, 140; regional, 171, 190, 192; situated, 156, 192
Kolodny, Annette, 18
Ku Klux Klan, 159

labor: in comparison to domesticity, 28; emotional, 41, 55–56, 86; in progressive politics, 85; transient, 110; wage, 106, 110
Ladies Home Journal, 30
Lamont, Victoria, 8, 18, 31
The Lamplighter (Cummins), 42
"The Land of the Free" (Sui Sin Far), 148
"Leaves from the Mental Portfolio of an Eurasian" (Sui Sin Far), 123, 146
liberal guilt, 34, 132
liberalism: American, 13, 23, 37–38, 45, 149; anxieties, 27, 29; as contradictory, 212; democracy, 24, 28; failed, 205–6; global, 73–74
liberal personhood, 38, 121; in comparison to slavery, 86; and

domesticity, 87, 112; and women, 40, 45, 52, 63, 66, 109
liberal philosophy, 118
liberty: and sentimental women writers, 44; in the West, 209, 210; women's lack of, 55, 58, 61, 63, 65
"Life" (Dunbar), 170
Lincoln, Abraham, 46
Link, Eric Carl, 123, 130, 135
Locke, John, 13
London, Jack, 122, 130, 134
Louisiana, 210
Lowe, Lisa: *The Intimacies of Four Continents*, 23, 28, 45, 86, 201, 223n23, 224n24, 236n4; and intimacy, 118, 121; and "liberal forgetting," 195; and "political economy of intimacies," 119, 149

Macellaro, Kimberly, 230n68
Madison, James, 220n22
Malcolm X, 31, 159, 176, 197
Manifest Destiny: history of, 12, 20, 24, 28, 86, 153; and imperialism, 107, 112; and John O'Sullivan, 97–98; rhetoric of, 22, 28, 47, 76, 89–90, 160, 173; and the sentimental novel, 42, 116
"Manifest Domesticity" (Kaplan), 55, 58, 231n79
marriage plot, 59, 66, 69
masculinity: Anglo-American, 67–68, 121–22, 133, 138; and the West, 9, 18, 138
McClellan Air Force Base, 202
Mead, Rebecca, 14–15
Mexal, Stephen J., 13–14, 22

Mexican American War, 12, 28, 35, 36
Miss Brooks (White), 125
Molina, Natalia, 39
Monterey CA, 30
Montreal Daily Witness, 148
Morrison, Toni, 11, 180, 201
Morse, Ephraim W., 27, 66
Mostern, Kenneth, 161

The Nation, 105
national identity, 20–21, 24; homogenous, 20–22, 122, 134, 138; literary, 22
nationalism, 20, 21; American, 22, 38, 69, 108; white, 116
Native Americans, 27, 59–60; autonomy of, 93, 101–2, 103; labor of, 111; removal of, 82, 115, 153; representations of, 98
Native Californians, 27
naturalism, 118, 123, 128, 129, 130, 135
neurasthenia, 107
newspaper industry, 148
New Woman, 117
New Yorker, 7
New York Times, 33, 35, 37, 60, 77, 92
No Crystal Stair (Rutland), 30
Norris, Frank, 122, 123, 127, 128, 130, 228n18
"Notes from a Native Daughter" (Didion), 199
the novel, 124, 128

Obama, Barack, 5, 202
"On Morality" (Didion), 209
O'Sullivan, John, 97–98

INDEX 249

Overland Monthly, 14, 23

Page Law, 122
pattern of forgetting, 10–12, 195
Pattillo, Mary, 158, 186
Pease, Donald, 125, 229n24
Perkins Gilman, Charlotte, 40
Phillips, Kate, 225n58
pioneer(s): elite, 8, 17; history, 1, 3, 9, 11, 16, 161; myth, 12, 15, 161; narrative, 9, 98, 110, 153–54, 161; spirit, 9, 28, 76; woman, 7–8
Pita, Beatrice, 42, 47
Playing in the Dark (Morrison), 201
Plessy vs. Ferguson, 122
policing, 179
politics of respectability, 157, 181, 182–83, 186, 198
popular literature, 96, 98
populism, 213
postmodernism, 203
Powell, Douglas, 160–61, 232n10
Pratt, Mary Louise, 26, 43, 52, 74, 80–81
print capitalism, 20–21
progress: ambivalent, 80; California, 1–2, 8, 203; history of, 162; illusion of, 183–84; narratives of, 6, 10, 15, 24, 154, 211–12; rhetorical, 16, 24, 28, 167, 176, 203, 208, 214–15; and the sentimental novel, 73; U.S., 90, 164, 205, 216; western American, 2–3, 4, 7, 8, 17, 33, 155–57, 166
Progressive Era, 132, 170, 213
progressivism: ambivalent, 193; historical, 190; as identity, 147, 156, 215; literary, 27, 80, 83, 84, 85, 89, 110, 113–16, 132, 134, 144; political, 28, 129; rhetorical, 24, 194, 196, 204; western American, 15, 31–32, 81, 87, 151, 161, 165, 169, 172, 191–92, 195, 207, 209, 213
Pryse, Marjorie, 17, 232n10
"Psychoanalyzing the Narrative Logics of Naturalism" (Pease), 229n24
public school politics, 183–84, 187–88
Publisher's Weekly, 174

Quinton, Amelia Stone, 89

racism, 31, 56; contemporary, 151; and labor, 86, 110–11; and literary production, 131, 135; and region, 192; and sex, 193; in the West, 171, 177
Ramona (Jackson), 27, 79, 81, 84
realism, 21, 29, 126, 130, 213; as democratic, 122, 123; as following Victorian sentimentalism, 106; and imperialism, 125, 129; and observation, 118, 124, 125, 129, 141, 144–45; and realist subjects, 139, 142, 149; and romanticism, 123, 145–46; and third-person limited narration, 126–27, 129
Reconstruction, 82, 107, 138, 158, 169
Redbook, 30
regionalism, 21, 24–25, 31
Republican motherhood, 101, 103–4, 106, 108
Republican Women of Southwest Louisiana, 212
reservations, 92, 102, 103, 112, 115

respectability, 176, 185
"The Responsibilities of the Novelist" (Norris), 128, 228n18
rhetoric of care, 169, 179, 197
rhetoric of motherhood, 180, 197
Rich, Nathaniel, 33, 214
Rocky Mountains, 153
Roediger, David, 226n102
Roosevelt, Franklin, 9
Roosevelt, Theodore, 9, 222n78
Ruiz de Burton, María Amparo, 23, 25–26, 35–36, 37, 46, 47–48
Run River (Didion), 5–9, 15–17, 126, 200
Rutland, Bill, 29
Rutland, Eva, 29–31, 153, 199, 236n12

Sacramento CA, 1, 5, 10–11, 17, 29, 153, 165, 177, 181, 199
Sacramento Union, 173
Sánchez, Rosaura, 42, 47
San Diego CA, 27
San Diego History Center, 27
San Francisco CA, 135
Saturday Evening Post, 202
Sedgwick, Catherine Maria, 25
seduction plot, 59, 67
the self-made man, 120
Sensational Designs (Tompkins), 41
sentimentalism, 25–26; as contractual, 85; and conventional heroines, 26, 43, 49, 53; as gendered, 83; as genre, 115–16; in novels, 28, 37, 41, 58, 71, 85; and sentimental domesticity, 36–37; and sentimental heroes, 59; and sentimental liberalism, 26; as shifting to realism, 106

Serra, Junipero, 90
settler colonialism, 75, 102
Sixteenth Street Baptist Church bombing, 197
the sketch, 124, 128, 136, 137, 144, 230n64
slave narrative, 163, 172
slavery, 31, 46, 87–88, 169; in comparison to Spanish missions, 91, 94; history of, 171, 194
"Slouching Towards Bethlehem" (Didion), 32, 202–3, 204–6
"The Smuggling of Tie Co" (Sui Sin Far), 126–30
South, American, 33–34
South and West (Didion), 33, 214
Spanish missions, 90, 91, 93
speechlessness, 5, 200
Spelman College, 29
The Squatter and the Don (Ruiz de Burton), 36, 42
squatters, 73–77, 79, 82, 87, 94
Stover, Johnnie, 162, 163, 164
Stowe, Harriet Beecher, 18, 25, 36, 43–44, 84, 104
Strangers in Their Own Land (Hochschild), 33, 210
"strategic motherhood," 159–60, 163, 165, 167, 171
"The Strenuous Life" (Roosevelt), 222n78
Sui Sin Far, 22, 28–29, 136, 137, 154, 170–71

Thirteenth Amendment, 104
"Tian Shan's Kindred Spirit" (Sui Sin Far), 126
Tompkins, Jane, 18, 41, 49
Topsy (character), 36

Transamerica Building, 206, 209, 211
Traub, James, 213
Treatise on Domestic Economy (Beecher), 40
Treaty of Guadalupe Hidalgo, 26, 39, 71
The Trouble with Being a Mama (Rutland). See *When We Were Colored* (Rutland)
Trump, Donald, 210
Turner, Frederick Jackson, 36
Tuskegee Airmen, 29
Tuttle, Jennifer S., 106
2020 presidential election, 215

Uncle Tom's Cabin (Stowe), 18, 36, 43, 85
University of Oregon, Eugene, 30

The Valley of the Moon (London), 134–36
Victorian womanhood, 7, 95, 109, 112–13
violence: against immigrants, 130, 149, 151; against Native Americans, 116; against women, 64–66, 126; imperial, 36, 51, 54; racial, 36, 171–73; representational, 49, 126, 142; rhetorical, 6, 158; settler-colonial, 37, 56, 112; in the West, 18

Wages of Whiteness (Roediger), 226n102
Warner, Charles Dudley, 105
Warner, Susan, 42
Washington, Booker T., 162
Weaver, James, 225n58

West, American: arrival in, 12–13, 19, 153, 191, 196; in comparison to South, 3–4, 165, 167, 189, 210; discursive, 156; globalization of, 206; ideal, 8, 161, 202, 209; identity, 199; literary representations of, 77; myth, 7, 12, 15, 23, 67, 153; paradox, 9, 155; resources, 70, 98; as romantic, 35; women in the, 94–95, 196, 200, 209
western American women writers, 18–19, 20, 22, 196, 200
Westerns: A Woman's History (Lamont), 8
What Was Liberalism? (Traub), 213
When We Were Colored (Rutland), 30, 154, 157, 199
Where I Was From (Didion), 1
White, Eliza Orne, 125
The White Album (Didion), 206
Who Would Have Thought It? (Ruiz de Burton), 36, 41, 47
The Wide, Wide World (Warner), 42
Wild West, 8, 98
Williams, Raymond, 236n4
Women and Economics (Perkins Gilman), 40
women's culture, 41, 54–55, 72–73, 85
Women's Day, 30
Women's National Indian Association (WNIA), 89, 90
Writing Out of Place (Fetterely and Pryse), 232n10

xenophobia, 131, 135, 151